Psychology in Litigation and Legislation

Master Lectures in Psychology

Psychology in Litigation and Legislation

Master Lecturers

Julie Blackman
Wayne F. Cascio
Stephen J. Ceci
Gary B. Melton
Michael Owen Miller

Edited by
Bruce D. Sales
and Gary R. VandenBos

AMERICAN PSYCHOLOGICAL ASSOCIATION
WASHINGTON, DC

Published by the
American Psychological Association
750 First Street, NE
Washington, DC 20002

Copies may be ordered from
APA Order Department
P.O. Box 2710
Hyattsville, MD 20784

In the UK and Europe, copies may be ordered from
American Psychological Association
3 Henrietta Street
Covent Garden, London
WC2E 8LU England

Typeset in Cheltenham by Easton Publishing Services, Inc.,
Easton, MD

Printer: BookCrafters, Chelsea, MI
Technical/Production Editor: Mark A. Meschter

Library of Congress Cataloging-in-Publication Data

Psychology in litigation and legislation / edited by Bruce D.
  Sales and Gary R. VandenBos
        p.   cm.
    Includes bibliographical references.
    ISBN 1-55798-247-3
    1. Psychology, Forensic.   2. Evidence, Expert—United
States.   3. Children as witnesses—United States.   4. Law—
Psychology.   I. Sales, Bruce Dennis.   II. VandenBos, Gary R.
KF8965.P78   1994
347.73'67—dc20
[347.30767]   93-17321
                                                                 CIP

British Library Cataloguing-in-Publication Data
A CIP record is available from the British Library

Printed in the United States of America
First edition

CONTENTS

PREFACE

THE VALUE OF PSYCHOLOGY TO THE LAW AND LAW TO PSYCHOLOGY

S ince the first Master Lectures in Psychology focusing on psychology and law were given more than a decade ago (Scheirer & Hammonds, 1983), interest in using psychological knowledge, and in involving psychologists in the legal process, has continued to grow. For example, among other involvements, psychologists provide assessment, treatment, and intervention services in jails and prisons and in the community for court-referred clients; serve in administrative capacities in a variety of state and federal administrative agencies; work for law enforcement agencies helping both police officers and their families avoid and overcome the stress that the profession engenders while advising law enforcement officials on how to deal with suspects and offenders on issues ranging from negotiating the successful release of hostages to defusing domestic altercations; aid the executive branches of state and federal governments in policy analysis and planning a variety of service and intervention programs; serve government agencies and legislatures as evaluators of legally mandated service and entitlement programs; provide consulting services to lawyers on litigation strategy; and provide expert testimony in courts and legislatures on numerous psychological issues. In addition, psychological research of relevance to the law continues to expand, as does research directly focused on psycholegal issues. The creation of a new journal by the American Psychological Association, *Psychology, Public Policy, and Law*, is but one indicator of the significance of this expansion.

It is appropriate, therefore, that another volume in the Master Lecture in Psychology series be devoted to the interface of psychology and law. But in doing so, it was necessary to limit the coverage to manageable terrain. The field today encompasses concerns ranging from environmental policy (e.g., Pitt & Zube, 1987; Ribe, 1989) to mental health policy (e.g., Shah & Sales, 1991; Tor & Sales, in press) and from sexual harassment in the workplace (e.g., Gutek & O'Connor, in press) to psychological distress in law students and lawyers (e.g., Benjamin, Darling, & Sales, 1990; Benjamin, Kaszniak, Sales, & Shanfield, 1986). Thus, the Master Lecture Series, and the chapters in this volume, can no more cover all of the major issues in psychology and law than they could cover all of the issues in any other major subfield of psychology (e.g., clinical psychology, social psychology).

The decision was made, therefore, to focus on a range of critical issues that have been raised by the intersection of psychology with two of the most visible legal systems—the courts and legislatures—and with two critical legal processes—adjudication and the creation of legislation. Because the Master Lectures in Psychology and the ensuing publications are typically limited to five presentations, this volume cannot cover the full range of issues even in this subdomain. On the other hand, the topics selected for inclusion admirably raise fundamental issues that should be of concern to psychologists who interact with lawyers, judges, and juries in litigation and who interact with legislators in drafting legislation.

Relevance of Psychological Science to Litigation and Legislation

Litigation provides an opportunity for parties to resolve a dispute when less adversarial means have failed. Because it often involves disagreement over what the true facts that are involved in a case may be, the resolution of this issue can constitute an important part of the trial. In many instances, the factual disputes revolve around behavioral or social issues (hereinafter called *social facts*). Social-fact questions ranging from the conditions under which an operator of complex equipment is least likely to make errors in her or his work to various predictions about human behavior (e.g., who is likely to be a better parent in a particular case) may be under dispute in a trial.

Similarly, legislators, when considering and drafting statutes, are confronted with a variety of complex social-fact questions. For example, in drafting legislation dealing with the construction of new prisons, legislators will face such questions as whether large prisons are safer for the public than community-based correctional programs, whether publicly operated correctional facilities are more efficient and effective than privately operated units, whether large prisons are more likely to foster rehabilitation than smaller units; legislators may also be concerned with causal explanation for whatever answers are received. As another example, consider proposed legislation to require detailed labeling on food products. Some of the social-fact questions involved when considering this proposed law include whether consumers will attend to the labels, be informed by them, and change their buying behavior or use of the products based on the information presented; and the characteristics of labels that will make them most useable and used by consumers (Hadden, in press).

The level of sophistication and expertise that is relevant to answering fact questions will vary. In some situations, the expertise asked for will be to provide information about "legislative facts"—facts that are used to create or modify a rule of law and establish the validity of factual assumptions on which fundamental questions of law are decided. In other situations, the facts under question will be "adjudicative"—facts that are relevant to a specific case or situation (Davis, 1942). For example, asking whether jurors are likely to experience difficulty in understanding the substantive instructions that judges read to them at the end of trials is an example of legislative fact-finding, whereas asking whether the jurors in a particular case showed poor comprehension of the instructions exemplifies adjudicative fact-finding (e.g., Elwork, Sales, & Alfini, 1982).

Answering both legislative and adjudicative social-fact questions may be difficult for attorneys, judges, juries, and legislators, who probably have little or no training in the social sciences. Psychologists, however, possess unique skills to aid in the resolution of social-fact disputes. Psychologists can draw on the existing theoretical and empirical knowledge base within psychology to answer some of the questions, and they can draw on their arsenal of methodological and statistical skills to carry out new research that would be directly relevant to the issues under consideration (Sales, 1983).

Quality of the Expert Information Conveyed in Courts and Legislatures

As experts in human behavior, it is only logical that psychologists should want to share their knowledge so that the resolutions of social-fact disputes are based on scientific evidence rather than lay opinion and personal values. Conversely, given the expertise—and perceived expertise—of psychologists, it also is not surprising that lawyers, judges, and legislators look to psychologists for information that can help in resolving these issues.

Indeed, for psychologists to build a knowledge base that is unknown or unused is ineffectual and counterproductive for the discipline. Yet, despite the laudatory intention of psychologists to share their knowledge with lawyers, judges, juries, and legislators, it is important that psychologists ask whether the data/information that they plan to share is appropriate for the issue under consideration in the policy arena—that is, if the data to be imparted are of sufficient quality that it is reasonable to have them be used by the trier of fact (jury, or judge when there is no jury) in litigation or to drive policy decisions in legislatures (Wursten & Sales, 1988). In the first chapter in this volume, Ceci raises this issue by discussing the recent research showing that the validity of children's testimony of prior sexual abuse is highly dependent on the suggestiveness of the questioning that the child has been subjected to, amongst other factors.

Conversely, the law also has a role to play in keeping out nonexpert "experts" and nonscientific "scientific" information. Evidence law provides criteria for the judge to use in deciding whether the expert and the proffered information should be admitted into evidence in the trial. Consideration of the admissibility of the expert, and the information that she or he wishes to impart, is different from the trier of fact's evaluation of a witness' credibility once the evidence is admitted. Because psychologists have traditionally focused on how to be an effective expert witness—which is a consideration of credibility (e.g., Brodsky, 1991; Whobrey, Sales, & Elwork, 1981)—a consideration of admissibility is appropriate and timely.

Melton, in this volume's second chapter, discusses a recent United States Supreme Court decision, *Daubert v. Merrell Dow Pharmaceuticals, Inc.* (1993), which considers the standard for the admissibility of scientific information in federal courts and is likely to have a significant impact on many states as well. At least theoretically, admissibility rules can provide the courts with an important means to prevent bad science from finding its way into case law. This gate-keeping function is important when one realizes that the expert testimony may be based on valid and reliable research, a combination of science and professional experience, professional experience alone, or personal values that become masked as professional opinion (e.g., Sales & Simon, 1993).

Relevance of Professional Knowledge to Litigation and Legislation

There is an admissibility issue that is particularly important for psychologists that is not addressed by *Daubert*. Although a court may reject testimony that is offered by a scientist because of its lack of scientific quality, the court may still accept that same information from a practitioner who does not cloak her or his testimony in the mantle of science, but rather presents it as opinion that is based on professional experience (Sales, Shuman, & O'Connor, in press). This creates an ironic twist for litigation; information that is excludable because it does not meet the law's criterion for evidentiary reliability can be admitted by casting it as professional opinion and not science. Wouldn't both types of presentation equally persuade the fact-finder? Thus, bad science, or no science for that matter (e.g., a situation in which research has never been conducted on the issue under consideration), may be introduced in court cases by psychologists.

This is not minimize the importance and value of professional opinion to litigation; psychology's value to the law is not, and should not be, limited to sharing research knowledge. The law, including its adversarial and legislative processes, relies on professional psychologists to aid in its administration in a variety of ways. As already noted, in addition to serving as expert witnesses in trials and before legislative committees, psychologists provide assessments of litigants at the request of courts and attorneys, treat persons who are under court order, and critically review the extant literature and suggest policy recommendations at the request of legislators.

Advocating for Psychological Knowledge in Courts and Legislatures

Given that judges, juries, and legislators may not be able to easily distinguish when an expert's testimony is straying from science to professional opinion or personal values, an important concern for psychologists who are involved in the adversarial or legislative processes should be over what they are advocating. Although advocacy is a relatively simple concept (i.e., to promote something), this notion becomes particularly problematic when used in litigation and legislation. No one would argue with the proposition that psychologists should advocate for empirically derived knowledge that is valid and reliable. But it is possible for less-than-expert "experts" not to be aware of the current scientific information and thereby advance poor science in the public forum.

What if the information presented and advocated for is based on theories that have not yet been empirically validated? To the extent that the scientist notes the limits in the support for his or her proposition, he or she would be acting ethically and responsibly (Sales & Simon, 1993). Would the same result ensue, however, if the psychologist was advocating for personal values and not scientific or professional knowledge? To the extent that the judge or jury in a trial, or the legislator in a legislative hearing, is listening to the expert because of his or her doctoral training in the discipline of psychology, it is deceptive to advocate for personal values under the guise of expertise. Melton makes note of this issue in his chapter in this volume.

Relevance of Psychological Standards to Litigation and Legislation

But there is a larger issue to be recognized here. To what extent should psychologists rely on legal standards for the admissibility of their information and expert testimony, rather than on standards internal to the profession, such as ethical principles and standards (Sales & Shuman, 1993). Because litigation and science search for truth in different ways, it would be naive to assume that standards for admissibility of evidence would be sufficient for guiding what psychologists should do in the courtroom. Indeed, lawyers' needs to resolve cases forces them to seek immediate answers from experts even when there are none. This same problem holds true for legislatures. Where is the psychologist to turn then to ensure that his or her testimony is appropriate?

The ethical principles (American Psychological Association, 1992) provide an excellent starting point (e.g., Sales & Shuman, 1993). It cautions about the importance of competence when providing services (Principle A), of promoting the integrity of psychological science (Principle B), and of contributing to the welfare of others by performing one's role in a responsible fashion that avoids or minimizes harm to others (Principle E). To the extent that the psychologist is not familiar with the current scientific information about which he or she is testifying, he or she is not competent to testify and should not be testifying. To the extent that the psychologist is not advocating for the knowledge base of the science and the profession, he or she is not promoting the integrity of the discipline and should not be testifying. To the extent that the psychologist is being seduced by an attorney to advocate for a client's cause rather than scientific/professional knowledge, he or she is not performing the role as an expert witness in a responsible fashion and is unfairly increasing the harm that may result to the other litigant or litigants in a case. Thus, the ethical principles (American Psychological Association, 1992) provide an excellent complement to the law controlling the admissibility of expert testimony, and they promote high standards of behavior for psychologists who are involved in the adversarial or legislative processes.

Understanding and applying the ethical principles and standards is critical for another reason. They, in combination with other professional standards (e.g., Committee on Ethical Guidelines for Forensic Psychologists, 1991), provide sources of guidance to psychologists about appropriate professional behavior. Adherence to their mandates will provide protection against professional liability from malpractice actions and other legal suits (e.g., for breach of contract). Ignorance or disregard of them can result in costly and destructive outcomes for psychologists and their clients.

Relevance of Law to Psychological Practice

Knowledge of the law, including statutory and case law, that affects one's practice provides another important source of information for guiding psychologists in their practice (Sales & Miller, 1986–1994). When evaluating a litigant for an attorney, and when testifying in the case, the psychologist is being asked to assess the person in comparison to a legal standard. Without knowledge of the law, it is all too easy to perform an evaluation that is inappropriate for the legal issue under consideration. The result is that the psychologist performs an inappropriate service and could be subject to a malpractice claim.

Although it occurs relatively infrequently, when claims are brought against psychologists, they may need to testify in their own defense. Becoming a defendant in a lawsuit is a sure way to impress upon someone the need to know the law that affects them and the legal process that controls the litigation against them. In the third chapter in this volume, Miller discusses the causes of malpractice litigation against psychologists and highlights protective actions that they can take.

The law affects psychological practice in another way. It creates opportunities for psychologists to provide services. As Cascio's chapter in this volume instructs, in its desire to protect the rights of disabled persons, the law has generated significant opportunities for psychologists to aid employers in complying with the law's mandates regarding the hiring and employment of disabled persons, in assessing whether an employer complied with the law's behavioral demands, and in responding to important questions that can only be answered by psychological research.

Values That Color Science and Law

Blind adherence to standards and laws can also create problems because these written statements can embody values that create needless suffering for others. Blackman, in this volume's fourth chapter, explores the way the law and psychology have relied on a set of male-dominated values that feminist scholars in both fields are appropriately questioning today. The fact that a male-dominated society created law and analytical frameworks that were based on male prejudices is not surprising. Wexler (1981) reported the outrageous case of a 19-year-old Mexican–American woman who was committed to the Territorial Asylum for the Insane in Phoenix, Arizona, on January 23, 1912, for what amounted to "mental problems as being supposedly caused by 'bathing in cold water at menstrual period' [as quoted from court papers] and as probably being 'only temporary' [as quoted from court papers] in nature...." (p. 2). The woman was still there in 1971, then 78 years of age. What Blackman reveals are the new analytical frameworks that are being applied today to generate the insights that are essential to neutralizing science of inappropriate values and biases and to ensuring that biased "facts" and beliefs are repudiated by the law.

Values can also distort one's views to the point that important issues are completely ignored. For example, laws that require extraordinary, life-saving care for disabled infants are laudable in isolation. But what if the same lawmakers who created this law ignore the financial implications for the single, unemployed parent who is responsible for the child? Is the state going to underwrite the cost of services? If so, are appropriate and needed services available? Issues such as this are also part of the focus of Blackman's justifiable concern with the way that society selects the questions to ask about women and the ways that society structures laws that control women's behaviors.

Ultimately, once values are clarified, society will be forced to deal with the most difficult questions. What is it that society values, in what order of priority, and how much is society willing to pay for the legal choices. The feminist literature from psychology will help society to focus on these critical questions, and in the process, we hope empower those who have found little or no voice in either psychology or law.

Conflicts in Values Between Psychology and Law

One must remember, however, that minimizing the biasing values that may cloud psychologists' questions, perspectives, and research does not necessarily mean that courts or legislatures will follow feminist advice. Although psychology takes a utilitarian, consequentialist perspective that focuses on understanding some truth and achieving some end, the law is partially deontologically driven, adhering to normative values, such as those embodied in the Constitution. For the feminist movement to achieve its goals that are dependent on the law, it will have to find avenues of redress that do not violate normative principles that the law strongly holds.

This same admonition equally applies to psychology's teachings in general that are relevant to the law (e.g., Sales & Shuman, 1994). For example, because psychologists can empirically test the validity of behavioral and social assumptions underlying the law, they have the power to point out invalid assumptions and make suggestions for how to restructure laws that minimize undesirable consequences and maximize the chance that the law will achieve its goals (Sales, 1983). Thus, the psychologist can approach lawmakers with powerful tools and information. This does not mean, however, that the lawmakers will follow the advice. Constitutional mandates concerning due process, for instance, may conflict with the recommendations and override the lawmakers' ability to follow the advice.

What is important is not that psychologists control the ultimate policy decision in the courthouse or the chambers of legislatures. That responsibility appropriately belongs to those who have been duly elected or selected for the job. Rather, it is important that psychologists share their scientific and professional expertise on issues that are relevant to the courts and legislatures so that ambiguities over social facts are decreased or lessened and behavioral and social options are made known and clarified. The achievement of this goal will best serve to acquit psychology's social responsibility, while promoting the integrity of the discipline.

BRUCE D. SALES, PhD, JD
GARY R. VANDENBOS, PhD

References

American Psychological Association. (1992). Ethical principles of psychologists and code of conduct. *American Psychologist, 47*, 1597–1611.

Benjamin, G. A. H., Kaszniak, A., Sales, B., & Shanfield, S. B. (1986, spring). The role of legal education in producing psychological distress among law students and lawyers. *American Bar Foundation Research Journal*, 225–252.

Benjamin, A., Darling, E., & Sales, B. (1990). Prevalence of depression, alcoholism, and cocaine abuse among United States lawyers. *International Journal of Law and Psychiatry, 13*, 233–246.

Brodsky, S. L. (1991). *Testifying in court*. Washington, DC: American Psychological Association.

Committee on Ethical Guidelines for Forensic Psychologists. (1991). Specialty guidelines for forensic psychologists. *Law and Human Behavior, 15*, 655–665.

Daubert v. Merrell Dow Pharmaceuticals, Inc., 113 S. Ct. 2786 (1993).

Davis, K. C. (1942). An approach to problems of evidence in the administrative process. *Harvard Law Review, 55*, 364–425.

Elwork, A., Sales, B. D., & Alfini, J. (1982). *Making jury instructions understandable*. Charlottesville, VA: Michie.

Gutek, B. A., & O'Connor, M. (in press). The empirical basis for the reasonable women standard in sexual harassment law. *Journal of Social Issues*.

Hadden, S. G. (in press). Labeling as advertising. In J. P. Lipton & B. D. Sales (Eds.), *Advertising, law and the social sciences*. New York: Plenum.

Pitt, D. G., & Zube, E. H. (1987). Management of natural environments. In D. Stokols & I. Altman (Eds.), *Handbook of environmental psychology* (Vol. 2, pp. 1009–1042). New York: Wiley.

Ribe, R. G. (1989). The aesthetics of forestry: What has empirical preference research taught us? *Environmental Management, 13*, 55–74.

Sales, B. D. (1983). The legal regulation of psychology: Professional and scientific interactions. In C. J. Scheirer & B. L. Hammonds (Eds.), *The master lecture series: Vol. 2. Psychology and the law* (pp. 5–36). Washington, DC: American Psychological Association.

Sales, B. D., & Miller, M. O. (Series Eds.). (1986–1994). *Law and mental health professionals series*. Washington, DC: American Psychological Association.[1]

Sales, B. D., & Shuman, D. (1993). Reclaiming the integrity of science in expert witnessing. *Ethics and Behavior, 3*, 223–229.

Sales, B., & Shuman, D. (1994). Mental health law and mental health care. *American Journal of Orthopsychiatry, 64*, 172–179.

Sales, B. D., Shuman, D. W., & O'Connor, M. (in press). In a dim light: Admissibility of child sexual abuse memories in court. *Applied Cognitive Psychology*.

Sales, B. D., & Simon, L. (1993). Institutional constraints on the ethics of expert testimony. *Ethics and Behavior, 3*, 231–249.

Scheirer, C. J. & Hammonds, B. L. (Eds.). (1983). *The master lecture series: Vol. 2. Psychology and the law*. Washington, DC: American Psychological Association.

Shah, S. A., & Sales, B. D. (Eds.). (1991). *Law and mental health: Major developments and research needs*. Washington, DC: U.S. Government Printing Office. (National Institute of Mental Health Monograph)

Tor, P., & Sales, B. (in press). A social science perspective on the law of guardianship: Directions for improving the process and practice. *Law and Psychology Review*.

Wexler, D. B. (1981). *Mental health law: Major issues*. New York: Plenum.

Whobrey, L., Sales, B. D., & Elwork, A. (1981). Applying social psychological research to witness credibility law. In L. Bickman (Ed.), *Applied social psychology annual* (Vol. 2, pp. 189–210). Beverly Hills, CA: Sage.

Wursten, A., & Sales, B. (1988). Community psychologists in state legislative decision making. *American Journal of Community Psychology, 16*, 487–502.

---

[1]A series of authored books, with supplements to maintain currency, devoted to covering the law affecting mental health professionals in each of the 50 states, the District of Columbia, and the federal jurisdictions. Volumes covering Arizona, Minnesota, New Jersey, New York, Massachusetts, and Texas are currently in print or in press. Volumes covering California, Georgia, Washington, the District of Columbia, and Wisconsin are drafted and undergoing final revisions before going into production. Volumes covering 20 other jurisdictions are currently under development.

STEPHEN J. CECI

COGNITIVE AND SOCIAL FACTORS IN CHILDREN'S TESTIMONY

S tephen J. Ceci is the Helen L. Carr Professor of Developmental Psychology at Cornell University, where he has been a professor for the past 15 years. He received his doctorate in developmental psychology from the University of Exeter, England, in 1978.

Ceci's honors include a Senior Fullbright–Hayes Award, a Research Career Development Award from the National Institute for Child Health and Human Development, the Mensa Senior Research Award, an IBM Supercomputing Prize for Social Sciences, and the Arthur R. Rickter Award. He has been a member of eight editorial boards, including *Developmental Psychology*, *Child Development*, *Journal of Experimental Child Psychology*, *Law and Human Behavior*, and *Psychological Bulletin*.

Ceci is a member-at-large of the Executive Committee of Division 7 of the American Psychological Association (APA), a fellow of Divisions 1, 3, 7, and 41 of APA, a fellow of the American Psychological Society, and past program chair of Divisions 1 and 7 of APA. He is currently an advisor to the Science Directorate of APA and a member of the Council of Editorial Advisors of APA. In 1990, Ceci received an endowment chair at Cornell University.

Ceci has conducted research on children's testimonial issues for over a decade, as part of his 20-year-old research on children's cognitive development. Since receiving his doctorate in 1978, he has published

150 articles, chapters, and books. His writings range from children's intellectual development to factors that influence their testimonial accuracy. During the past few years, Ceci has given invited addresses at the British Psychological Society, APA, the Eastern Psychological Association, and the Midwest Psychological Association as well as at colloquia at approximately 50 universities. Ceci is currently working on a long-term project involving methods of maximizing children's reporting accuracy; the project is being funded by the National Science Foundation.

COGNITIVE AND SOCIAL FACTORS IN CHILDREN'S TESTIMONY

T here is an emotional battle being waged today in our nation's court-rooms, universities, and professional societies. It revolves around the credibility of children's testimony.

To listen to one side, one would think that everything that a child tells a social worker or therapist must be believed: Because it is hard for children to reveal the details of their victimization, when they do so, we must believe them. To listen to the other side in this battle, one would think that because young children are more vulnerable to erroneous suggestions and social demands than older children and adults, they should not be believed when they claim to have been sexually molested.

I think that this battle over children's suggestibility boils down to whether one focuses on "numerators" or "denominators." One who focuses on numerators sees the issue from the perspective of the prosecution, aware of the large numbers of sexual assaults that are never reported or are reported but never prosecuted. One who focuses on denominators sees the issue from the perspective of the defense, aware of the error component contained in the large number of allegations. To see these competing perspectives in stark contrast, consider the numerators first: Approximately 40% of all reports of child abuse and neglect that are made to state central registrars each year are "substantiated" following a perfunctory investigation (National Center for Child Abuse and Neglect, 1993). These substantiated cases form the numerator and are regarded by some as an index of true allegations.

Although I assume that most of the 40% of cases that come to be substantiated are true allegations of sexual abuse, I also assume that some portion of these cases may not be true, and although I have no way of knowing if this portion is large, in terms of the sheer number of cases, it may be nontrivial in magnitude. Denominators focus on the proportion of substantiated cases that are constituted by true cases.

Thus, numerators emphasize the large number of children who are truly abused each year and the ineffectiveness of law enforcement in prosecuting and protecting these children. Pope and Hudson (1992) estimated "prevalence rates of 27%–51% for narrowly defined childhood sexual abuse by an older perpetrator (e.g., sexual assaults), and 31%–67% if noncontact experiences are included" (p. 460). Even skeptics of these numbers (e.g., Kutchinsky, 1992; Wexler, 1990) agree that no matter which figures one accepts, the problem of sexual abuse is enormous given that even the lower figure still places the absolute number of abuse cases at over 100,000 children per year.

Denominators, on the other hand, emphasize the possibility that at least some claims of sexual abuse are false. The size of this portion is anyone's guess, and I am personally unimpressed by past attempts to quantify these estimates—they are almost certainly little more than guesses. Those who emphasize the numerator put a pro-prosecution spin on the scientific and clinical findings (e.g., arguing that children may be suggestible in relation to some things but are not nearly as suggestible concerning salient events, particularly those occurring to their own bodies). To focus on the denominator, on the other hand, prods one to put a pro-defense spin on the data (e.g., seeing suggestibility under every rock). Thus, although those who view the denominator decry the suggestive questioning of young children, the use of multiple interviews for a child who has refused to disclose abuse on prior occasions and the use of fantasy play, imagery inductions, hypnotic regression, and "memory work" that make it easier for the child to disclose, those who view the numerator argue that many abused children will not disclose the details of their victimization in the absence of some of these techniques. In fact, the latter rightly point to the probability that many instances of true abuse go unsubstantiated because of lack of aggressive and persistent questioning.

My colleague Maggie Bruck came up with an interesting analogy to this battle between numerators and denominators: Suppose that you have invented a drug that is an effective cancer treatment for some people. But suppose this drug will create cancer in some individuals who are cancer-free. Assuming that you have no way of knowing which individuals have cancer and which do not, would you administer drug to everyone? Obviously not. Would you administer it only to those individuals whom you suspect might be at high risk for cancer, say a 4 out of 5 chance of having it? Probably not, because the risk of infecting the 20% who did not have the disease is too great a price to pay.

I hope to convince you that the situation regarding children's suggestibility is somewhat like the cancer analogy. Those viewing the numerator are right in pointing out that children who have been victimized often do not disclose the details of their victimization easily: If they are simply asked open-ended questions such as "Is there something you wish to tell me?", many will never disclose. Unless these children are pursued over multiple interviews, using leading questions and "memory work" techniques (e.g., visually guided imagery), then true instances of abuse will go undetected, and these children will remain vulnerable to revictimization.

On the other hand, there is reason to fear that if one pursues children who were not abused in this same manner (i.e., with multiple interviews, "memory work" techniques, and repeated suggestive questions), there is at least a chance that this will result in their making false disclosures. Later, I describe research in this area, but for now the point that I wish to make is simply that there seems to be a dilemma between doing all we can do to elicit disclosures of actual abuse (i.e., treating cancer in a child) and simultaneously avoiding anything that might increase the risk of false disclosures (i.e., inducing cancer in a healthy child). Fortunately, there are steps midway between these two poles that can and should be adhered to. I comment on these in the conclusion to this chapter.

As both a scientist who has studied children's reports for nearly 20 years and as the father of a first grader, I think it would be truly awful to ever lose sight of the enormity of child abuse in the United States today. We rightly recoil at an earlier generation's denial of the pervasiveness of the problem, but I also think that we cannot ignore the possibility of false allegations. We must always denominate the reality of true disclosures with the risk of false disclosures. All of this is my way of saying that although I think that false claims exist, and perhaps in nontrivial numbers, I also believe that, in absolute numbers, the numerator (true accusations) is frighteningly large.

I am asked each year to enter court as an expert witness in hundreds of cases (503 in 1992), including most of the high-profile day-care cases involving allegations of mass abuse and the acrimonious custody disputes between celebrities that appear in the national media. I almost never agree to do this because I believe that the role I can play as an educator of juries, attorneys, and policymakers is easier to accomplish in my writings than under cross-examination in an adversarial system more geared to scoring clever debate points than arriving at the truth. In my few experiences as an expert witness, I declined a fee, suggesting that both sides make a donation to my university or to a charity of their choice.

Why am I telling you this about me? Because once I begin describing my recent studies, you may wonder if I am someone who puts an advocacy spin on my research to profit by serving as an expert for one side or another. I am not. But I also do not make any apologies for being a denominator; my best reading of the corpus of scientific research leads me to worry about the possibility of false allegations. It is not a tribute to one's scientific integrity to walk down the middle of the road if the data are more to one side. As I hope to show, the data are somewhat off-center, although not so egregiously as to discredit children from testifying. Later, I outline conditions that increase my confidence that a child witness is presenting an accurate disclosure. But first I share the basis of my beliefs in the real possibility of false accusations.

Historical Trends

From the earliest times, society has been conflicted over whether young children can resist the suggestions of an adult who attempts to mislead them. Although some early commentators expressed the opinion that young children are hopeless sponges, soaking up the suggestions of manipulative adults (e.g., Then we will no longer be infants tossed back and forth by the cunning and craftiness of men and their deceitful scheming; Ephesians 4:14), others oppositely opined that children were uniquely able to resist all forms of adult contamination (e.g., Out of the mouth of babes and nursing infants you have perfected praise; Matthew 21:16).

Scientists have not been immune to the conflict over children's proneness to suggestibility: Research on children's eyewitness testimony is both contradictory and confusing, even for those who work in this area (for a review see Ceci & Bruck, 1993b).

In this chapter, I focus on the two primary factors that influence children's suggestibility, namely, cognitive and social influences. Each of these influences is composed of a family of specific variables, which I touch on as I review early and modern studies of suggestibility and present the results of five recent interview studies that my colleagues and I conducted. Before doing so, however, it is necessary to say something about the construct of suggestibility itself.

What is meant by suggestibility? Traditionally, suggestibility has been conceptualized in terms of information being incorporated into memory (e.g., Andrews, 1964; Loftus, 1979). According to this account, *suggestibility* is defined as "the extent to which individuals come to accept and subsequently incorporate post-event information into their memory recollections" (Gudjonsson, 1986, p. 195; see also Powers, Andriks, & Loftus, 1979). This definition implies that (a) suggestibility is unconscious (i.e., postevent information is unwittingly incorporated into memory); (b) suggestibility results from the provision of information following an event as opposed to preceding it—hence, the adjective *postevent*; and (c) suggestibility is a memory-based phenomenon, as opposed to a social one—thus, it results from the unconscious incorporation of suggested information into the memory trace, in contrast to conscious deceit.

However, my colleagues and I have argued for a more inclusive definition of suggestibility, one that is more in accord with both legal and lay usage. According to this account, suggestibility concerns the degree to which children's encoding, storage, retrieval, and/or reporting of events can be influenced by a range of internal and external factors (Ceci & Bruck, 1993b). This definition implies that

- it is possible to accept erroneous information and yet be fully conscious of its divergence from a perceived event, as in the case of "confabulation," acquiescence to social demands, or lying; hence, these forms of suggestibility do not involve the alteration of memory
- suggestibility can result from the provision of information either preceding or following an event (in the former case, the provision of stereotypes may influence how information gets processed)
- suggestibility can result from social factors (e.g., bribes, threats) as well as cognitive ones.

This broader view of suggestibility encompasses all of the ways that one can be influenced by subtle suggestions, expectations, stereotypes, and leading questions that can unconsciously alter reports, as well as by explicit bribes, threats, and other forms of inducement that can consciously alter reports. Any of these factors may be involved when a child comes to court to tell his or her story. Because each of these factors is associated with unique developmental and individual differences, no simple recipe can be given regarding the presumed suggestibility of an entire age group; such a determination requires a case-by-case analysis to decide whether a particular child in a particular case is suggestible, determined on the basis of the specific cognitive and social factors operative in that case and in that child.

In this chapter, I describe several studies of children's reports that I think raise more questions than they answer, especially if we try to extrapolate principles from them to the world of children's testimony. One might wonder why I would choose to spend time on studies that do not seem to be generalizable to the courtroom. I do so because although these studies do not supply definitive answers, they do serve an extremely important purpose: They debunk myths that have been circulating among expert witnesses in child-abuse cases and in the pages of many journals. For this reason, these studies should be valuable to those who testify in court or who prepare documents for admission to court. Before describing these studies, however, it is useful to place them in both historical and contemporary context.

Early Studies of Suggestibility

The first experiments on children's suggestibility were conducted at the close of the 19th century by Maurice Small (1891–1897), a student of G. Stanley Hall. Small reported that when asked if they smelled a perfume sprayed from an atomizer into the air, first graders were more likely than older children to claim that they could smell a fragrance even though it was only distilled water. Small also reported that first graders were more suggestible on a variety of other tasks. Without exception, the early 20th-century European studies agreed with Small's findings of the extent to which children were prone to report distortion. Beginning in the early 20th century with the experiments of Alfred Binet (Binet, 1900; Lipmann, 1911; Stern, 1910; Varendonck, 1911) and concluding in the 1920s and early 1930s with empirical studies (Aveling & Hargreaves, 1921; Messerschmidt, 1933; Otis, 1924; Sherman, 1925), these early researchers expressed the view that children were extremely susceptible to leading questions and could not be trusted to resist an adult interviewer's suggestions. A typical study of this epoch involved asking children about the color of the beard of a man who visited their school. Although the man had no beard, many children nevertheless supplied a color.

In his first of three reviews in the *Psychological Bulletin*, Whipple (1909) summarized the work of Binet, Stern, Lobsien, Borst, and Plüschke and concluded that according to these reports, children were in every way inferior to adults as reflected by their suggestibility: "The child ... observes not so much what is placed before him as what his instincts and interests prompt him to observe" (p. 163).

However, on the basis of Borst's work, Whipple was optimistic that children could be trained to become more reliable reporters. Two years later, Whipple (1911) reviewed the dispute between a German pediatrician named Baginsky, who declared that children "are the most dangerous of all witnesses and ... that their testimony be excluded from court record whenever possible" (p. 308), and his Hungarian counterpart, Gross, who criticized Baginsky's conclusion because it was based on unsystematic observation of small numbers of children and failed to take into consideration adult baselines of unreliability. Gross suggested that children make errors that are different from but not more serious than those of adults, who may be influenced by prejudice, emotion, and intoxication. Although the other experts cited in this debate (Dupree and Binet) favored Baginsky's position, Whipple (1911) was cautious, concluding "that the whole matter could be very simply cleared up by an appropriate experiment. Why not subject observers of different ages to a graded series of event-tests?" p. 308). It was not until the 1980s that his suggestion was taken up with any seriousness by psychologists.

Whipple's (1912) third review in the *Psychological Bulletin* referred to a series of studies on the effects of training and elicitation methods on the accuracy of children's reports (e.g., the works of Bèaden, Frankel, Lipmann, and Vos). The results of these studies were mixed and, according to Whipple, open to interpretation. In this article, Whipple described the work of Varendonck (1911), a Belgian psychologist who "conducted a half dozen striking experiments upon school children to demonstrate the unreliability of their reports when implicative and expectative questions are employed" (p. 268). Varendonck used his data to throw doubt on the testimony of two young girls who had accused a man of murdering their playmate. Whipple expressed unbridled enthusiasm for the validity of Varendonck's research and its forensic application: "The presentation of his testimony reached the jury and induced a verdict of 'not guilty.' The psychology of testimony has, therefore, found its way formally into the court room and saved a man's life" (p. 268).

Whipple (1912) provided additional European examples of the unreliability of children's testimony. For example, Märbe (1913) testified as an expert witness against German school girls who provided the court with detailed and "decidedly incriminating" testimony that their teacher had made sexual advances toward them. Märbe convinced the jury that the young girls' testimony was unreliable because all but two of their claims became self-contradictory under cross-examination and because although the remaining statements were consistent, they were not supported by medical evidence. Along similar lines, the German psychologist Mehl testified against a 13-year-old girl who claimed that a boarder in her family's house had made improper advances toward her. Mehl reviewed the girl's statements, examined the house, and concluded that she was a mental defective whose story was untrue. By the conclusion of his final *Psychological Bulletin* review, Whipple was no longer cautious; he had become a staunch advocate of the position that young children are highly suggestible and capable of making serious errors in their testimony, even when they testify about matters of great personal importance.

Whipple's reviews are still cited as definitive summaries of early research (e.g., Baxter, 1990; Ceci & Bruck, 1993b; Goodman, 1984; Lindberg, 1991). And, because these reviews were the only translations available of the European research, they had enormous influence on the English-speaking scientific and legal communities, aptly expressed in a popular law text of the time: "Create, if you will, an idea of what the child is to hear or see, and the child is very likely to see or hear what you desire" (Brown, 1926, p. 133).

A careful reading of Whipple's articles, however, gives rise to several concerns. First, it is often not clear whether he is merely citing opinions of expert witnesses or whether his conclusions are supported by empirical data. Even in the latter case, his summaries are so brief that the reader is often left with no clear idea of the experimental procedures or outcomes of these early European studies. Second, the paradigms used by these early researchers are open to challenge on ecological grounds: Put simply, they lack the force and salience of the events that bring children to court. It is one thing for a child to be susceptible to adult suggestions about the color of a stranger's beard or the length of a line, but it is another matter to claim that children are prone to suggestions about whether their bodies were touched and by whom. Hence, researchers have been reluctant to generalize these early European results to the forensic arena. Although there has been concern about the testimonial competence of preschoolers, not one study in the first 80 years of this century included preschool-aged subjects. (In recent years, this void has begun to be filled; since 1980, over 30 studies relevant to the suggestibility of children's eyewitness testimony have included a preschool sample.) The awareness of the limitations of the early research on children's suggestibility has spawned a cottage industry of research examining children's reports about salient events. (See Ceci & Bruck, 1993b, for a more comprehensive account of this research.)

How does a researcher conduct an ethically acceptable suggestibility experiment that contains conditions that are similar to those experienced by an actual child witness? Of course, it would be unacceptable to see if an interviewer could persuade children who had been abused that the abuse had never occurred. Similarly, it would be unacceptable to determine if nonabused children could be led to falsely "remember" being sexually abused. In the past several years, however, a number of researchers have developed new paradigms that, although they do not mirror all of the conditions that bring children to court, do contain important elements of these conditions. I describe two lines of research that illustrate these new paradigms and discuss what they tell us about the role of basic research in understanding children's eyewitness testimony. The two new lines of research are (a) movement away from controlled laboratory settings to naturally occurring settings that are imbued with high levels of stress, loss of control, possible embarrassment, and personal participation (as opposed to mere observation) and (b) movement away from focusing on the child's role in suggestibility to focusing on both the child and the interviewer.

Modern Studies of Children's Suggestibility

In response to the criticism that earlier studies were not forensically relevant because they did not examine how children respond to questions about stressful events that involve their own bodies or about other salient events that are personally experienced, a number of researchers have designed studies in which children are asked misleading questions about being touched, including on their genitals. In some studies, children are questioned about their previous interactions with an experimenter in which they actually participated in versus only observed an experience (e.g., Rudy & Goodman, 1991), whereas in other studies children are questioned after being inoculated by a physician (Bruck, Ceci, Francoeur, & Barr, in press; Goodman, Hirschman, Hepps, & Rudy, 1991) or given genital examinations by their pediatrician (Bruck et al., in press; Saywitz, Goodman, Nicholas, & Moan, 1991).

For example, Saywitz et al. (1991) examined 5- and 7-year-old girls' memories of medical examinations. Half of each age group had a scoliosis examination (for curvature of the spine), and the other half had a genital examination. Children were interviewed at either 1 or 4 weeks after their examination. They were asked suggestive and nonsuggestive questions that were abuse related (e.g., How many times did the doctor kiss you?) or nonabuse related (e.g., Didn't the doctor look at your feet first?) Although, initially, the older children were more accurate than the younger children on most questions, some of these age differences disappeared after the 4-week delay. Most important, although there were age differences on suggestive abuse questions, only a few children actually gave incorrect responses.

Saywitz et al. (1991) concluded that children's inaccurate reports usually involved errors of omission rather than those of commission. That is, children in the genital-examination condition frequently did not disclose their genital contact (i.e., errors of omission) unless specifically asked to do so with leading questions (e.g., Did the doctor touch you here?). In the scoliosis-examination condition, when children were asked the same questions (which were misleading in this condition), the incidence of false reports (i.e., errors of commission) was very low:

> Leading questions were often necessary to elicit information from children about actual events they had experienced (genital touching).... The children ... were generally accurate in reporting specific and personal things that had happened to them. If these results can be generalized to investigations of abuse, they suggest that normal children are unlikely to make up details of sexual acts when nothing abusive happened. They suggest that children will not easily yield to an interviewer's suggestion that something sexual occurred when in fact it did not, especially if nonintimidating interviewers ask questions children can comprehend. (Goodman & Clarke-Stewart, 1991, pp. 102–103)

There are two clear conclusions from this research. First, children who have been exposed to genital touching may not disclose this unless they are pursued with leading questions and other suggestive techniques.

Second, earlier studies of children's suggestibility may have overestimated the extent to which children are suggestible because of the studies' reliance on events and settings that are unimportant to children and on events in which the children acted as passive observers as opposed to actual participants. On the basis of these findings, some have claimed that even very young children are quite resistant to erroneous suggestions about personally experienced events that are salient, in contrast to the historical literature that depicts children as highly suggestible:

> There is now no real question that the law and many developmentalists were wrong in their assumption that children are highly vulnerable to suggestion, at least in regard to salient details. Although some developmentalists may be challenged to find developmental differences in suggestibility in increasingly arcane circumstances, as a practical matter who really cares whether 3-year-old children are (more) suggestible about peripheral details in events that they witnessed than are 4-year-old children? Perhaps the question has some significance for developmental theory, but surely it has little or no meaning for policy and practice in child protection and law. (Melton, 1992, p. 154)

Even among researchers who work in medical settings, however, it is important to point out that there are contradictory results. For example, Ornstein, Gordon, and Larus (1992) found that when children were later questioned about their memories of a visit to the pediatrician, 3-year-olds were more prone than 6-year-olds to make false claims in response to suggestive questions about silly events that involved bodily contact (e.g., Did the nurse lick your knee?). Oates and Shrimpton (1991) also found that preschoolers were more suggestible than older children concerning previously experienced events that involved bodily touching, and Bruck et al. (in press) found that preschoolers were suggestible concerning the identity of the individual who inoculated them if they were subjected to repeated erroneous suggestions about that person. Thus, there is some evidence that the conclusions from the early European studies that characterized young children as highly suggestible sometimes apply when the events are salient, involve bodily touching, and are personally experienced. The most recent research findings seem to reinforce this conclusion.

Interviewer Dynamics

In addition to the move away from laboratory studies to everyday settings in which children's bodies are touched for medical reasons, the second research innovation has been a focus on examining the effects of various components of the memory interview. This has arisen in response to the concern that the interviewing procedures of earlier studies were less intense than those that bring children to court, so much so as to result in an alleged underestimation of children's suggestibility (Raskin & Esplin, 1991; Steller, 1991). According to researchers with this contention, the interviewing procedures that have been used in traditional laboratory studies differ in three ways from those that are used in the forensic arena.

First, children who come to court are frequently questioned weeks, months, or even years after the occurrence of an event (as opposed to the very brief delays that are common in most memory studies). Second, it is rarely the case that actual child witnesses are interviewed only one time by one interviewer under relaxed conditions. Most child witnesses are officially interviewed between 3.5 and 11 times before appearing in court (Gray, 1993; McGough, in press), and some children are interviewed weekly for years about the same event prior to testifying in court (e.g., they may have been involved in suggestive practices in therapy sessions). Some researchers have suggested that the incessant use of leading questions and suggestions in these repeated interviews may result in a qualitatively different type of report distortion than that arising from a single misleading question in a single postevent interview. Both implicit and explicit suggestions can be contained in the interview through the use of bribes, threats, repetition of certain questions, or the induction of stereotypes and expectancies (Ceci & Bruck, 1993b). Finally, in actual forensic situations, children are questioned by parents, therapists, and legal officials (i.e., adults who carry status and power in the child's eyes). In such situations, children may be more likely to comply with the suggestions of the interviewers than in analogous experimental situations, where interviewers are generally less important or less imposing to them.

Although it is very difficult to create experimental conditions that reflect the confluence of forensically relevant variables (e.g., stressful episodes, repeated and suggestive questioning, questioning over prolonged periods by interviewers who possess status in the child's eyes), researchers are beginning to examine how children's reports are influenced by the repetition of suggestions in multiple interviews prior to and following the occurrence of an event. In addition, researchers have focused on the potential effects that a particular interviewer bias may have on the reports elicited from young children. In what follows, I confine the discussion to several studies conducted at Cornell and McGill Universities by my colleagues and me designed specifically to address these issues.

Several Recent Interview Studies

A review of therapy transcripts and law-enforcement interviews with children suspected of having been abused in several mass-allegation day-care cases reveals that it is common for a child in these cases to make his or her first "disclosure" about abuse in a therapy session in which the therapist is pursuing a single hypothesis about the basis of the child's difficulties (see portions of transcripts in Ceci & Bruck, 1993a, 1993b). Such single-minded pursuit by a therapist usually entails techniques that are potentially suggestive and stereotype inducing (e.g., fantasy inductions, "self-empowerment" training, hypnotic age regressions, visually guided imagery inductions, role playing, symbol interpretation).[1] Following sustained periods of therapy, some children make disclosures that are then pursued in multiple law-enforcement and child protective services interviews. My colleagues and I patterned some of our experimental manipulations after materials that we collected over the past decade from court transcripts and therapy tapes, albeit in an attenuated form. Thus, we built into our studies the following factors: multiple suggestive interviews, over very long retention intervals, involving recollections of stressful experiences, entailing bodily events. We have come to believe that the majority of cases of children's suggestibility in actual criminal investigations and acrimonious custody adjudications bear little resemblance to the research studies that have tested suggestibility for a single leading question posed for the first time during a single interview. Given that child witnesses usually are interviewed by therapists, social workers, and law-enforcement professionals many times (and informally interviewed even more times by parents and siblings), we sought to build this factor into our experiments as well.

Study 1: The Effect of Repeated Suggestions on Children's Reports

From a theoretical standpoint, Dawes (1992) argued that the failure to test alternative hypotheses that are believable (on the basis of prior

---

[1] I am not claiming that all or even most therapists behave in this manner. The transcripts that I have been sent by attorneys and law-enforcement personnel that exhibit these problems are undoubtedly a highly select subgroup. However, I received 503 requests from attorneys to examine transcripts during 1992, and approximately one third of them could be characterized this way. (This year the number of requests from attorneys is running at an even higher rate because of several media appearances I made. If I can project this phenomenon to colleagues of mine who are also requested to examine transcripts or audio or video tapes of interviews, the numbers quickly add up.) So, although only a small number of therapists may behave in this manner, numerically, it could nevertheless be nontrivial.

knowledge) can pose serious risks to obtaining a scientifically adequate answer. This point is just as true for forensic investigators and therapists as it is for scientists. Failure to test an alternative to one's initial hypothesis can lead one to ignore inconsistent evidence and can shape an experiment toward eliciting consistent information. In decision research, this is termed a *confirmatory bias*.

Interviewer Hypotheses. In the study I report here, we examined how an interviewer's hypothesis can influence the accuracy of young children's reports. In our analysis of interviews conducted by therapists, police, and social workers, we observed what many others have also observed, namely, that interviewers and therapists rarely test alternative hypotheses. (For reviews of the evidence that therapists rarely test alternatives and often fall prey to illusory correlations and confirmatory biases, see Alloy & Tabachnik, 1984; Brehm & Smith, 1986; Kayne & Alloy, 1988; Maddux, 1993). Instead, many if not most interviewers exhibit a confirmatory bias, seeking to elicit support for their hypotheses about what the child experienced and engaging in little questioning about events that are inconsistent with their hypotheses. As a particularly telling example of this, consider the following interview from a recent court case (*State of New Jersey v. Margaret Kelly Michaels*, 1993, pp. 45–50). The interviewer was an experienced social worker and was occasionally joined in the interview by a police detective. I comment between sections to illustrate a number of inadvisable practices that I frequently observe in interviews by social workers, law-enforcement professionals, and therapists.

I (interviewer):	We have gotten a lot of other kids to help us since I last saw you.
C (child):	No. I don't have to.
I:	Oh come on. Did we tell you she is in jail?
C:	Yes. My mother already told me.

It is obvious that this interviewer is not neutral regarding the defendant's guilt, insinuating that because she is now jail, the child need not be afraid of her (if he ever was, which is not clear).

I: Well, we can get out of here real quick if you just tell me what you told me last time.

There is no desire on the part of this interviewer to test an alternative hypothesis; rather, he seeks to have the child to reaffirm on tape what he said in an earlier interview.

C: I forgot.
I: No you didn't. I know you didn't.

C: I did, I did.
I: No, come on.
C: I forgot.
I: I thought we were friends last time.
C: I'm not your friend any more.
I: How come?
C: Because I hate you.
I: Is it because we are talking about stuff you don't want to talk about? What, are you a monster now? Huh?

This interviewing borders on being coercive. There is little respect for the child's wish not to discuss the matter.

I: We talked to a few more of your buddies—we talked to everybody now. And everyone told me about the nap room, and the bathroom stuff, and the music room stuff, and the choir stuff, and the peanut butter stuff, and nothing surprises me any more.

This is further evidence that no alternative hypothesis is being tested. The interviewer essentially tells the child that his friends have already told on the defendant and that he, the child, should do the same.

C: I hate you.
I: No you don't.... You just don't like talking about this, but you don't hate me.
C: Yes, I do hate you.
I: We can finish this real fast if you just show me real fast what you showed me last time.
C: No.
I: I will let you play my tape recorder.... Come on, do you want to help us out? Do you want to help us keep her in jail, huh? ... Tell me what happened to (three other children). Tell me what happened to them. Come on.... I need your help again, buddy. Come on.

C: No.
I: You told us everything once before. Do you want to undress my dolly? Let's get done with this real quick so we could go to Kings to get Popsicles.... Did (defendant) ever tell you she could get out of jail?

The interviewer comes close to bribing the child for a disclosure by implying that the aversive interview can be terminated as soon as the child repeats what he said earlier. Popsicles and playing with a tape recorder are offered as rewards

P (police detective): She could never get out.
C: I know that.
P: Cause I got her.... She is very afraid of me. She is so scared of me.
I: She cries when she sees him (indicating the police detective) because she is so scared.... What happened to (another child) with the wooden spoon? If you don't remember in words, maybe you can show me.

There is no attempt to test the hypothesis that the defendant did not do what the interviewers believe she did. Instead, we see further attempts to vilify the defendant to make it more likely the child will confirm their hypothesis about her.

C: I forgot what happened, too.
I: You remember. You told your mommy about everything, about the music room, and the nap room. And all the stuff. You want to help her stay in jail, don't you? So she doesn't bother you any more.... Your mommy told me that you had a picture of yourself in your room and there was blood on your penis. Who hurt you?
C: (Child names the defendant).
I: So, your penis was bleeding, oh. Your penis was bleeding. Tell me something else: Was your hiney bleeding, too?
C: No.
I: Did (defendant) bleed, too?
C: No.
I: Are you sure she didn't bleed?
C: Yes.... I saw her penis, too.
I: Show me on the (anatomical) doll.... You saw that? Oh.
C: She doodied on me.... She peed on us.
I: And did you have to pee on her at all?
C: Yeah.
I: You did? And who peed on her, you and who else?
C: (Child names a male friend)
I: Didn't his penis bleed?
C: Yes.
I: It did? What made it bleed? What was she doing?
C: She was bleeding.
I: She was bleeding in her penis? Did you have to put your penis in her penis? Yes or No?
C: Yeah.... And I peed in her penis.
I: What was that like? What did it feel like?
C: Like a shot.
I: Did (friend) have to put his penis in her penis, too?
C: Yes, at the same time.

I: At the same time? How did you do that?

C: We chopped our penises off.

I: So, she was bleeding in her penis and you had your penis and your friend's inside her penis.

C: At the same time.

This type of exchange is very common in the transcripts I am sent: When the child says something that is not part of the interviewer's hypothesis (in this case, that the children chopped off their penises), the interviewer ignores it. There is no attempt to pursue it, probably out of fear that the child may embellish this claim with even more incredible claims.

At this point, the child and interviewer began discussing a stream of events in which the child alleged that the defendant urinated in his mouth and he urinated in her mouth; he and others were made to walk in her urine and to slide on the classroom floor in her urine. Nowhere in this interview was there any evidence that an alternative hypothesis was being tested. Specifically, there was no attempt by this interviewer to try to get the child to assent to an incompatible hypothesis (e.g., one in which the child's pediatrician put his penis in the child's mouth, or the sheriff made him drink his urine, or the child was just teasing about the defendant bleeding). As can be seen, there is no attempt to encourage the child to deny that any of this happened. Although it is not possible to know how much of what the child reported was accurate, there is a certain suspiciousness about his disclosures, which was even more troubling in the interviews of some of his classmates. Partly, this is due to the heavy-handed use of coercive tactics (e.g., "If you tell me real quick, we can go get popsicles"; refusal to believe that the child has forgotten or has a legitimate motive for not wanting to repeat an earlier remark he allegedly made to his mother), but partly there is an absence of incredulity on the part of the interviewer. I think this often results from a confusion among advocates between taking everything the child says seriously and believing everything a child says. If this type of interviewing is widespread, then it raises some real concerns because, as I show, we are beginning to understand that even mild versions of such interview techniques can increase the risk of eliciting false reports, especially if they are conducted over long delay intervals.[2] Finally, such interviews

---

[2]There is another reason why I am troubled by such interviews. As a parent, I have seen how easily my daughter and her friends lapse into scatological humor with the slightest encouragement from an adult. One wonders if the interviewers realize this about some children. In fact, one wonders why they often tout themselves as specializing in "child-centered" or "developmentally sensitive" interviewing practices. This often seems to mean little more than couching questions in a language structure that the child can understand. Nowhere is there any evidence that this type of interviewer appreciates the child's theory of mind or suggestibility or the salient social factors operative in the child's life. Hence, as a developmentalist, the nomenclature *developmentally sensitive* strikes me as a gratuitous presumption.

are impeachable in courts of law because they not only challenge common sense about the suggestibility of young children, but they violate state and national codes of interviewing practices such as the following:

> During the interview process, the interviewer must remain open-minded and try not to be influenced by any preconceived ideas. . . . As an interviewer, you must remain open, neutral, and objective, and beware of any reactions which could be interpreted as reinforcing certain responses ... Avoid leading questions. . . . Never threaten or try to force a reluctant child to talk or continue an interview. (National Center for the Prosecution of Child Abuse, 1987, p. 473)

Interviewer's Hypotheses. In the study that I describe next, preschoolers were exposed to an event and then interviewed 1 month later. The interviewer, a trained social worker, was given a 1-page report containing information that she was told might have occurred. She was asked to conduct an interview to determine what the child could, in fact, still recall. The only instruction given to the social worker was that she should begin by asking the child for a free narrative of what had transpired, avoiding all forms of suggestions and leading questions. Following this, she was allowed to use any strategies that she felt necessary to elicit the most accurate recollection from the child. The report contained two types of information about the event that the children allegedly had experienced: accurate information and erroneous information. For example, if the event involved Child A touching Child B's nose and Child B rubbing her own stomach, the interviewer might be told that Child A had touched Child B's toe and that Child B had in turn rubbed her own stomach.

The information in the report influenced the interviewer's hypothesis about what had transpired and strongly influenced the dynamics of the interview, with the interviewer eventually shaping some of the children's reports to be consistent with her hypothesis, even when it was inaccurate. When the interviewer was accurately informed, she elicited recall that was 70–100% correct. However, when she was misinformed, 34% of the 3- and 4-year-olds and 18% of the 5- and 6-year-olds corroborated one or more events that the interviewer falsely believed had occurred. It is interesting that the children seemed to appear more credible as their interviews unfolded. Many children initially stated details inconsistently or reluctantly, but as the interviewer persisted in asking leading questions about events that had not occurred but were consistent with her hypothesis, a significant number of these children abandoned all contradictions and hesitancy and endorsed the interviewer's erroneous hypothesis.

One month later, we gave the social worker's notes from this interview to another interviewer and asked her to reinterview the child.

The original interviewer's notes ended up serving the same function as the report given to the first social worker, namely, they helped the second interviewer form a hypothesis. The second interviewer not only got the children to continue to assent to erroneous statements consistent with her hypothesis but children did so with increasing levels of confidence and in increasing numbers. If we had continued to reinterview the children in this study, each time passing along the notes of the prior interviewer to the new interviewer, there is no telling how far astray the children might have been lead. After two such interviews, children gave detailed but false accounts of bodily touching (e.g., their knees being licked and marbles inserted into their ears).

Ideally, a forensic interview should be a form of scientifically guided inquiry. And, as already asserted, a hallmark of such an inquiry is the attempt to disprove a hypothesis by giving alternative hypotheses a fair chance of confirmation. Simply put, scientists try to arrive at truth by ruling out rival hypotheses—particularly the most reasonable rivals—and by attempting to falsify their favored hypothesis (Ceci & Bronfenbrenner, 1991; Dawes, 1992). Similarly, for interviewers to obtain the most reliable information, they should also attempt to rule out rival hypotheses rather than exclusively attempt to confirm their favored hypothesis. Because of the needs of child protective service interviewers, however, it is not feasible or even desirable to insist that they generate and test all conceivable hypotheses or, conversely, be "blinded" from all relevant information that pertains to the prosecutor's main hypothesis. The latter could result in missed opportunities whenever an interviewer does not recognize the relevance of a given piece of information provided by the child. But, as I have described, the failure to test a rival hypothesis can result in various types of errors (e.g., suggestibility effects, misattributions, source confusions).

What relevance do these findings have for therapists? I have discussed this question with dozens of experienced clinical psychologists and psychiatrists, and although their answers are as numerous and varied as they are, a few commonalities emerge. Most claim that therapeutic goals are quite different from forensic goals, with some even purporting to be interested not at all in the latter but only in their client's feelings and interpretations about what may have happened. In contrast, the forensic interviewer wants only the facts and the context in which they occurred, not the witnesses' feelings about what may have happened. Clinicians do not usually see themselves as conducting law-enforcement interviews, and their goal may be to bring to fruition some intrapsychic material that they believe is at the root of their young client's problems. If this is their goal, then many techniques that are potentially suggestive (e.g., visually guided imagery inductions, fantasy play, role playing) may be suitable. A problem arises, however, when the client or the therapist gives testimony after many months of such therapy. I can make clearer these risks by describing another experiment, one conducted to illuminate the effects of visually guided imagery on young children's reality monitoring. Young children were asked repeatedly to visualize a scenario that could result in some of them subsequently claiming that they experienced it even though they did not.

Study 2: Effect of Repeated Visualizations on Children's Free Narratives

I asked children to think about events that were both actual events that they had experienced in their distant past (e.g., an accident that eventuated in stitches) and fictitious events that they had never experienced (e.g., getting their hand caught in a mousetrap and having to go to the hospital to get it removed).

There is a theoretical construct called *source-misattribution error* that refers to the problems that all people have in separating the sources of their memories. Occasionally, all people experience source misattribution difficulties. For example, if I showed you a mug book of photos and asked if you recognized someone who staged a mock theft minutes earlier and if the actual "thief's" photo was not in this mug book, you would probably correctly state that you could not find the thief's photo. But if a week later I ask you to examine a line-up that contained one of the individuals whose photo was in the mug book that you had inspected, you would be likely to incorrectly attribute this familiarity to actually having observed this person commit the mock crime. His face would be familiar, but you would misattribute the source of the familiarity to the crime rather than to the mug book. The questions I wished to pursue were whether young children exhibit source misattributions when they are encouraged to think about events that never occurred and whether they come to think that they actually experienced events that they only thought about. Although the analogy to therapy is imperfect, I think that such a study has relevance for the testimony of a child who has been in a certain type therapy for a long time, engaging in similar imagery inductions and "memory work."

Each week for 10 consecutive weeks, preschool children were individually interviewed by a trained adult. The adult showed the child a set of cards, each containing a different event. The child was invited to pick a card, and then the interviewer would read it to the child and ask if the event had ever happened to him or her. For example, when the child selected the card that read "Got finger caught in a mousetrap and had to go to the hospital to get the trap off," the interviewer would ask "Think real hard, and tell me if this ever happened to you. Can you remember going to the hospital with the mousetrap on your finger?" This is obviously a very simple procedure. Each week, the interviewer asked the child to think hard about each actual and fictitious event, with prompts to visualize the scene.

After 10 weeks, these preschool children were given a forensic interview by a new adult. All of these interviews were videotaped. The interviewer began by gaining the child's rapport, discussing events that were unrelated to the event in question, and giving the child the expectation that the interviewer wanted elaborated answers, not simple yes or no ones. Initially, the interviewer asked "Tell me if this ever happened to you: Did you ever get your finger caught in a mousetrap and have to go to the hospital to get the trap off?" Following the child's reply, the interviewer asked for additional details (e.g., "Can you tell me more?"). When the child indicated that he or she had no additional details, the interviewer asked a number of follow-up questions that were based on the child's answers. For instance, if the child said that she did go to the hospital to get the mousetrap off, the interviewer asked how she got there, who went with her, and what happened at the hospital.

I have been doing memory research with preschool children for 19 years, and I cannot recall being as surprised by the findings of another study as much as I was by the results of this experiment. I had anticipated that asking children to think about events repeatedly would result in later confusion about whether they had actually participated in the events, but I had no expectation that this would result in the sort of highly detailed, internally coherent narratives that the children produced. Fifty-eight percent of the children produced false narratives to one or more of the fictitious events, with 25% of the children producing false narratives to the majority of them. What was so surprising to me was the elaborateness of the children's narratives. They were very embellished, describing an internally coherent account of the context in which their finger got caught in the mousetrap as well as the affect associated with it.

Watching the children describe these fictitious events gave me an idea. Why not show the videotapes of these children to professionals and see if they could determine which events had actually occurred and which were fictitious. When I showed these videos to psychologists who specialize in interviewing children at two recent conferences, the results were sobering: Professionals were fooled by the children's narratives. They were not reliably different from chance at detecting which events were real because they could imagine such plausible, internally coherent narratives being fabricated. However, I agree with these professionals that the accounts did not appear to be fabrications if by fabrication one means "a conscious attempt to mislead a listener about the truth as one understands it" (Ceci & Bruck, 1993b). Although I cannot prove it in any scientifically satisfying manner, I believe that many of the children had come to believe what they were telling the interviewer. This is why they were so believable to professionals who watched them. They exhibited none of the typical signs of duping, teasing, or tricking. They seemed sincere, their facial expressions and affect were appropriate, and their narratives were filled with the kind of low-frequency details that make accounts seem plausible (e.g., "My brother Colin was trying to get Blowtorch [an action figure] from me, and I wouldn't let him take it from me, so he pushed me into the wood pile where the mousetrap was. And then my finger got caught in it. And then we went to the hospital, and my mommy, daddy, and Colin drove me there, to the hospital in our van, because it was far away. And the doctor put a bandage on this finger").

As can be seen, the child in this example supplied a plausible account, not simply yes or no answers. One can imagine how believable such children might be to someone who was not told the ground truth about this experiment—someone who was merely shown these children's "disclosures" and asked to judge their authenticity.

One further bit of evidence supports the contention that at least some of these children had come to believe that they had actually experienced the fictitious events. When ABC's news program *20/20* heard about this study, they requested to visit my lab and film some of these children. I agreed to allow them to do this and called some parents to ask if they would bring their children back for an interview with John Stossel, the *20/20* interviewer. One parent came in with her 4-year-old son and reported to us that she and her husband had thought that the experiment was over and had therefore explained to their son that the story about the mousetrap was fictitious and had never happened. She said that her son initially refused to accept this debriefing, claiming that he remembered it happening when the family lived in their former house. She and her husband continued to explain that the whole story was just in his imagination, that nothing like this had ever happened. Two days later, when the child came to do the *20/20* interview, Stossel asked the child if he had ever got his finger caught in a mousetrap and had to go to the hospital to get it off. The child's mother was shocked at the child's reply. He stated that he remembered this happening, and he proceeded to supply a richly detailed narrative. When Stossel challenged him, asking him if it was not the case that his mother had already explained that this never happened, the child protested, "But it really did happen. I remember it!" Although this child's insistence, in the presence of his mother, is not proof that he believed what he was saying about this fictitious event, it does suggest that he was not duping us for any obvious motive, given that the demand characteristics were all tilted against his claiming that he remembered this. I am presently pursuing this hypothesis with a new set of experiments, but it is too early to draw from them any conclusions.

Study 3: Effect of Repeated Suggestions

In many court cases, a constellation of factors has co-occurred. Children in these cases are given an expectancy about the defendant (e.g., the defendant might be an estranged parent who is criticized by the custodial parent in the child's presence, and the child comes to accept these criticisms as stable aspects of the estranged parent's character). As an example, in 1990 I was asked to write a stay of execution brief in a death row case in El Paso, Texas, in which the most important testimony at the original trial had been given by a child who claimed that she remembered seeing the defendant with blood on his shirt at his trailer. It was known that the child's mother had told her on numerous occasions that the defendant was a bad man and that she should not be friendly with him—long before he was accused of murder. From interviews with the child, it was clear that she possessed a stereotype about the defendant. Another ingredient that had occurred in this case, and occurs in others like it, was the relentless pursuit of the child's memory in a series of highly suggestive interviews extended over several months.

One wonders whether combining a negative expectancy about a defendant with repeated suggestive interviews seriously reduces the accuracy of the child's report. In the El Paso case, the child later gave three sworn depositions, at least one of which had the effect of recanting her courtroom testimony. She said that the repeated interviews had confused her and that she had said things that she thought were wrong because she wanted to help the adults and because she knew that this man was bad. This statement, made 12 days before the defendant's scheduled execution, resulted in a stay of execution. (Ultimately, the defendant was freed.)

To examine this issue experimentally, my colleague Mickey Leichtman at Harvard and I conducted an experiment called the *Sam Stone Study*. A stranger named Sam Stone paid a 2-minute visit to preschoolers (ages 3–6 years) in their day-care center. Following Sam Stone's visit, the children were asked for details about the visit on four different occasions over a 10-week period. During these four occasions, the interviewer refrained from using suggestive questions and simply encouraged children to describe Sam Stone's visit in as much detail as possible. One month after the fourth interview, the children were interviewed a fifth time by a new interviewer who used forensic procedures (e.g., first acclimating the children, then eliciting a free narrative, then using probes, urging the children to say when they did not recall, taking breaks). This interviewer asked about two "nonevents," which involved Sam soiling a teddy bear and ripping a book. In reality, Sam Stone never touched either item.

When asked in the fifth interview "Did Sam Stone do anything to a book or a teddy bear?", nearly all children correctly replied no. Only 10% of the youngest (3–4 years old) children's answers contained claims that Sam Stone did anything to a book or a teddy bear. When asked if they actually saw him do anything to the book or teddy bear, as opposed to thinking or hearing that he did something, now only 5% answered that anything had occurred. Finally, when these 5% were gently challenged ("You didn't really see him do anything to the book/teddy bear, did you?"), only 2.5% still insisted on the reality of the fictional event. None of the older (5–6 years old) children claimed to have actually seen Sam Stone do either of the fictional things. We considered this condition a control against which we could assess the effects of the use of repeated suggestive questioning, especially about characters who were the object of children's stereotypes.

A second group of preschoolers were presented a stereotype about Sam Stone before he ever visited their school. We did this to mimic the sort of stereotypes that some child witnesses have about a defendant. Each week, beginning a month prior to the visit, the children were told a new Sam Stone story in which Sam was depicted as very clumsy.[3] For example,

> You'll never guess who visited me last night. [pause] That's right. Sam Stone! And guess what he did this time? He asked to borrow my Barbie and when he was carrying her down the stairs, he tripped and fell and broke her arm. That Sam Stone is always getting into accidents and breaking things!

Following Sam Stone's visit, these children were treated identically to those in the control group; that is, they were interviewed four times, avoiding all suggestions, and were then given the same forensic interview by a new interviewer, starting with free narrative, then proceeding to questions about anything happening to the book or teddy bear.

The stereotyping had an effect for the youngest children, 42% of whom claimed Sam Stone ripped the book or soiled the teddy bear in response to suggestive probes. Of this 42%, 19% claimed they saw Sam Stone do the misdeeds (i.e., not just heard that he did these things). But, after being gently challenged, only 11% continued to claim that they witnessed him doing these things. In contrast, older preschoolers were significantly more resistant to the influence of the stereotype; their error rates were approximately half of those of the younger children.

A third group of children were assigned to a suggestion-only condition that involved the provision of suggestive questions during the four interviews following Sam Stone's visit. However, rather than the clumsy stereotype, each suggestive interview contained two erroneous suggestions, one having to do with ripping a book and the other with soiling a teddy bear (e.g., "Remember that time Sam Stone visited your classroom and spilled chocolate on that white teddy bear? Did he do it

---

[3] In earlier versions of this study, we also used other stereotypes besides clumsy, including being a thief. The results were essentially the same as for clumsy, although we never reported these results because of small sample sizes and their exploratory nature.

on purpose or was it an accident?"; "When Sam Stone ripped that book, was he being silly or was he angry?").

Ten weeks later, when the forensic interviewer probed these children about these events (e.g., Did anything happen to a book? Did anything happen to a teddy bear?), 52% of the younger children's answers and 38% of the older children's answers contained claims that Sam Stone was responsible for one or both misdeeds.

Thirty-five percent of the younger children's answers contained the claim that they had actually witnessed him do these things, as opposed to just being told that he did them. Even after being gently challenged, 12% of these children continued to claim that they saw him do one or both misdeeds. The older children were also susceptible to these suggestive interviews, although somewhat less so.

Finally, a fourth group of children were assigned to a condition that combined the features of the stereotype and the suggestion-only conditions. During the fifth (i.e., forensic) interview conducted 10 weeks later, 72% of the youngest preschoolers claimed that Sam Stone did one or both misdeeds, a figure that dropped to 44% when asked if they actually saw him do these things. The figure further dropped to 21% when these children were gently challenged. There was still cause for concern with the older preschoolers, 11% of whom insisted that they saw him do the misdeeds, even when gently challenged.

Some researchers have opined that the presence of perceptual details in children's reports is one of the indicators of an accurate memory, as opposed to a confabulated one (Loftus & Hoffman, 1989; Raskin & Yuille, 1989). In the study discussed earlier, as well as in this study, however, the presence of perceptual details was no assurance that the report was accurate. In fact, it was surprising to see the number of false perceptual details that children in the combined stereotype-plus-suggestion condition provided to embellish the nonevents (e.g, claiming that Sam Stone took the teddy bear into a bathroom and soaked it in hot water before smearing it with a crayon). This may be another difference between this study and many other studies in the suggestibility literature that are based on single leading questions over brief durations and without stereotypes.

It is one thing to show that children can be induced to make errors and include perceptual details in their reports, but it is quite another to show that such faulty reports are convincing to an observer, especially a highly trained one. To examine the believability of the children's reports, we showed videotapes of the children during the final interview to over one thousand researchers and clinicians who work with children. These researchers and clinicians (including psychiatrists) were simply told that all of the children observed the visit of a man named Sam Stone to their day-care centers. They were asked to watch the tapes carefully and to decide which of the things that were alleged by the children actually transpired during Sam Stone's visit. After viewing the tape, they were asked to rank the children in terms of their overall accuracy and to rate the accuracy of specific statements that the children had made.

Strikingly, the majority of these highly trained professionals were very inaccurate. Our analyses indicated that experts who conduct research on children's testimonial competence, who provide therapy to children suspected of having been abused, and who carry out law-enforcement interviews with children failed to detect which children were accurate, despite being confident in their mistaken opinions. The overall credibility ratings they made of individual children were highly inaccurate; the very children who were least accurate were rated as being most accurate. Despite claims from some to the contrary, our data attest to the fact that even extensive training does not always make it possible to detect the validity of young children's reports when they have been subjected to persistent erroneous questioning over long delay intervals.

Study 4: Children's Reports of an Inoculation

It could be argued that the Sam Stone Study is not relevant to evaluating the reliability of a child witness who reports personally experienced events that involve his or her own body, especially when the experience involves some degree of distress or potential embarrassment. Furthermore, some might argue that the Sam Stone data are not germane to testimony about predictable and scripted events. In cases in which the event involves a child's own body, is somewhat stressful, and is predictable, it is often thought that children may be resistant to suggestion (Goodman, Rudy, Bottoms, & Aman, 1990).

To determine whether children could be misled under such circumstances, we examined the influence of postevent suggestions on children's reports about two specific pediatric visits (Bruck et al., in press). I briefly describe two studies that we conducted. The first study had two phases. In the first phase, the 5-year-olds visited their pediatrician for an annual check-up. The visit was scripted as follows: First, the pediatrician examined the child. Then the child met a research assistant who talked about a poster that was hanging on the wall in the examining room. Next, with the research assistant present, the pediatrician gave the child an oral polio vaccine and a diphtheria inoculation. Immediately after the inoculation, the pediatrician left the room. The research assistant then gave the child feedback about how he or she had acted when receiving the inoculation. Some children were given pain-affirming feedback: They were told that it seemed as though the shot really hurt them, but that that was okay because shots hurt even big kids (hurt condition). Other children were given pain-denying information, that is, they were told that they acted like the shot did not hurt much and that they were really brave (no-hurt condition). Finally, some children were merely told that the shot was over (neutral condition). After giving the feedback, the research assistant gave each child a treat and then read the child a story. One week later, a second research assistant asked each child to indicate through the use of various rating scales how much he or she cried when receiving the shot and how much the shot hurt.

The children's reports during this interview did not vary as a function of feedback condition. Essentially, the children's reports about the stressful, personally significant, and physically invasive check-up procedures were not rendered less accurate by the suggestive questions. These findings resemble those of other researchers who have studied the effects of providing children with suggestions about personally relevant, stressful past experiences in a single interview.

The picture changed, however, when we reinterviewed the children three more times approximately 1 year after the shot. During these three interviews, the children were provided with repeated suggestions about how they had acted when they received their inoculations. Thus, as in the first phase of the study, some children were told how brave they had acted when they got their shot, whereas other children where not given any information about how they had acted. (For ethical reasons, we did not continue with the pain-affirming feedback in case it had the effect of making children doctor phobic.) When the children were visited for a fourth time and asked to rate how much the shot had hurt and how much they had cried, there were large suggestibility effects. Those who had been repeatedly told that they had acted brave and did not cry reported significantly less crying and less pain than did children who were not provided with any information about how they had acted. Thus, these data indicate that under certain circumstances, children's reports concerning stressful events involving their own bodies can be influenced by erroneous postevent suggestions.

We also provided children with different types of misleading information about the agents of actions that occurred in the pediatrician's office during the original inoculation visit. Some children were falsely reminded (on three occasions) that the research assistant had given them the inoculation and the oral vaccine, whereas the control-group children were merely reminded that someone did these things. Other children were falsely reminded that the pediatrician had shown them the poster, had given them treats, and had read them a story, whereas the control-group children were merely reminded that someone did these things. According to some researchers, children should not be open to suggestion concerning such central and important events, particularly involving shifting the gender of the person who administered the inoculation. The male pediatrician had never given them treats or read them a story, and the female research assistant had never inoculated them.

Contrary to these predictions, the children were misled. In the fourth interview, when asked to tell what happened to them when they had visited their doctor, 45% of the misled and 22% of the control subjects reported that the pediatrician had shown them the poster, given them treats, and read them a story. For children who had been told that the research assistant had given them the shot and the vaccine, 38% of their reports, versus only 10% of the control children's reports, were consistent with this suggestion. In fact, 38% of the misled children and none of the control children said that the research assistant had performed other scripted events that were not accurate (e.g., checked their ears and nose), although these events had not been suggested.

Hence, our suggestions to these children influenced not only their reports of personally experienced, central events but also their memories for nonsuggested scripted events that were related to the suggested events. One final aspect of these data are of interest: Children in this study often produced errors of commission in their free recall, something rarely reported in the literature (Ceci & Bruck, 1993b).

In summary, these data indicate that under certain circumstances, preschool children's reports concerning stressful events involving their own bodies can be influenced. As in the Sam Stone Study, two important factors included in this study were repeated suggestions over multiple interviews and a long delay interval. These same two factors were independently confirmed as important determinants of suggestibility by Warren and Lane (in press) and Bjorklund and Cassell (1992) in their respective studies of children's reports of a theft.

The results of this study are therefore consistent with those of the Sam Stone Study, even though the events and experiences about which children were misled were different. In the Sam Stone Study, repeated suggestions and stereotypes led to convincing claims of witnessing nonoccurring events. In the inoculation study, misleading information given in repeated interviews after a long delay influenced children's memories of personally experienced, salient, and predictable events.

Study 5: Using Anatomical Dolls to Symbolically Represent Actions

The final study was an effort to determine whether the report errors that we observed in these other studies could be extended to sexualized events. To approach this issue in an ethically permissible manner, we took advantage of 70 naturally occurring pediatric visits to the offices of our colleagues, two of whom are professors of pediatrics. The procedure involved a pediatric examination in which 35 3-year-old girls were given a genital examination and 35 were given a nongenital examination. Five minutes after the examination, with the child's mother present, the child was asked to describe in her own words where the doctor touched her. Following this, the child was presented with anatomical dolls and asked once more to tell where the pediatrician had touched her. The major conclusion from this study was that 3-year-olds ought not to be interviewed with anatomical dolls. The majority of the children who were not touched in the genital region correctly refrained from saying they were touched—but only when they were interviewed without the dolls. When the dolls were used, nearly 60% of these children indicated genital insertions and other acts that could be cause for concern. This goes against the common beliefs of most people that children will not indicate sexual events with such dolls. Although research by Goodman and colleagues (e.g., Goodman & Aman, 1990; Goodman & Clarke-Stewart, 1991; Goodman, Levine, Melton, & Ogden, 1991; Goodman et al., 1990) did not find that 5-year-olds made errors of commission with the dolls, they also did not find that the dolls were beneficial in eliciting information. Thus, it seems best not to use the dolls with 3-year-olds until and unless their incremental validity can be demonstrated, which at this point seems unlikely. If anything, it appears that the use of dolls may actually reduce the validity of reports with 3-year-olds when they are added to a predictive equation. We are in the process of extending this research with a large sample of older children, but we have not decided whether we will replicate the claims of others or whether we will modify stories already used. These concerns point to the need for the American Psychological Association Council of Representatives to review their 1991 statement on the benefit of doll use by experienced clinicians.

To give you an idea of how 3-year-olds used these dolls in our study, I am going to describe the activities of a child who was given a nongenital examination in which her underpants were never removed and the pediatrician never touched her genital or anal areas. Five minutes after the examination, the child made two errors: She inserted her finger in the doll's vagina, and she incorrectly used a measuring tape on her own head and on the doll's ankle. Other than these two errors, she responded correctly to all questions about where the doctor touched her, and she correctly demonstrated the other props (stethoscope, light, reflex hammer) on herself and on the doll.

The following day, however, this child made several more errors, including inserting her finger in the doll's vagina and anus and demonstrating two very interesting uses of the props used during the examination. She inserted a stick that the pediatrician had used to tickle her foot into the doll's vagina and then hammered it in violently with the reflex hammer. When the interviewer asked "Eva, did Dr. Emmett really do this to you?" the child replied that he did. A follow-up question by her father elicited a similar claim. Finally, when the father pointed out that her mother did not see Dr. Emmett do this to her, the child replied that he did it when the mother left the room. The majority of these 3-year-olds used the dolls inappropriately immediately following the nongenital examination.

Summary of Current Literature

The five studies that I have described in this chapter highlight the different techniques that researchers use to examine suggestibility in children. As mentioned earlier, the most recent studies, in contrast to the older literature, are somewhat more equivocal in their conclusions about children's testimonial competence. As a result, it is as easy to locate in the recent literature studies claiming that young children are quite resistant to suggestion (e.g., Marin, Holmes, Guth, & Kovac, 1979; Saywitz et al., 1991) as it is to find studies claiming the opposite (Ceci, Ross, & Toglia, 1987; Cohen & Harnick, 1980; King & Yuille, 1987). This has resulted in a confusing juxtaposition of claims and counterclaims (and newspaper headlines).

However, a careful reading of the scientific literature suggests that there are reliable age differences in suggestibility, with preschool children's reports being more readily impeded by the presence of erroneous suggestions by an interviewer than those of older children. Table 1

Table 1
Summary of Studies That Compared Suggestibility of Preschoolers to That of Older Children or Adults

Study	Reliable age effects for suggestibility
Ceci, Leichtman, & White (in press)	+
Ceci et al. (1987, Experiment 1)	+
Ceci et al. (1987, Experiment 2)	+
Delamothe & Taplin (1992)	0
Goodman & Aman (1990)	+
Goodman et al. (1990, Experiment 4)	+
Goodman, Hirschman et al. (1991, Experiment 3)	+
Goodman, Hirschman et al. (1991, Experiment 2)	+
Goodman, Hirschman et al. (1991, Experiment 4)	+
Goodman & Reed (1986)	+
Gordon et al. (1991)	+
Howe (1991)	0
Marin et al. (1979)	0
Oates & Shrimpton (1991)	+
Ornstein et al. (1992)	+
Rudy & Goodman, 1991	+
Saywitz et al. (1991)	+

Note. A plus sign denotes that preschoolers were significantly more impaired by misleading questions than older subjects. A zero denotes no significant age differences in the suggestibility effect. Adapted from Ceci & Bruck, 1993b. Copyright 1993 by the American Psychological Association.

(adapted from Ceci & Bruck, 1993b) shows the basis for this claim: In 14 of 17 modern studies, suggestibility was greater among preschoolers than among older children or adults. To be sure, there are many caveats that accompany this conclusion. For example, some researchers have claimed that age differences in suggestibility are evident principally with nonparticipating children (i.e., bystanders as opposed to children who were the recipients of some action) and principally on nonsexual questions (Rudy & Goodman, 1991). Others, however, have claimed that pronounced age differences can also be found for sexual questions (e.g., Study 5), as well as when the child is a participant in a stressful event (e.g., Study 4). The safest conclusion is probably that suggestibility effects can be and have been found for all types of events, but perhaps they are somewhat harder to find when the event is salient for a child.

There is an important difference that I have not yet mentioned between the conditions created in the studies I have described and those that occur in actual therapeutic and law-enforcement investigations. Namely, the latter are seldom as sanitized of affect or as lacking in motives as the former. High levels of stress, assaults to a victim's body, and the loss of control are characteristics of events that motivate forensic investigations. Although these factors are at play in some of our other studies,[4] we will never mimic experimentally the assaultive nature of acts perpetrated on child victims. Even those studies that came closest to reality, such as the medical studies, were socially and parentally sanctioned, unlike sexual assaults against children.

Notwithstanding this caveat, our work does allow us to state with confidence the following: The majority of children are neither as hypersuggestible and coachable as some pro-defense advocates have alleged nor are they as resistant to suggestions about their own bodies as some pro-prosecution advocates have claimed. Children can be led to incorporate false suggestions even into their accounts of intimate bodily touching if these suggestions are made by powerful adult authority figures and are delivered repeatedly over prolonged periods. Children also can be amazingly resistant to false suggestions and be able to provide highly detailed and accurate reports of events that transpired weeks or months ago (e.g., Baker-Ward, Gordon, Ornstein, Larus, & Clubb, in press). This underscores the need for great care in accepting

---

[4]Elsewhere, we have used emotionally laden events to examine issues related to the role of affect and bodily touching in producing misinformation effects, including suggestions about being kissed while naked (Ceci, DeSimone, Putnick, & Nightengale, 1993), witnessing parents violate norms, hurting other to protect loved ones (also see Ceci & Bruck, 1993a), and painful and/or potentially embarrassing medical procedures (e.g., inoculations and genital examinations). Children's accuracy and resistance to suggestions are sensitive to all of these factors (and others). No single research program has attempted to put all of these factors into a single experiment, and until one does, there should be caution about how any single child will behave in any given situation.

the claims by those who are eager to put a one-sided spin on data. Unfortunately, some of the better known figures in this area of research have exhibited a partisanship that prods them to discuss their findings without making clear the limits and alternate interpretations.

Therapeutic Concerns

A central concern of many critics of research on the suggestibility of children's recollections involves the relevance of this research for therapists and law-enforcement professionals. Admittedly, the types of studies that I have described are quite unlike the conditions that bring children into therapy and into the courts. All of our events are either neutral (e.g., Sam Stone's visit) or socially sanctioned (e.g., getting inoculated or receiving a genital examination).

Thus, it would be imprudent to claim that we have created an analog to child abuse. We have not. And yet because science is fallibilistic and because we often do not possess definitive knowledge, we must base our understanding on the best available evidence that we have at the time, regardless of how indirect it is. I believe that we now have enough indirect evidence to raise concerns about professionals interacting with very young children in ways similar to our experimental manipulations. Although it is ethically impermissible to see if preschoolers can be misled into believing that they have been molested by using these same techniques (e.g., having them repeatedly create images about being sodomized by a baby-sitter), the evidence documenting children's suggestibility in other realms makes it impossible not to question children's suggestibility in the realm of sexual abuse. Theoretically, there is nothing in the corpus of research that mitigates against this possibility. But claiming that such certain techniques might elicit false reports is not the same as asserting that children who experience less intense forms of suggestion will provide false reports. Similarly, one would never maintain that preschoolers who are suspected of having been abused should not receive therapy until the matter is fully adjudicated. This would be both inhumane and unreasonable. A young child who has been torn from his or her home, neighborhood, and kindergarten on an emergency court order and placed a foster home is in dire need of counseling to help get through the coming months. Regardless of how expeditious the juvenile and criminal justice proceedings are in child-abuse cases, they are never speedy enough. This is because the needs of both sides to prepare, take depositions, engage in elaborate "discovery" contests, and the like necessitate long delays between the allegation and its legal resolution. During this time, children are in need of mental health services, and I would be sad if anything that I have written in this chapter were to be misconstrued to imply otherwise. However, on the basis of what we now know, it would be imprudent to advise fantasy inductions, imagery play, or memory work during pre-trial sessions if there is an expectation that the case may end up in court. These practices can be saved for after the legal disposition. Perhaps prior to the legal resolution of a case, therapy could be restricted to working on everyday coping strategies that cannot be challenged by the defendant's counsel as creating false memories.

Some of my colleagues who are therapists do not like this suggestion and have told me so in stout words. I am sorry that they do not like it; I do not like it either. But I would like it even less if a child's legitimate claims of abuse were discredited because of the suggestive techniques used in therapy or if a child made an illegitimate claim as a result of an interviewer's using such techniques. Moreover, the need to engage in these techniques before legal resolution seems unwarranted. After all, there is not a single treatment outcome validity study that I am aware of that has demonstrated that these techniques are critical to achieving a positive mental health outcome for children who have been abused. So, until there is such evidence, the possible consequences of using these potentially suggestive techniques in therapy with very young children seems to outweigh their presumed benefits. However, because I am a pragmatist, I would be willing to reevaluate this suggestion if researchers provided compelling, carefully controlled studies showing that visually guided imagery, hypnosis, repeated retrieval probing, and the like added incremental validity to treatment outcomes with pre-school children suspected of being abused.

I would like to make two final points regarding the relevance of these findings for therapists. First, it sometimes happens that one will find his or her way into court and be asked to testify about a child's status, even if this seemed unlikely at the start of therapy. (It is beyond the scope of this chapter to delve into the sundry forms that this testimony can take.) When this occurs, therapists should restrict their expert testimony to those topics about which they are truly expert. I apologize for offending anyone who sees this as a gratuitous statement, but I have been sent many transcripts of testimony or court documents that therapists have been commissioned to prepare that go beyond the bounds of their expertise. Mason (1991) reviewed 122 appellate court cases in which expert testimony was given in child sexual-abuse cases. Clinical psychologists, social workers, pediatricians, and psychiatrists occasionally gave testimony that was decidedly beyond the limits of their knowledge, or anyone's for that matter. They testified about

- the suggestibility of children's memory
- about children's penchant for deception
- about the suggestive nature of anatomical dolls
- about the role of amnesia versus repression in posttraumatic stress

- about child sex-abuse accommodation syndrome
- that preoccupation with anatomical doll genitals is consistent with sexual abuse
- that avoidance of anatomical doll genitals is consistent with sexual abuse
- that the dolls are only a single part of the larger diagnostic picture, implying that they were aware of evidence that demonstrates that the dolls add any incremental prediction beyond other techniques used
- that children's memory for central details and bodily touching is highly suggestible
- that children's memory for central details and bodily touching is impervious to suggestion.

Besides giving our profession a "black eye," these examples could impede justice. When psychologists are called on to testify, it is imperative that we make clear the basis of our knowledge and its limits. For example, if we are testifying about a matter for which there exists systematic research, such as the suggestibility of children's recollections, then we need to make clear to the court the basis of our testimony. Are we up-to-date on the scientific studies? How about the literature on theory of mind, deception, and the like? Although everyone I present these precautions to denies knowing anyone who acts otherwise, the transcripts sent to me, as well as those that formed the basis of Mason's (1991) analysis, indicate that at least some of our colleagues honor this enjoinder more in breech than in spirit.

The second point worth noting is the potential incompatibility between the therapeutic role and the forensic role, a point made by Lindsay and Read (in press). Although I have already touched on this issue, it is important enough to warrant reiteration. Forensic investigators have the obligation to obtain the facts and their context. They ought to do nothing that might taint the child's production of these facts. On the basis of the five studies that I reviewed in this chapter, I believe that some of the things that we might do in therapy could taint a child's understanding of the past. If therapists are aiming to bring intrapsychic material to fruition and if the methods involve memory work, imagery inductions, and fantasy play, then this may be incompatible with forensic goals. To the extent that such techniques actually overwrite part of a child's biography and to the extent that an accurate knowledge of a child's past is important to achieving the therapeutic goals, the use of potentially suggestive techniques with preschoolers would seem to have costs beyond the forensic ones alluded to. But there are many variables, and I leave it to you to judge the weight of these risks.

Conclusion

Notwithstanding the findings of the five studies I described, it is clear that children—even preschoolers—are capable of recalling much that is forensically relevant. For example, when there was no attempt by the interviewers in the Sam Stone Study to mislead them, even 3-year-olds recalled large amounts of information accurately. The same is true when the social worker interviewer in the first study was not herself misled into misleading the child; in such conditions, even very young preschoolers do well. In this chapter, I have focused on preschoolers' weaknesses under specific conditions, namely when the adults who have access to them pursue their memory in a persistently suggestive manner over long periods of time—usually months. I have focused on these weaknesses rather than on preschool children's strengths, which are many, because these weaknesses are real and because they may not be obvious given the recency of much of the relevant research (some is still in press and will not appear in print for a while). Although research findings may always be modified by subsequent research, this does not imply that it is safe to dismiss them. In some of these studies, age was a more potent variable in accounting for suggestibility effects than any other variable that we have studied (i.e., gender, IQ, or personality). However, the fact that preschool-age children's reports are more vulnerable to postevent distortion than those of older children and that preschoolers can be induced more easily to make false reports in response to certain practices or motives is not meant to imply that these children are incapable of providing accurate testimony. In many of the studies that have been reported during the past decade, young children have accurately recollected the majority of the information that they observed, even when they have not recalled as much as older children. They may be more likely than older children or adults to succumb to erroneous suggestions, but their vulnerability is a matter of degree only. Even adults are vulnerable to suggestion (Belli, 1989; Belli, Windschitl, McCarthy, & Winfrey, 1992; Loftus, 1979; Loftus & Hoffman, 1989), and in the absence of persistently misleading suggestions from powerful adults, the effect size for age is often modest—at times, nonexistent. Thus, the question ought not be whether children are vulnerable to suggestion but whether their level of vulnerability is so much greater than an adult's as to render them an obstacle to the court's truth-seeking process when they serve as witnesses. On the basis of the evidence reviewed in Ceci and Bruck (1993b), the answer appears to be a qualified no. I say qualified because although my colleagues and I believe that the available evidence indicates that children can report much that is accurate and that when they differ from older subjects it is often by a degree that is forensically trivial, there are circumstances in which they report significantly less accurately than do older witnesses. For example, in some studies of facial identification that have used perpetrator-absent photo parades or line-ups, preschoolers selected innocent foils from these blank line-ups in over 70% of the cases despite cautions that the perpetrator may not be in the line-up and that they should not choose a photo unless they are sure it belongs to the person they saw (e.g., Peters, 1991).

My claim that children's testimonial behavior is not ineluctably an obstacle to the truth-finding function of courts may appear to be inconsistent with the thrust of this chapter. In view of the general unreliability of young children's testimony under conditions I have described and given the inability of experts to detect errors of omission or commission (Leichtman & Ceci, in press) that may cause them to mislead a jury (e.g., Horner, Guyer, & Kalter, 1993), one might wonder why a judge should ever admit their testimony. If an expert has given testimony about characteristic behaviors of sexually abused children, then other expert testimony can be offered about the inherent reliability problems of such testimony, as well as testimony about the conditions under which the child's original testimony was elicited (similar to the way that hypnotically induced testimony is challenged). In addition, judges can give juries cautionary instructions about the reliability risks of expert testimony.

Researchers are beginning to turn their attention to creating optimal conditions for fostering accurate reports of children. Although there is still much to learn about optimizing the accuracy of children's testimony, we already know some techniques that ought to be taken into consideration by interviewers. For example, young children's disproportionate vulnerability to suggestive questions can be reduced by instructions from the interviewer to be wary of suggestions (e.g., Warren, Hulse-Trotter, & Tubbs, 1991) or by arranging the retrieval context so that the child experiences less anxiety (Peters, 1991). In our recent work, my colleagues and I experimented with different forms of social support to see if a particular configuration aids preschoolers' resistance to the kinds of suggestions I have described in this chapter. Although it is too early to draw conclusions, we already know that if children are provided with a supportive interview atmosphere, they appear to be less vulnerable to suggestion (Goodman et al., 1990). Moreover, if they are interviewed carefully, with an interview format that is conducive to accurate reporting (e.g., elicitation of free narratives prior to using specific and leading questions, the testing of alternative hypotheses by the interviewer, and the avoidance of repeated questions and imagery inductions), and if adults who have access to the children prior to their testimony are not motivated to distort their recollections through relentless and potent suggestions and outright coaching, then young children appear to be capable of providing a great deal of information that is forensically relevant and accurate. And, above all, if law-enforcement officials, therapists, and social workers maintain neutrality during the interview or therapy process, attempting to test alternative hypotheses, then there is every reason to believe that even very young children can provide courts with valuable, accurate information. To a significant degree, we have discovered that what one gets out of an interview with a preschooler is as much a function of what the interviewer brings to the situation as what the child brings to it, hence, the focus in all of these studies on the potential weaknesses in both parties, not only the child.

In view of these conclusions, extreme negative opinions proffered throughout this century about young children's abilities to resist leading questions are unwarranted. Earlier assertions such as "Create, if you will, an idea of what the child is to hear or see, and the child is very likely to see or hear what you desire" (Brown, 1926, p. 133) are needlessly ungenerous depictions of the young child's capabilities, as are statements that were made during the middle years of this century, such as Lord Goddard's (*R. v. Willwork*, 1958) dictum about a 5-year-old witness who claimed that she had been falsely imprisoned and sexually assaulted:

> The jury could not attach any value to the evidence of a child of five ... to call a little child of the age of five is most undesirable, and I hope it will not occur again.... Of this there can be no doubt: that many, if not all, of the difficulties that subsequently beset the trial ... flow directly from the fact that the complainant was a child of extremely tender years. (see *R. v. Willwork*, 1958)

In light of the data reviewed here, these extreme opinions are not supported by the available research. The research shows that children are able to encode and retrieve large amounts of information (e.g., the control-group children in the Sam Stone Study were highly accurate), especially when it is highly meaningful to them. Equally true, however, is the fact that no good will be served by ignoring that part of the research that demonstrates potentially significant social and cognitive hazards to young child witnesses if adults who have access to them attempt to usurp their memories, wittingly or unwittingly, through the persistent use of suggestive questions, fantasy play, and visualization exercises. Inattention to the full corpus of empirical data will only forestall efforts to improve the way in which child witnesses are treated and delay needed research into ways of optimizing the accuracy of young children's testimony through better interviewing techniques and judicial reform.

References

Alloy, L. B., & Tabachnik, N. (1984). Assessment of covariation by humans and animals: The joint influence of prior expectations and current situational information. *Psychological Review, 91*, 112–149.

Andrews, J. A. (1964). The evidence of children. *Criminal Law Review, 64*, 769–777.

Aveling, F., & Hargreaves, H. (1921). Suggestibility with and without prestige in children. *British Journal of Psychology, 11*, 53–75.

Baker-Ward, L., Gordon, B., Ornstein, P. A., Larus, D., & Clubb, P. (in press). Young children's long-term retention of a pediatric examination. *Child Development.*

Baxter, J. (1990). The suggestibility of child witnesses: A review. *Journal of Applied Cognitive Psychology, 3*, 1–15.

Belli, R. F. (1989). Influences of misleading postevent information: Misinformation interference and acceptance. *Journal of Experimental Psychology: General, 118*, 72–85.

Belli, R. F., Windschitl, P., McCarthy, T., & Winfrey, S. (1992). Detecting memory impairment with a modified test procedure: Manipulating retention interval with centrally presented event items. *Journal of Experimental Psychology: Learning, Memory, and Cognition, 18*, 356–367.

Binet, A. (1900). *La suggestibilité [The suggestibility].* Paris: Schleicher Freres.

Bjorklund, D. F., & Cassell, W. S. (1992, April). *Tell me about . . . Don't you remember? . . . Isn't it true? . . . : Developmental patterns of eyewitness responses to increasingly suggestive questions.* Paper presented at the annual meeting of the Conference on Human Development, Atlanta, GA.

Brehm, S. S., & Smith, T. W. (1986). Social psychological approaches to psychotherapy and behavior change. In S. L. Garfield & A. Bergin (Eds.), *Handbook of psychotherapy and behavior change* (3rd ed., pp. 69–116). New York: Wiley.

Brown, M. R. (1926). *Legal psychology.* Indianapolis, IN: Bobbs-Merrill.

Bruck, M., Ceci, S. J., Francoeur, E., & Barr, R. (in press). "I hardly cried when I got my shot": Young children's reports of their visit to a pediatrician. *Child Development.*

Ceci, S. J., & Bronfenbrenner, U. (1991). On the demise of everyday memory: The rumors of my death are greatly exaggerated. *American Psychologist, 46*, 27–31.

Ceci, S. J., & Bruck, M. (1993a). The child witness: Translating research into policy. *SRCD Social Policy Report, 7*(3), 1–30.

Ceci, S. J., & Bruck, M. (1993b). The suggestibility of the child witness: A historical review and synthesis. *Psychological Bulletin, 113*, 403–439.

Ceci, S. J., DeSimone, M., Putnick, M., & Nightengale, N. (1993). Age differences in suggestibility. In D. Cichetti & S. Toth (Eds.), *Child witnesses, child abuse, and public policy* (pp. 117–138). Norwood, NJ: Ablex.

Ceci, S. J., Leichtman, M. D., & White, T. (in press). Interviewing preschoolers: Remembrance of things planted. In D. Peters (Ed.), *The child witness in context: Cognitive, social, and legal perspectives.* Norwell, MA: Kluwer Academic.

Ceci, S. J., Ross, D., & Toglia, M. (1987). Age differences in suggestibility: Psycholegal implications. *Journal of Experimental Psychology: General, 117*, 38–49.

Cohen, R. L., & Harnick, M. A. (1980). The susceptibility of child witnesses to suggestion. *Law and Human Behavior, 4*, 201–210.

Dawes, R. (1992). The importance of alternative hypothesis and hypothetical counterfactuals in general social science. *General Psychologist, spring,* 2–7.

Delamothe, K., & Taplin, E. (1992, November). *The effect of suggestibility on children's recognition memory.* Paper presented at the annual meeting of the Psychonomic Society, St. Louis, MO.

Goodman, G. (1984). Children's testimony in historical perspective. *Journal of Social Issues, 40,* 9–31.

Goodman, G., & Aman, C. (1990). Children's use of anatomically detailed dolls to recount an event. *Child Development, 61,* 1859–1871.

Goodman, G. S., & Clarke-Stewart, A. (1991). Suggestibility in children's testimony: Implications for child sexual abuse investigations. In J. L. Doris (Ed.), *The suggestibility of children's recollections* (pp. 92–105). Washington, DC: American Psychological Association.

Goodman, G. S., Hirschman, J. E., Hepps, D., & Rudy, L. (1991). Children's memory for stressful events. *Merrill Palmer Quarterly, 37,* 109–158.

Goodman, G. S., Levine, M., Melton, G., & Ogden, D. (1991). Child witnesses and the confrontation clause: The American Psychological Association brief in Maryland v. Craig. *Law and Human Behavior, 15,* 13–30.

Goodman, G. S., & Reed R. S. (1986). Age differences in eyewitness testimony. *Law and Human Behavior, 10,* 317–332.

Goodman, G. S., Rudy, L., Bottoms, B., & Aman, C. (1990). Children's concerns and memory: Issues of ecological validity in the study of children's eyewitness testimony. In R. Fivush & J. Hudson (Eds.), *Knowing and remembering in young children* (pp. 249–284). New York: Cambridge University Press.

Gordon, B., Ornstein, P. A., Clubb, P., & Nida, R. E. (1991, November). *Visiting the pediatrician: Long-term retention and forgetting.* Paper presented at the annual meeting of the Psychonomic Society, San Francisco, CA.

Gray, E. (1993). *Unequal justice: The prosecution of child sexual abuse.* New York: Macmillan.

Gudjonsson, G. (1986). The relationship between interrogative suggestibility and acquiescence: Empirical findings and theoretical implications. *Personality and Individual Differences, 7,* 195–199.

Horner, T. M., Guyer, M. J., & Kalter, N. M. (1993). Clinical expertise and the assessment of child sexual abuse. *Journal of the American Academy of Child and Adolescent Psychiatry, 32,* 925–931.

Howe, M. L. (1991). Misleading the children's story recall: Forgetting and reminiscence of the facts. *Developmental Psychology, 27,* 746–762.

Kayne, N. T., & Alloy, L. B. (1988). Clinician and patient as aberrant actuaries: Expectation-based distortions in assessment of covariation. In L. Y. Abramson (Ed.), *Social cognition and clinical psychology: A synthesis* (pp. 171–194). New York: Guilford.

King, M., & Yuille, J. (1987). Suggestibility and the child witness. In S. J. Ceci, D. Ross, & M. Toglia (Eds.), *Adults' perceptions of children's testimony* (pp. 24–356). New York: Springer-Verlag.

Kutchinsky, B. (1992). The child sexual abuse panic. *Nordisk Sexoligi, 10,* 30–42.

Leichtman, M. D., & Ceci, S. J. (in press). The effect of stereotypes and suggestions on preschoolers' reports. *Developmental Psychology.*

Lindsay, D. S., & Read, J. D. (in press). Psychotherapy and memories of childhood sexual abuse. *Applied Cognitive Psychology.*

Lindberg, M. (1991). A taxonomy of suggestibility and eyewitness memory: Age, memory process, and focus of analysis. In J. L. Doris (Ed.), *The suggestibility of children's recollections* (pp. 47–55). Washington, DC: American Psychological Association.

Lipmann, O. (1911). Pedagogical psychology of report. *Journal of Educational Psychology, 2,* 253–261.

Loftus, E. F. (1979). *Eyewitness testimony.* Cambridge, MA: Harvard University Press.

Loftus, E. F., & Hoffman, H. (1989). Misinformation and memory: The creation of new memories. *Journal of Experimental Psychology: General, 118,* 100–104.

Maddux, J. E. (1993). The mythology of psychopathology: A social cognitive view of deviance, difference, and disorder. *General Psychologist, 29,* 34–45.

Märbe, K. (1913). Kinderaussegen in einem Sittlichkeitprozess [Child testimony in a sex abuse cases]. *Fortschrifte der Psychologie, 1,* 375–396.

Marin, B. V., Holmes, D. L., Guth, M., & Kovac, P. (1979). The potential of children as eyewitnesses. *Law and Human Behavior, 3,* 295–305.

Mason, M. A. (1991). A judicial dilemma: Expert witness testimony in child sex abuse cases. *Journal of Psychiatry and Law, winter,* 185–219.

McGough, L. (in press). *Fragile voices: the child witness in American courts.* New Haven, CT: Yale University Press.

Melton, G. (1992). Children as partners for justice: Next steps for developmentalists. *Monographs of the Society for Research in Child Development, 57* (Serial No. 229), 153–159.

Messerschmidt, R. (1933). The suggestibility of boys and girls between the ages of six and sixteen. *Journal of Genetic Psychology, 43,* 422–437.

National Center for Child Abuse and Neglect. (1993). *National Child Abuse and Neglect Data System, 1991: Summary data component.* Gaithersburg, MD: U.S. Department of Health and Human Services.

National Center for the Prosecution of Child Abuse. (1987). *Manual of the National Center for the Prosecution of Child Abuse.* Washington, DC: Author.

Oates, K., & Shrimpton, S. (1991). Children's memories for stressful and nonstressful events. *Medicine, Science, and the Law, 31,* 4–10.

Ornstein, P. A., Gordon, B. N., & Larus, D. (1992). Children's memory for a personally experienced event: Implications for testimony. *Applied Cognitive Psychology, 6,* 49–60.

Otis, M. (1924). A study of suggestibility in children. *Archives of Psychology, 11,* 5–108.

Peters, D. P. (1991). The influence of stress and arousal on the child witness. In J. L. Doris (Ed.), *The suggestibility of children's recollections* (pp. 60–76). Washington, DC: American Psychological Association.

Pope, H. G., & Hudson, J. I. (1992). Is childhood sexual abuse a risk factor for bulimia nervosa? *American Journal of Psychiatry, 4,* 455–463.

Powers, P., Andriks, J. L., & Loftus, E. F. (1979). Eyewitness accounts of females and males. *Journal of Applied Psychology, 64*, 339–347.

R. v. Willwork. (1958). (British Court Record)

Raskin, D., & Esplin, P. (1991). Witness statement analysis: Credibility assessment. In J. L. Doris (Ed.), *The suggestibility of children's recollections* (pp. 153–164). Washington, DC: American Psychological Association.

Raskin, D., & Yuille, J. (1989). Problems in evaluating interviews of children in sexual abuse cases. In S. J. Ceci, D. Ross, & M. Toglia (Eds.), *Adults' perceptions of children's testimony* (pp. 184–207). New York: Springer-Verlag.

Rudy, L., & Goodman, G. S. (1991). Effects of participation on children's reports: Implications for children's testimony. *Developmental Psychology, 27*, 527–538.

Saywitz, K. J., Goodman, G. S., Nicholas, E., & Moan, S. F. (1991). Children's memories of a physical examination involving genital touch: Implications for reports of child sexual abuse. *Journal of Consulting and Clinical Psychology, 59*, 682–691.

Sherman, I. (1925). The suggestibility of normal and mentally defective children. *Comparative Psychology Monographs, 2*.

Small, M. H. (1896–1897). The suggestibility of children. *Pedagogical Seminary, 4*, 176–220.

State of New Jersey v. Margaret Kelly Michaels. (1993). Superior Court, Appellate Division. Docket No. 199–88T4. Supplementary Appendix, Vol. 1.

Steller, M. (1991). Commentary. In J. L. Doris (Ed.), *The suggestibility of children's recollections* (pp. 106–109). Washington, DC: American Psychological Association.

Stern, W. (1910). Abstracts of lectures on the psychology of testimony and on the study of individuality. *American Journal of Psychology, 21*, 270–282.

Varendonck, J. (1911). Les temoignages d'enfants dans un proces retentissant [The testimony of children in a famous trial]. *Archives de Psychologie, 11*, 129–171.

Warren, A., & Lane, P. L. (in press). Effects of timing and type of questioning in eyewitness accuracy and identification. In M. Zaragoza, J. Graham, G. Hall, R. Hirschman, & Y. Ben-Porath (Eds.), *Memory and testimony in the child witness*. Beverly Hills, CA: Sage.

Warren, A. R., Hulse-Trotter, K., & Tubbs, E. (1991). Inducing resistance to suggestibility in children. *Law and Human Behavior, 15*, 273–285.

Wexler, R. (1990). *Wounded innocents: The real victims of the war against child abuse*. Buffalo, NY: Prometheus.

Whipple, G. M. (1909). The observer as reporter: A survey of the psychology of testimony. *Psychological Bulletin, 6*, 153–170.

Whipple, G. M. (1911). The psychology of testimony. *Psychological Bulletin, 8*, 307–309.

Whipple, G. M. (1912). Psychology of testimony and report. *Psychological Bulletin, 9*, 264–269.

GARY B. MELTON

EXPERT OPINIONS: "NOT FOR COSMIC UNDERSTANDING"

G ary B. Melton is director of the Institute for Families in Society and professor of neuropsychiatry, law, and psychology at the University of South Carolina. A Fellow of the American Psychological Association (APA) and seven of its divisions, Melton is past president of the American Psychology-Law Society and the APA Division of Child, Youth, and Family Services and a former member of the Council of Representatives. He has recently served as a member of the U.S. Advisory Board on Child Abuse and Neglect, the American Bar Association (ABA) Commission on Mental and Physical Disability Law, the ABA working group on the United Nations Convention on the Rights of the Child, and the national board of directors of Parents Anonymous. He formerly served on APA's Task Force on Psychology and AIDS, and he was twice chair of the APA Committee for the Protection of Human Participants in Research (now known as the Committee for Standards in Research).

The author of approximately 200 publications, Melton has testified several times before the U.S. Congress, and he has served as a consultant to numerous state social service, mental health, legislative, and court-administrative agencies. As director of the Consortium on Children, Families, and the Law—an association of eight interdisciplinary university-based centers and three nonacademic centers (e.g., the Office of Public Policy of APA)—he has organized a regular Congressional briefing series. Melton's work has been cited by courts at all levels, including the U.S. Supreme Court.

Among the awards Melton has received are the APA Award for Distinguished Contributions to Psychology in the Public Interest (1985), the Harold Hildreth Award from the APA Division of Psychologists in Public Service (1992), the Nicholas Hobbs Award of the APA Division of Child, Youth, and Family Services (1992), the Donna Stone Award from the National Committee to Prevent Child Abuse (1992), and the Frederick Lewis Award of Psi Chi (1993).

From 1989 to 1990, Melton was a Fulbright Scholar at the Norwegian Center for Child Research at the University of Trondheim. He has been an invited lecturer in Australia, Germany, Israel, Italy, The Netherlands, Norway, and Scotland; he is currently conducting research in the Czech Republic and Estonia. In 1991, he led a Citizen Ambassador delegation on child protection to Czechoslovakia, Poland, and Russia.

Melton was educated at the University of Virginia (BA with high distinction, 1973) and Boston University (MA, 1975, and PhD, 1978, in clinical–community psychology). He has held faculty appointments at the Universities of Hawaii, Minnesota, Nebraska, and Virginia and at Morehead State University (Kentucky).

EXPERT OPINIONS: "NOT FOR COSMIC UNDERSTANDING"

There can be no doubt that the usefulness of expert opinions[1] in the legal process is a matter of considerable controversy, a fact that should come as no surprise to even casual readers of *American Psychologist*, *Science*, or journals in psycholegal studies.[2] Indeed, the question of proper use of scientific evidence is sufficiently important, complex, and debatable that its consideration now forms the foundation for entire courses in law schools (e.g., Areen, King, Goldberg, & Capron, 1984; Monahan & Walker, 1985, 1990).

---

[1] In this context, I am referring not only to formal admission of expert testimony but also to admission of expert opinion into the decision-making process, whatever the mechanism for doing so. Some of the structures and procedures for doing so are discussed later in this chapter.

[2] Compare, for example, Barrett and Morris (1993) and Saks (1993) with Fiske, Bersoff, Borgida, Deaux, and Heilman (1993); J. Goodman (1993), Faust and Ziskin (1988a, 1988b), and Ziskin and Faust (1991) with Fowler and Matarazzo (1988) and Matarazzo (1990, 1991); Elliott (1991) with Ellsworth (1991); Gardner, Scherer, and Tester (1989) with Melton (1990a); G. Goodman, Levine, and Melton (1992) with Underwager and Wakefield (1992); Grisso and Appelbaum (1992, 1993) with Litwack (1993); and Loftus (1983) with Elliott (1993) and McCloskey and Egeth (1983). See generally, for example, "Expert testimony" (1989); Golding (1992); Grisso (1987); Grisso and Saks (1991); Koshland (1993); McCloskey, Egeth, and McKenna (1986); Melton (1987a); Roesch, Golding, Hans, and Reppucci (1991); and Tremper (1987).

These scholarly debates are mirrored by popular concerns. Many critics of the purported litigation explosion (cf. Saks, 1992) believe that it is being fed by "junk science" proffered by experts who, for a fee, will find evidence of almost anything (Begley, 1993; Bernstein, 1993; Huber, 1991). Moreover, highly publicized cases in which criminal defendants have "gotten off"—or even tried to obtain such a result—through a psychological defense have led many in the general public to question the objectivity and expertise of the mental health professions (Slater & Hans, 1984). Since the earliest explicit use of social science in judicial opinions (e.g., *Brown v. Board of Education*, 1954; *Muller v. Oregon*, 1907), commentators have worried that psychologists and sociologists were using the legal process to undermine the political judgments of less liberal legislators elected by the people.

The intense concerns of the general public and of legal scholars and practitioners about the usefulness of expert opinions have not matched the ferocity of the debate among social science researchers and mental health professionals about the preservation of scientific and professional integrity in the legal process. To some degree, the debate reflects the fact that courtrooms are foreign territory for psychologists. The legal rules for admission and consideration of evidence do not necessarily conform to the norms of mental health practice and scientific inquiry. The resulting culture clashes create ambiguity and conflict about the standards to be applied: Does forensic work inevitably result in some compromise of psychologists' principles or at least their mode of operation?

The stakes involved in the answer to this question are often high for the parties involved. With their potentially profound consequences for litigants, the conflicts of interest and of principle in forensic work are sufficiently common (Pope & Vettner, 1992) and thorny (Melton, Petrila, Poythress, & Slobogin, 1987, § 3.05) that the most recent version of psychologists' ethical code includes a special section on forensic activities (American Psychological Association [APA], 1992, § 7). After an elaborate process of comment and debate, the American Psychology-Law Society (AP-LS; APA Division 41) adopted a detailed set of guidelines on such issues (Committee on Ethical Guidelines for Forensic Psychologists, 1991).

The significance of the public and private interests directly involved in litigation accounts for some of the intense concern by psychologists about their own and their colleagues' conduct in relation to legal matters. Much of the emotion is traceable, though, to the fact that public perceptions—and, to some degree, self-perceptions—of the science and the profession appear closely tied to their status in courtrooms and judges' chambers. On the one hand, lack of recognition by legal authorities is perceived to challenge the usefulness of psychology. On the other hand, acceptance of psychological opinions that are not consensually accepted in the field is perceived to threaten the explicit and implicit canons of science and practice and thus to undermine the discipline itself.

The fundamental nature of this conflict was illustrated when Ziskin and Faust (1988, 1991; Faust & Ziskin, 1988a, 1988b) argued in prestigious journals that clinical opinions are insufficiently reliable and valid to warrant their use in the legal arena. In a remarkable professional brouhaha, those articles not only stimulated special symposia at professional meetings but also provoked replies by the chief executive officer and the then-president of APA (Fowler & Matarazzo, 1988; Matarazzo, 1990, 1991). It is hard to imagine many topics about which a gadfly article would evoke such an institutional response.

I believe, though, that this dispute and other controversies about use of psychological evidence in the legal process have been blown out of proportion and that they reflect a misunderstanding of the purpose of expert evidence and the standard for its admission. To make this point, I review the prevailing legal rules, discuss a recent Supreme Court decision, and consider the implications for psychologists. I then turn to special problems in the use of psychological research in judicial decision making.

In the second half of this chapter, I change the focus to practical concerns. Although much of the energy of scholars and practitioners in psychology and law has been invested in debate about what opinions should be kept from legal decision makers, the more difficult problem may be developing systems that ensure the availability of useful information. The philosophical and practical issues are related in that the clarity and breadth of standards for admission and consideration of expert evidence affect the willingness of judges, lawyers, and psychologists to facilitate easy access by legal authorities to psychologists' opinions. Even when doctrinal ambivalence is not an issue, though, practical problems of work in and with the legal system can be significant obstacles, so I will offer some ideas about optimal structures for provision of both clinical and research evidence.

The Standard for Admissibility of Expert Opinions

Specialized Knowledge

Theoretical foundation. Before considering the standard for admission of expert opinions, I offer a caveat. I focus on the Federal Rules of Evidence, which were enacted by Congress in 1975. Most states have adopted the federal framework; indeed, many states have so fully incorporated the Federal Rules that the rule numbers in their own codes are identical to the federal counterparts. Even some states that have embraced the Federal Rules, however, have not done so in toto. Also, as I show, interpretations of the rules are not uniform, and some state courts have recognized additional standards even when the state evidence code mimics the Federal Rules. Therefore, psychologists should be sure to learn the prevailing standards before becoming involved in expert testimony in state courts.

Consideration of the admissibility of relevant expert opinions begins with Rule 702 (see Table 1), which permits the admission of a qualified expert's opinion into evidence only if it is based on *specialized knowledge* and will *assist the trier of fact* (the judge or the jury). The fact that an opinion is given by an expert does not imply that it is admissible as an expert opinion because the opinion may not aid the trier of fact in understanding the evidence or in determining a fact at issue. As I discuss, determination of assistance to the trier of fact requires attention not only to the level of validity of an opinion but also to the particular legal context in which the opinion is offered.

Rule 702 is derived in part from the democratic premise that professional education in itself does not confer special status in the legal system. In principle, everyone is equal before the bar of justice. It follows that occupational status should not infringe the societally designated authority of the judge or jury to decide the case at hand (Federal Rule of Evidence 704, Advisory Committee's note).

The allocation of authority for fact finding is the foundation for the rule severely limiting witnesses' ability to offer opinions when they testify (Federal Rule of Evidence 701; see Table 1). Experts should be able to go further than lay witnesses in offering opinions only if doing so would assist the trier of fact in understanding the evidence as it is presented. That this exception is present at all reflects a desire to facilitate justice—to promote reliable and valid decision making and to enable the parties to make their best case—while preserving the institutional role of the trier of fact.

The rules of evidence not only protect the integrity of legal institutions but they also provide guidance to experts in maintaining fidelity to their role. In particular, the specialized-knowledge requirement for admissibility of opinions offers a convenient heuristic for psychologists in avoiding a violation of the ethical prohibition of reaching beyond one's expertise in the formation of professional opinions (APA, 1992, especially Principle A and Standards 1.04, 3.03, 7.01, and 7.04; Committee on Ethical Guidelines for Forensic Psychologists, 1991, Guideline III). When a psychologist offers an opinion pursuant to a legal proceeding, he or she is making an implicit representation that the opinion is derived from expertise as a psychologist, not common sense or legal analysis.[3]

---

[3]Although *specialized knowledge* offers a heuristic for both courts and experts themselves in defining the bounds of admissible opinions (see footnote 4), it is effectively subsumed within *assistance to the trier of fact*. By definition, opinions that are not based on specialized knowledge are within the province of the fact finder.

Table 1
Federal Rules of Evidence Pertaining to Opinions and Expert Testimony

Rule 701
Opinion Testimony by Lay Witnesses

If the witness is not testifying as an expert, the witness's testimony in the form of opinions or inferences is limited to those opinions or inferences which are (a) rationally based on the perception of the witness and (b) helpful to a clear understanding of the witness's testimony or the determination of a fact in issue.

Rule 702
Testimony by Experts

If scientific, technical, or other specialized knowledge will assist the trier of fact to understand the evidence or to determine a fact in issue, a witness qualified as an expert by knowledge, skill, experience, training, or education may testify thereto in the form of an opinion or otherwise.

Rule 703
Bases of Opinion Testimony by Experts

The facts or data in the particular case upon which an expert bases an opinion or inference may be those perceived by or made known to the expert at or before the hearing. If of a type reasonably relied upon by experts in the particular field in forming opinions or inferences upon the subject, the facts or data need not be admissible in evidence.

Rule 704
Opinion on Ultimate Issue

(a) Except as provided in subdivision (b), testimony in the form of an opinion or inference otherwise admissible is not objectionable because it embraces an ultimate issue to be decided by the trier of fact.

(b) No expert witness testifying with respect to the mental state or condition of a defendant in a criminal case may state an opinion or inference as to whether the defendant did or did not have the mental state or condition constituting an element of the crime charged or of a defense thereto. Such ultimate issues are matters for the trier of fact alone.

Rule 705
Disclosure of Facts or Data Underlying Expert Opinion

The expert may testify in terms of opinion or inference and give reasons therefor without first testifying to the underlying facts or data, unless the court requires otherwise. The expert may in any event be required to disclose the underlying facts or data on cross-examination.

Accordingly, an expert can minimize ethical violations through self-monitoring of the foundation for one's opinion to ensure that it is based on specialized knowledge.[4]

Ultimate-issue opinions. In this regard, there is near-unanimity among scholarly commentators (e.g., Melton, Petrila, Poythress, & Slobogin, 1987, §§ 1.04 and 14.05 and citations therein) that experts should not offer, and that the courts should not seek, opinions about ultimate legal issues,[5] although the provision of such opinions unfortunately remains widespread. Ultimate-issue opinions inherently require legal and moral judgments that are outside the expertise of mental health professionals and that are properly reserved to judges and juries. This principle applies as well to penultimate questions involving the elements of the ultimate issue (e.g., whether the defendant appreciated the wrongfulness of his or her conduct; whether the respondent in a civil commitment proceeding is dangerous to others). Direct answers to such questions require legal judgments about, for example, the nature and level of risk that is subsumed within "dangerousness" in a civil commitment statute.

The view that ultimate-issue opinions should be withheld as a matter of professional ethics and excluded as a matter of law is widely held in spite of Rule 704 (see Table 1), which appears to permit such opinions except in regard to defendants' mental state at the time of the offense.[6] Three points are noteworthy in this regard. First, the framers of the Federal Rules generally took a "liberal" approach to evidence law in which they desired to avoid artificial constraints on the evidence available to triers of fact, who were trusted in most circumstances to give appropriate weight to the various evidence presented. Thus, Rule 704 was intended to avoid artificial constraints on expert testimony. For example, where *mental illness* is an element of the legal standard at

---

[4]In this respect, legal and ethical standards overlap. A psychologist should not assume, however, that lawyers' failure to object to an opinion or a court's failure to sustain an objection implies that the opinion is within the bounds of the psychologist's competence. The psychologist bears personal responsibility for monitoring whether an opinion is based on specialized knowledge as a psychologist and for withholding any opinion that does not meet such a standard. If the court nonetheless demands an opinion outside psychological expertise—for example, an opinion that calls for a conclusion of law (see Committee on Ethical Guidelines for Forensic Psychologists, 1991, Guideline IV[F])—the psychologist should qualify the opinion accordingly (see Melton, Petrila, Poythress, & Slobogin, 1987, § 14.05[c]).

[5]Examples include whether a respondent meets the criteria for civil commitment, whether a defendant was insane at the time of the offense, whether a child's best interests require a particular custody or visitation arrangement, and whether a defendant is competent to stand trial.

[6]In 1984, Congress added the prohibition of opinions on the ultimate question of insanity or diminished capacity as part of its response to the *Hinckley* verdict. In doing so, Congress reflected widespread—and unrealistic—concern that mental health professionals often assist criminal defendants in avoiding justly deserved punishment (Slater & Hans, 1984).

issue, or where the legal test is expressed in functional terms (e.g., *the defendant's ability to assist counsel in his or her own defense*), it is relatively difficult to provide an opinion without addressing the ultimate issue. In some other domains (e.g., opinions about whether victim-witnesses' allegations were truthfully made), the courts generally have excluded experts' ultimate-issue opinions, notwithstanding Rule 704. Even in the instances in which the legal and mental health terms appear to be coextensive, though, experts should clarify that their use of the terms at issue should not be perceived as conclusions about their meaning in law.

Second, careful examination of Rule 704 shows that it does not open the door to ultimate-issue opinions in general. Consistent with the drafters' intent noted in the preceding paragraph, it limits such opinions to those that are otherwise admissible. Given the strictures of Rule 702 (in particular, the specialized-knowledge requirement), ultimate-issue opinions thus still should be barred in most circumstances.

Third, even if admissible, ultimate-issue opinions should not be offered because they involve provision of opinions outside mental health professionals' expertise. If absolutely commanded by the courts to give ultimate-issue opinions, clinicians should emphasize that the opinion being presented is based on their understanding of the law and that the ultimate inference is a product of legal (not psychological) analysis.[7]

In that regard, Slobogin (1989) indicated that he would approve ultimate-issue testimony *if* there is a vigorous adversary process. His logic is that an ultimate-issue opinion may help the trier of fact to organize the testimony cognitively and that little harm is done if the opinion is subject to zealous cross-examination (cf. Rogers, Bagby, & Chow, 1992; Rogers, Bagby, Crouch, & Cutler, 1990; Rogers & Ewing, 1989). Leaving aside the reality that there are relatively few circumstances in which clinicians' opinions are tested in such a manner, Slobogin misses the central point that such opinions push experts beyond their expertise. Even if there is no harm in admitting ultimate-issue opinions, psychologists are ethically bound not to offer them.

Assistance to the Trier of Fact

The context as a factor. Determination of whether an opinion is based on specialized knowledge requires a straightforward determina-

---

[7]Once courts understand the reason for declining to reach the ultimate issue, my experience is that they generally accept it, especially when they are provided with rich clinical information on which to base their decision. In one hearing in which I testified, attorneys for both the defense and the prosecution repeatedly asked for my opinion of whether the defendant was competent to stand trial. In response, I repeatedly described the defendant's strengths and weaknesses in understanding the proceedings and assisting counsel, and I explained my reluctance to draw a legal conclusion. Finally, the judge dryly and correctly observed, "I think that he wants me to decide."

tion of whether the opinion is derived from the witness's professional training and expertise. By contrast, the criterion of *assistance to the trier of fact* relates only partially to the scientific merit of an expert's position. In considering this point, it is useful to turn to more general rules of evidence. Any evidence is admissible only if its probative value—its tendency to prove a fact at issue—outweighs its prejudicial or misleading effect (Federal Rule of Evidence 403).

Therefore, an opinion that is based on a large body of well-designed research still should be excluded if "the aura of special reliability and trustworthiness" (*State v. Saldana*, 1982, p. 230) attached to an expert's opinion is apt to result in the fact finder's placing undue weight on it. For example, such a situation may arise (although courts seldom so rule) in circumstances such as cases on civil commitment (e.g., Hiday, 1977, 1981; Stier & Stoebe, 1979; Turkheimer & Parry, 1992) and competency to stand trial (e.g., Roesch & Golding, 1980), in which mental health professionals' opinions often are dispositive.

Similarly, a solid scientific foundation may be outweighed by a tendency to mislead—a situation that I believe occurs when profile evidence is presented. Even when such evidence is presented carefully, the difficulty that most people have in processing base rates (e.g., Kahneman & Tversky, 1973) is likely to result in erroneous conclusions. In particular, victim profiles are apt, on balance, to prejudice fact finders and in my view should not be admitted. Table 2 presents a hypothetical case in which an extraordinarily valid profile of a sexually abused child— far more valid than anything currently available—still would result in only a 32% probability that a randomly selected child showing the profile would have recently been abused.

With similar logic, Slobogin (1984) argued that a mental health professional's opinion about a defendant's[8] dangerousness should be admissible only if the defendant submits such evidence first. Slobogin's article on this point predated the recent, "second-generation" research on assessment of risk of violence that has broadened the contexts and variables for such research, in large part as a result of the work of the MacArthur Network on law and mental health (Monahan & Steadman, in press-a, in press-b). Although such research has shown that the accuracy of clinical predictions of violent behavior is often better than chance, no research yet has contradicted the proposition that the validity of even short-term clinical predictions of violent behavior typically is modest (see Lidz, Mulvey, & Gardner, 1993; McNiel & Binder, 1991).[9]

---

[8]This discussion refers not only to criminal defendants facing sentencing but also to respondents facing dispositions in juvenile delinquency or civil commitment proceedings and *insanity acquittees* facing decisions about confinement or conditions of release.

[9]There also is some evidence to suggest that use of a broader array of conceptually derived predictor variables may increase the level of validity substantially. For example, one study showed that 92% of insanity acquittees who did not comply with a medication

Table 2
Probability That a Child Fitting a Hypothetical Profile of a Sexually Abused Child Actually Has Been Recently Abused

1. There are about 65 million children and youth in the United States.
2. Assume that 5% have been recently sexually abused.[a]
3. Therefore, 3.25 million children and youth have been recently sexually abused; 61.75 million have not.
4. Assume that 90% of the children fitting the profile of a sexually abused child on the Melton Magnificent Measure (MMM) have recently been sexually abused; 90% of those children who do not fit the profile have not.[b]
5. Sally Doe fits the MMM profile.

What is the probability that Sally has been recently sexually abused?

3.25 million × 0.90 = 2.925 million true positives (TPs)
61.75 million × 0.10 = 6.175 million false positives (FPs)
2.925 million TPs + 6.175 million FPs = 9.1 million positives (Ps)
2.925 million TPs divided by 9.1 million Ps = 0.32

Therefore, the hypothetical probability (under a scenario of far more pronounced base-rate differences than is true in reality) is only about 1 in 3!

[a]This percentage probably substantially exceeds the actual base rate (see Melton, in press. [b]The development of a profile with such high validity is extremely unlikely given the great diversity of responses among victims of child sexual abuse (Conte & Berliner, 1987).

    The law apparently tolerates a high false-positive rate in predictions of violent behavior, even when the consequences of an error are especially grave (e.g., *Barefoot v. Estelle*, 1983). Nonetheless, Slobogin (1984) believes that the prejudicial impact of any predicted risk of violence and the threat to due process posed by a high false-positive rate are so great that fact finders should be required to decide questions of dangerousness on the basis of fact testimony (e.g., the defendant's history of violence) alone, unless the defendant opens the door to clinical opinions.

    Slobogin's (1984) proposed rule, analogous to that applied to character evidence (Federal Rule of Evidence 404), is designed, therefore, to limit prejudicial evidence. He favors such limitation even when such

---

regimen were readmitted to the hospital within 5 years after release, but only 36% of those who complied were readmitted (Cohen, McEwen, Williams, Silver, & Spodak, 1986). This study suggests that prediction of medication noncompliance under a predictable range of supervision might improve the prediction of dangerous—or at least decompensated or uncontrolled—behavior.

evidence is clearly relevant (as in sentencing and civil commitment hearings) and derived from well-designed psychological or sociological research. At the same time, Slobogin's rule would offer the defendant the opportunity to admit evidence that the odds are low that he or she will engage in violent conduct and, if such evidence is admitted, to permit the prosecution to submit rebuttal evidence.

The examples that I have described so far involve circumstances in which opinions that are at least potentially scientifically sound[10] are or ought to be excluded because of their prejudicial or misleading effect. Conversely, in a situation in which the probative value of an opinion is low (but not zero[11]) because of a weak scientific foundation, it still should be admitted if the fact finder will not exaggerate its significance. In such a circumstance, the opinion still will assist the trier of fact.

For example, a psychodynamic formulation about a defendant's state of mind may give the trier of fact a way of thinking about the evidence that is helpful. Evidence that is not scientifically validated may still extend beyond folk wisdom if it is based on specialized knowledge (see Bonnie & Slobogin, 1980). Consistent with the presumption of innocence, such evidence may enable a defendant to raise a reasonable doubt about his or her guilt. When taken with the proverbial grain of salt (as is likely in insanity cases; see Melton, Petrila, Poythress, & Slobogin, 1987, § 6.02) and given with forthright explanation of its uncertainty, a weakly grounded opinion may nonetheless assist the fact finder.[12]

In a 1993 brief presented to the Supreme Court, the solicitor general noted other circumstances in which scientific evidence that is of low validity should be admitted:

---

[10] Even if research is available on which to base an opinion, of course the opinion itself need not be scientifically valid. For example, translation of a statistically significant difference between abused and nonabused children into a conclusion about behavior observed in most abused children or in abused children, period, obscures the actual finding. Such an opinion would be both scientifically and ethically problematic.

[11] The Supreme Court recently noted in *Daubert v. Merrell Dow Pharmaceuticals* (1993) that *knowledge* "connotes more than subjective belief or unsupported speculation" but that it need not be "'known' to a certainty" (*Daubert*, 1993, p. 2796).

[12] Although juries often are skeptical about mental health professionals' opinions about criminal defendants' sanity, in some jurisdictions successful insanity defenses typically are the product of plea bargains (e.g., Petrila, 1982). The opinion of the state's own expert—most commonly, the psychiatrist or psychologist in the security unit of the state hospital—is typically dispositive, especially when the offense charged is relatively minor. Although expert testimony may not occur in such a context (because no trial takes place), special care should be taken to ensure that due caution is exercised in the reporting of opinions to the prosecutor and, ultimately, the court. When the practice is that prolonged confinement in sometimes draconian conditions can occur because of a mental health professional's essentially unchallenged opinion in regard to a defendant's plea of not guilty by reason of insanity or, worse, guilty but mentally ill (see Callahan, McGreevy, Cirincione, & Steadman, 1992; Slobogin, 1985), the clinician should self-censor speculative opinions—even informed speculation (cf. Bonnie & Slobogin, 1980)—that might be ethical and admissible in a truly adversary setting.

[E]ven a body of assertions generally viewed as manifestly unreliable, untrue or even superstitions for most purposes may be sufficiently reliable to be helpful in certain limited circumstances. Thus, while a judge would err in admitting the testimony of an astrologer to prove that certain events must have occurred as predicted by the horoscope, he would be justified in admitting testimony from the same witness in order to explain the pattern underlying the crimes of a zodiac killer. Similarly, evidence that is not sufficiently reliable to be considered helpful in proving the truth of a disputed fact may be reliable enough to impeach or corroborate the reliable evidence that is admissible to prove the point. An epidemiological study that produces statistically insignificant results, for example, might properly be used for the limited purpose of casting doubt on a more definitive study on the same question, provided the jury receives a suitable limiting instruction. (*Daubert v. Merrell Dow Pharmaceuticals* [hereinafter cited as *Daubert*], 1993, brief of United States, LEXIS p. 13)[13]

The duty to disclose uncertainty. Although the *specialized-knowledge* text offers a heuristic for self-monitoring the boundaries of one's expertise, that principle does not apply to determination of *assistance to the trier of fact*. Psychologists should remember that a properly admissible opinion is not necessarily a fully ethical one, and vice versa. The *assistance* test does provide a heuristic for effective fulfillment of the expert role, however. It should help experts to remember that their task is to be as helpful as possible to the fact finder. In that regard, obfuscating uncertainty, whether intentionally or inadvertently, does not assist the trier of fact in determining the weight to be given an expert's opinion.

I have argued, therefore, that experts should have an affirmative duty to disclose the objective level of certainty (not the subjective confidence) that is associated with their opinions (Melton, Petrila, Poythress, & Slobogin, 1987, § 1.03[b], especially p. 12). If properly applied, such a standard would often lead to admission that systematic data about the validity of an opinion do not exist—in effect, "meta-uncertainty" (e.g., uncertainty about the level of certainty of a prediction). To use what some may regard as an extreme example, even when research is available on the reliability and validity of clinical inferences (as often is not the case in regard to forensic opinions), the expert is likely to

---

[13]The reference to studies not resulting in statistically significant findings probably was based on notice of the fact that statistical analyses using confidence intervals (the evolving practice in public health research; see Rothman, 1986) rather than traditional tests of significance had suggested toxic properties of Benedectin. The circuit courts—and the district court panel that had heard *Daubert*—split on their willingness to hear opinions based on epidemiological studies that had not yielded statistically significant results (see Charrow, 1992; Christoffel & Teret, 1991).

lack systematic evidence about the reliability and validity of his or her own predictions. In other instances, research may be available but may have methodological flaws or questionable generalizability so that its application in a particular case is questionable.[14]

Much more problematic are circumstances in which there is a near-vacuum in directly relevant research. For example, despite the annual incidence of nearly three million reports of suspected child maltreatment, research on risk assessment and treatment efficacy in child-protection cases is sparse at best (U.S. Advisory Board on Child Abuse and Neglect [U.S. ABCAN], 1993; Wald & Woolverton, 1990; Wolfe, 1992). A clinician may still be able to assist the trier of fact in fashioning a conceptually based disposition by identifying precipitants of abusive or neglecting behavior (cf. Monahan, 1981) and indicating factors that are known to be related to child maltreatment and its effects (see generally U.S. ABCAN, 1993). In such a circumstance, though, the clinician should be careful to indicate the virtual absence of outcome research on which to base a prediction about the effectiveness of a proposed disposition. The opinion would be research based (in deriving a theory on which to base a dispositional possibility), but it would still be essentially a "best guess."

In other instances, there may be certainty about uncertainty. For example, well-designed and clearly apposite actuarial research may indicate low predictive validity. Although an opinion that a defendant is or is not dangerous raises the objections that I have noted about ultimate-issue testimony,[15] a carefully stated, empirically based statement of risk does not violate ethical principles in psychology. However, such a risk assessment does make the related policy dilemmas stark.

Thus, I agree with Grisso and Appelbaum's (1992, 1993) conclusion that an opinion about dangerousness is not per se unethical. Grisso and

---

[14] The problem here is related to Monahan and Wexler's (1978) point that the standard of proof and the substantive standard in predictive questions in law interact. The law might require proof of a low level of risk with a high degree of certainty and vice versa. Accordingly, if predictions of violent behavior have low validity (i.e., the probability of a true positive is low), dangerousness might still be proven beyond a reasonable doubt if (a) the variables involved in the predictive equation were well established, (b) the values on the variables associated with the case at hand were proven definitively, and (c) the level of risk required to pass the legal threshold for "dangerousness" was set at a low level.

[15] So do other conclusions of legally relevant status. Perhaps the most common contemporary variant of this error—although one that, fortunately, at least appellate courts typically appear unwilling to accept—is "diagnosis" of child sexual abuse (see Melton & Limber, 1989). For a particularly outrageous recent example of this phenomenon, see *State v. Cressey* (1993), in which a psychologist relied on human figure drawings (e.g., a child's choice of a person of the opposite sex as the first drawing) and an unnormed dissociative events scale to testify that two children had been sexually abused. Whether particular accounts by a child are truthful allegations or accurate signs of abuse is a matter of common sense, not specialized knowledge. Counterexamples that often are provided (e.g., young children's graphic descriptions of sexual activity) prove the point.

Appelbaum appear to base their position in part, however, on the legitimacy of restrictions on liberty derived from predictions with high false-positive error (see Grisso & Appelbaum, 1992, footnote 10). To the degree that they do so, they confuse questions of professional ethics with those of legal policy. Slobogin's (1984) defendant-first rule, for example, is based on an assumption that clinicians and researchers can present empirical evidence that has some probative value (and, I would add, ethical propriety) concerning the issues of dangerousness, but that, under most circumstances, its prejudicial impact should require its exclusion. I concur.

Conclusion

The Federal Rules clearly frame the question of admissibility of expert opinions as one of incremental, not absolute, validity. The central question is whether the admission of an expert opinion leads *marginally* to a better understanding of the evidence on a fact at issue. In this light, the much ballyhooed debate about whether psychological evidence meets a particular standard of reliability or validity has meaning only for those who wish to comment on the state of the field; it is largely irrelevant, however, to the question of admissibility of psychologists' opinions.

That question requires consideration not only of the scientific validity of a given opinion but also of the context in which it is proffered. Depending on the fact finder's knowledge and an opinion's potential to mislead, a highly valid opinion may be properly excluded, or a weakly valid opinion may be properly admitted. A psychologist should not assume either that an insult has been delivered in the former circumstance or that a pat on the back has been given in the latter.

The law's failure to apply a "pure" standard of scientific validity may offend some researchers, but the approach is a sensible one when viewed in light of the purposes of the legal process. An adversary system is based on the premise that justice generally will be promoted by permitting the parties to present their best cases, even if another, more inquisitorial procedure (like peer review) would result in a better approximation of the truth (Thibaut & Walker, 1978). An expert—or any other witness—who seeks to provide the "whole truth" is likely to have his or her answer stricken from the record as unresponsive to the question posed! Such embellishments interfere with the parties' control of the production of evidence. By the same token, evidence that a party proffers is generally admitted unless it has the clear potential to mislead (especially in the direction of unjustified deprivation of life, liberty, or property) or is so unreliable or irrelevant that its presentation will waste the court's time (Federal Rules of Evidence 402 & 403).

Because the rules of evidence are rooted in the theory of justice that underlies the legal system as a whole, they provide clues to the proper boundaries of the roles of the various actors within it. Although there is not a direct correspondence between rules of evidence and standards of professional practice, the connection is close enough that psychologists can monitor the ethics of their own behavior as expert witnesses by reference to Rule 702. Is a given opinion the product of expertise as a psychologist, not the moral sensibility or the common sense of a citizen? If the latter, the opinion should not be offered; if it is demanded, it should be described as a legal, moral, or commonsense judgment, not a psychological one. If the opinion does emanate from professional training and experience, is it being delivered in a manner (with appropriate indications of uncertainty) that will offer maximal assistance to the trier of fact?

In that regard, experts should exercise a level of caution in the provision of opinions that is commensurate with the seriousness of the questions that legal authorities must resolve. Although the law does not require perfect or even strong evidence, it does expect the best evidence (see G. S. Goodman, Levine, & Melton, 1992). The law seeks "to ensure that the trier of fact is presented with the most accurate evidence practicable in those situations where informed legal judgment has concluded that precision is essential" (Weinstein & Berger, 1987, ¶ 9.01[01]). Experts have a duty to provide as much precision in their testimony as is "practicable" so that fact finders can apply it as well as they can.

Daubert v. Merrell Dow Pharmaceuticals

Significance of the Case

Legal significance. Although Rule 702 has a strong conceptual basis, it is not an easy rule to apply. Courts do not have a bright-line standard. Rather, they must balance on a case-by-case basis the probative value of an expert opinion against its tendency to mislead and against the prior knowledge of the trier of fact.

Judges and lawyers often have been uncomfortable with this task. Many believe that judges and juries lack the background to evaluate the scientific merit of opinions. Even if judges and lawyers regard the general task as one that is within their ken, they also may view the time required to establish and explain the foundation for opinions as a luxury when they are trying to manage crowded dockets.

Accordingly, even after the adoption of the Federal Rules, the majority of states and federal circuits retained a version of the *Frye* rule to aid them in weighing the probative value of scientific evidence. Predating the congressional codification of the Federal Rules by more than half a century, the Circuit Court of Appeals for the District of Columbia held that admission of scientific evidence is conditioned on its being "sufficiently established to have gained general acceptance in the particular field to which it belongs" (*Frye v. United States*, 1923, p. 1014). Suspicious of "novel," "untested" ideas, many courts viewed the *Frye* test as an aid in screening scientific evidence for *reliability* (in legal terms, a synonym for scientific *validity*; see *Daubert*, 1993, footnote 9, and the brief in *Daubert* of amicus curiae A Group of American Law Professors, footnote 10). A lack of general acceptance would mean that an opinion would be too unreliable to be of any possible assistance to the trier of fact. Thus, even though *Frye* predated the adoption of the Federal Rules, many courts believed it still to be useful in applying Rule 702.

On the one hand, many commentators were critical of *Frye*, and many courts rejected it. The primary criticism was that *Frye* was unduly conservative. By requiring general acceptance, the *Frye* test resulted in exclusion of evidence that was novel but still reliable. On the other hand, general acceptance in a field with no scientific credibility (e.g., palm reading) is an invalid indicator of evidentiary reliability. The vagueness of the standard also was troubling: Which evidence is "scientific," which field is the "particular" field, how much acceptance is "general," how is general acceptance verified, and does it refer to the method used to reach an opinion or the conclusion actually reached?

Even if the standard resulted in exclusion of unreliable evidence without undue exclusion of evidence that would assist the fact finder, that relation would be irrelevant if the adoption of the Federal Rules preempted *Frye*. (Proponents of this view typically argued that *Frye* was in fact inconsistent with the liberal approach in the Federal Rules.)

The question of the current validity of the *Frye* rule (at least in federal courts) was recently decided by the U.S. Supreme Court in *Daubert v. Merrell Dow Pharmaceuticals* (1993), which now is unquestionably the leading decision on scientific evidence. *Daubert* focused on the admissibility of unpublished research relevant to allegations that maternal ingestion of Benedectin, a treatment for morning sickness, caused birth defects. Directly confronted with the possible preemption of *Frye* by the Federal Rules, the Court considered the propriety of the trial court's exclusion of the evidence (upheld by the Ninth Circuit Court of Appeals) because it had not been subjected to peer review and, therefore, had not obtained general acceptance in the field of epidemiology.

Political significance. Although the Supreme Court often considers scientific evidence,[16] the Court has rarely issued decisions focusing even

---

[16]Melton (1987a, p. 488) lists instances in which virtually every member of the Supreme Court had either approved of use of social-scientific evidence or had criticized other justices for failure to consider such evidence. APA's own prodigious involvement as amicus curiae in Supreme Court cases is another indicator of the significance that scientific evidence now has in the Court (Bersoff, 1987; Tremper, 1987).

tangentially on the circumstances under which such evidence can be admitted. When the Court decided to hear such a case, the result was a case example of the professional and political furor described in the introduction to this chapter. Reflecting the level of interest in the evidentiary, scientific, and ethical problems of expert testimony, *Daubert* elicited 22 amicus curiae (friend of the court) briefs, a number more common to abortion cases than tort litigation.

The list of amici curiae in *Daubert* looked to a large extent like a who's who of the scientific establishment: the American Association for the Advancement of Science (AAAS), the American Medical Association and a plethora of medical specialty organizations, the National Academy of Sciences, the *New England Journal of Medicine* and other prestigious medical journals, and numerous distinguished epidemiologists, specialists in forensic medicine, and philosophers of science. It may be the only time that AAAS and the National Academy have joined to speak out on a public issue (Marshall, 1993). Although the APA did not enter the case, several psycholegal scholars (Donald N. Bersoff, David L. Faigman, John Monahan, and Michael J. Saks) collaborated in a scholarly neutral brief filed by "A Group of American Law Professors."

Just as organized science believes its status and integrity to be at issue in expert testimony, the corporate sector regards the breadth of admissible expert evidence as a factor directly related to the scope of damages awarded plaintiffs. Accordingly, the remaining amici included the American Insurance Association, the American Tort Reform Association, the Chamber of Commerce, the Pharmaceutical Manufacturers Association, the Product Liability Council, the United States (Solicitor General), and the Washington Legal Foundation (a conservative legal advocacy group), all of whom filed briefs supporting Merrell Dow. Completing the list of corporate heavy hitters, former Solicitor General (now Harvard law professor) Charles Fried argued the case for Merrell Dow.[17] To some extent confirming the business groups' fear, the Association of Trial Lawyers of America—the plaintiffs' bar—filed a brief arguing, in support of Daubert, that scientific evidence should be admitted whenever it would assist the jury, regardless of whether peer reviewers had approved the proffered expert's opinion.

The Court's Analysis

The holding. As Chief Justice Rehnquist (joined by Justice Stevens) noted, the verbal free-for-all found in the two dozen briefs was "markedly

---

[17]The legal team for Merrell Dow included other legal luminaries. Charles Nesson, a well-known Harvard evidence scholar and occasional moderator of televised discussions, and Joel Klein, a Washington attorney who frequently has represented the American Psychiatric Association, also collaborated in Merrell Dow's brief.

different" from the debate usually before the Court, "in that large parts ... do not deal with decided cases or statutory language—the sort of material we customarily interpret. Instead they deal with definitions of scientific knowledge, scientific validity, and peer review—in short, matters far afield from the expertise of judges" (*Daubert*, 1993, p. 2799).

Not surprisingly, then, the opinion for the Court was assigned to its expert on scientific evidence, Justice Blackmun, a recipient of the AP-LS Distinguished Contributions Award, who was a math major at Harvard and general counsel to the Mayo Clinic (see Melton, 1990b; Schlesinger & Nesse, 1980). The central holding in *Daubert* was based, though, on the legislative history of adoption of the Federal Rules of Evidence, not an arcane epistemological analysis. Finding no evidence that Congress intended to fold the *Frye* rule into the Federal Rules, the Court unanimously held that the general-acceptance standard was superseded and therefore no longer controlling in federal courts.[18]

Although the core holding was based on a straightforward legal analysis, the multitude of amicus briefs heavily influenced the second half of the opinion, in which Blackmun was joined by six colleagues in providing dicta[19] about factors to be considered in weighing such evidence. By implication, that discussion provides guidance to experts and attorneys preparing the presentation of scientific opinions, although it also leaves new questions about the standards to be used in consideration of clinical opinions,[20] at least under federal law.

The balance involved in determining admissibility. In general, Blackmun supported the view that I presented in my analysis of the Federal

---

[18]Readers are again cautioned that the overruling of *Frye* is controlling only in regard to federal law. *Daubert* will undoubtedly be influential in many of the states whose evidence codes are copies of the Federal Rules and who, like several of the federal circuits, also had continued to follow *Frye*. Nonetheless, state courts are free to interpret their codes as encompassing a general-acceptance standard even if the language in the state code is identical to the Federal Rules.

[19]*Black's Law Dictionary* (Black et al., 1990) defines *dicta* as follows: The word is generally used as an abbreviated form of *obiter dictum*, "a remark by the way;" that is, an observation or remark made by a judge in pronouncing an opinion upon a cause, concerning some rule, principle, or application of law, or the solution of a question suggested by the case at bar, but not necessarily involved in the case or essential to its determination; any statement of the law enunciated by the court merely by way of illustration, argument, analogy or suggestion. (p. 454) Dicta thus have some precedential value because they indicate the thinking of a court and the analysis that it might apply if a particular issue related to the case at hand were before the court. Nonetheless, because dicta are not part of the holding in regard to the question litigated, they are not controlling on subsequent and inferior courts.

[20]I am not intending to suggest here that *clinical* opinions are devoid of a *scientific* foundation or to engage in one of APA's internecine guild battles. Rather, as I discuss later in this chapter, it is unclear whether the dicta in *Daubert* about *scientific knowledge* also apply to *technical and other specialized knowledge* under Federal Rule of Evidence 702 and, if not, how clinical opinions would be classified (see Table 1; see also *Daubert*, 1993, opinion of Rehnquist, joined by Stevens, concurring in part and dissenting in part).

Rules: Bright-line indicia of reliability (e.g., whether general acceptance has been obtained or even whether peer review has occurred) are inconsistent with the balancing test implicit in the requirement for specialized knowledge that will assist the trier of fact. Thus, the debate about a threshold standard of scientific reliability or expert credibility is misplaced. Those who would put expert opinions under an especially acute microscope of peer review ask too much of experts, but those who believe that the law should defer to clinical judgments without scrutiny ask too little.

On the one hand, Blackmun made clear that bright-line indicia of evidentiary reliability, such as the "austere" general-acceptance standard, are inconsistent with the "liberal" admission of evidence favored by the drafters of the Federal Rules (*Daubert*, 1993, p. 2794). The law relies on cross-examination to illuminate the weaknesses of most opinion evidence and the capacity of the jury to perceive and weigh it fairly.

On the other hand, Blackmun emphasized that it is proper for judges to exclude scientific evidence when its validity is so weak that it makes no demonstrable contribution to just resolution of the case at hand:

> [Some] suggest that recognition of a screening role for the judge that allows for the exclusion of "invalid" evidence will sanction a stifling and repressive scientific orthodoxy and will be inimical to the search for truth. It is true that open debate is an essential part of both legal and scientific analyses. Yet there are important differences between the quest for truth in the courtroom and the quest for truth in the laboratory. Scientific conclusions are subject to perpetual revision. Law, on the other hand, must resolve disputes finally and quickly. The scientific project is advanced by broad and wide-ranging consideration of a multitude of hypotheses, for those that are incorrect will eventually be shown to be so, and that in itself is an advance. Conjectures that are probably wrong are of little use, however, in the project of reaching a quick, final, and binding legal judgment—often of great consequence—about a particular set of events in the past. We recognize that in practice, a gatekeeping role for the judge, no matter how flexible, inevitably on occasion will prevent the jury from learning of authentic insights and innovations. That, nevertheless, is the balance that is struck by Rules of Evidence designed *not for cosmic understanding but for the particularized resolution of legal disputes.* (*Daubert*, 1993, pp. 2798–2799, emphasis added and footnote omitted)

In other words, the law does not require perfection or even a particular level of absolute validity. Accordingly, those who believe that the law expects "cosmic understanding" through a pristine scientific inquiry— a higher standard than may be customary in conventional science and practice—or even particular indicia of validity, such as peer-reviewed publication, are simply mistaken. The law's primary purpose is the pursuit of justice, not truth (Thibaut & Walker, 1978), and it accomplishes that result in part through predictability of decision making—"a quick, final, and binding legal judgment."

At the same time, those who believe that adherence to conventional norms of practice by an appropriately credentialed expert is a sufficient foundation for admission of the expert's opinion are also wrong. That an opinion is offered by an expert does not mean that it is an expert opinion within the meaning of the law. Reliance on professional credentials without consideration of scientific validity leaves "the professional guilds to decide what scientific evidence to admit. Admissibility of scientific evidence thus becomes a guild issue resolved not by legal principle, nor on the basis of the accuracy of the information, but instead by the internal politics of professional organizations" (*Daubert*, 1993, brief of A Group of American Law Professors, LEXIS p. 10).

Reliance on journal peer review has a similar curious result. As a group of amici who had studied the vagaries of the peer review process (e.g., Chubin & Hackett, 1990) observed,

> We ... think it odd ... that federal judges, who are pledged to uphold a Constitution that emphasizes such principles of due process of law as public access and accountability should be so eager to consign threshold questions of who can testify and what they can say to the self-selected editors of private journals, whose decisions are largely shrouded from view and totally insusceptible to appeals. (*Daubert*, 1993, brief of Chubin et al., footnote 5)

Factors for consideration. The *Daubert* dicta did make clear that to be "scientific," opinions must be based on "an inference or assertion ... derived by the scientific method" (*Daubert*, 1993, p. 2796). Determination of this threshold is susceptible to use of a neutral expert, as permitted by Federal Rule of Evidence 706 (*Daubert*, 1993, brief of Carnegie Commission on Science, Technology, and Government; cf. *Daubert*, 1993, brief of A Group of American Law Professors). Although appointment of a neutral expert for the court is often touted as a solution to the purported battle of the experts, the option is rarely used (Willging, 1986) in part because of fear that the court's choice will not be representative of experts on the particular issue. An opinion about whether a scientific method was used does not require substantive expertise on the specific topic at issue, however.

The Court further clarified in *Daubert* (1993) that the question of *assistance to the trier of fact* is primarily one of *relevance* or, in scientific terms, *generalizability*: "a valid scientific connection to the pertinent inquiry" (p. 2796). In summary, therefore, the trial court deciding the admissibility of scientific evidence must assess "whether the reasoning or methodology underlying the testimony is scientifically valid and . . . whether that reasoning or methodology properly can be applied to the facts in issue" (p. 2796). Although expressly noting that its list of factors was not exhaustive, the Court offered some criteria to use in forming such an impression: testability of opinions,[21] whether peer review has occurred (a "relevant, though not dispositive consideration"; *Daubert*, 1993, p. 2797), the error rate associated with methods used, and the level of acceptance of those methods by experts in the field. Blackmun emphasized that Rule 702 is intended to promote a "flexible" inquiry, with the "overarching" focus to be on "the scientific validity—and thus the evidentiary relevance and reliability—of the principles that underlie a proposed submission" (p. 2797). He further clarified that "the focus, of course, must be solely on principles and methodology, not on the conclusions that they generate" (p. 2797). Thus, new ideas not yet generally accepted in the scientific community are not barred from admission into legal decision making.

Implications for clinical testimony. Beyond the question whether the state courts will follow *Daubert*, the major confusion that is left by the case is the domain that it addresses. *Daubert* provides guidance to courts considering *scientific* evidence under Rule 702, but do its factors apply to *technical or other specialized knowledge*, too? If the standards are different, into which category does clinical evidence fall? If mental health professionals' opinions are "scientific," does the clinical inference process, as conventionally practiced, fall within the scope of the scientific method?

Note that if clinical decision making does not meet such a standard but if clinical opinions are classified as "scientific," then most clinical opinions would be properly excluded. Such a result is clearly contrary to the spirit of Rule 702 and its focus, when read as a whole, on incremental validity of decision making by the trier of fact. Accordingly, my hunch is that such opinions are considered technical rather than scientific, as *Daubert* defines the latter term.

Regardless, the Court's analysis of Rule 702 serves notice both that mere credentialing (in *Daubert*, 1993, journal editors' seal of approval) is insufficient for admissibility and that an absence of credentials is insufficient for exclusion of opinions. It thus gives additional authority for courts not only to conduct searching inquiries of the foundation for expert opinions but also to permit presentation of opinions that may provide novel but plausible ways of approaching the evidence.

---

[21] In dissenting from the *Daubert* dicta, Chief Justice Rehnquist admitted that he did not know what *falsifiability* means, much less how to judge it.

Standards for Consideration of
Psychological Research

Judicial Notice

Although maintenance of access to clinical expertise requires continuous efforts, the challenges may be even more formidable in assuring that courts have access to relevant findings of psychological research. Because they are case-specific, clinical opinions present fewer conceptual difficulties for courts than do research findings. Accordingly, trial court judges may prefer testimony by a clinician over that by a researcher even in regard to eyewitness issues (Poythress, 1983).

Whether the omission is purposeful or the result simply of lack of easy availability, appellate courts also often do not obtain scientific evidence to guide their decision making. That the *Daubert* case, for example, reached the Supreme Court at all may have resulted in part from the failure of the Ninth Circuit Court of Appeals (*Daubert v. Merrell Dow Pharmaceuticals*, 1991) to have done a more careful examination of scientific norms. As two groups of scholars on the philosophy and sociology of science lamented in their amicus briefs in the Supreme Court (*Daubert*, 1993, briefs of Chubin et al. and of Physicians, Scientists, and Historians of Science), the Ninth Circuit's categorical rejection of an unpublished reanalysis of published data was based on a single law review article, and its view that consensus and peer-reviewed publication are necessary for scientific validity relied exclusively on a popular book about "junk science" (i.e., Huber, 1991).

Part of the problem, about which I say more later, is that courts have little guidance about ways to obtain and then to weigh social science evidence. Undoubtedly, the most common means is *judicial notice*—admission, whether formally or tacitly, of evidence without testimony or other proof because it is already known to the court (see Perry & Melton, 1984). Judicial notice is a doctrine that permits courts to assume certain facts that are so obvious they do not require proof (e.g., visibility is reduced in the dark).

Although the propriety of judicial notice has been long established in the common law, the doctrine has expanded over the years. It has grown from that which everyone knows to that which is commonly known or readily verifiable through, for example, a trip to the library. Muddying the waters, though, is the fact that the evidentiary rule (Federal Rule of Evidence 201) that provides the authority and standard for judicial notice is expressly limited to *adjudicative* (case-specific) acts. Assumptions about principles of human behavior are not covered; indeed, there is no rule on this point at all.

Providing some guidance in *Daubert* (albeit in dicta; see footnote 6), the Supreme Court expressly approved use of judicial notice when "scientific law" is relevant (*Daubert*, 1993, p. 2796, footnote 11). If the Court's example (i.e., the laws of thermodynamics) is representative, however, then there may be few circumstances in which psychological facts are easily susceptible to judicial notice.

Monahan and Walker's Proposal

By far the most coherent and comprehensive—although, in my view, still not fully successful—rules for courts' use of social science evidence were proposed by University of Virginia law professors John Monahan and Laurens Walker (for summaries, see Monahan & Walker, 1988, 1991). In addition to purely clinical, case-specific evidence, Monahan and Walker posited three kinds of research evidence.

Social authority (Monahan & Walker, 1986) refers to research about empirical assumptions (e.g., children's competence as decision makers) used in creation or modification of a rule of law. Viewing social authority as similar to law itself in its generalizability beyond the instant case, Monahan and Walker argued that findings in regard to social authority should serve as precedent for subsequent and lower courts and that evidence that might ultimately be used in such findings should be submitted at both trial and appellate levels through briefs (not testimony). Moreover, just as judges at all levels may seek the law themselves (even if relevant authorities are not presented by the parties in arguments or briefs), appellate courts should be able to undertake de novo review of conclusions of social authority by lower courts.

In contrast to social authority, research on *social facts* (Walker & Monahan, 1988) is used to prove case-specific facts, such as the level of perceived similarity between two trademarks or of gender discrimination in hiring and promotion within a particular corporation. Although research is used as social authority by judges to determine the law, research on social facts is used by triers of fact (usually juries) to decide whether violations of law have occurred in particular cases. How research is to be designed and used is a legal standard in Walker and Monahan's view, so the appropriate methodology would be communicated by jury instruction. The application of the methodology of data collection to the case at hand would be presented in expert testimony.

Research on *social frameworks* (Walker & Monahan, 1987) provides triers of fact with general conclusions from social science to assist them in determining factual issues in a particular case. Examples include syndrome evidence and research on eyewitness identifications. As generalizable information, evidence on social frameworks would be presented by briefs (like law) and communicated to the jury through instruction.

I have two principal objections to the Monahan/Walker formulation. First, categories of expert evidence are not as neatly separable as Monahan and Walker imply. For example, research on particular trademarks may provide generalizable principles about perception. Similarly, clinicians are apt, expressly or implicitly, to present group evidence (social authority, in Monahan and Walker's approach) on which they rely to form their case-specific conclusions.

Second and more fundamentally, use of social science findings as legal authority is likely to result in increasing unreality in the law. When a court's impressions are demonstrably incorrect, why should lower courts be required to adopt a view of the world that is known to be wrong? Although judges certainly are not now immune from reliance on legal fictions, a requirement to institutionalize such mythical impressions (cf. Melton, 1987d; Perry & Melton, 1984) into the law is curious indeed. Although use of precedent builds predictability into the law, there is a logical error in assuming that social reality can be "found" through use of precedent. The opinions of rich old people are undoubtedly important in shaping public policy (and judicial opinions; see Rosen, 1984), but their purported superiority for determination of empirical truth is baffling.

Regardless, Monahan and Walker's formulation is an important first step that may provide courts with greater confidence in use of social science evidence. If it is to adopted, however, systematic efforts to educate the judiciary about the standards themselves and their application (including means of finding relevant research) will be necessary. Although Monahan and Walker's influence thus far has been more in the academy than the courts and legislatures, it is likely that their view eventually will result in even greater momentum for the rapidly growing use of Brandeis briefs.[22]

Enhancing Forensic Practice: The Case for Specialization

Of course, determination of the standard for admission and consideration of psychological evidence does not fully resolve the problem of courts' informed use of expert opinions. For example, once the conclusion is reached that some clinical opinions can be offered ethically and admitted legally, the next question is who should provide such expert assistance. In that regard, my preference is for use of forensic specialists whenever possible.

---

[22]*Brandeis briefs* are briefs that are intended primarily to inform courts about relevant social phenomena. The label refers to the briefs submitted by Louis Brandeis (prior to his appointment to the Supreme Court) that consisted primarily of extralegal authority and that established the practice of judicial notice of social authorities (see *Muller v. Oregon*, 1907).

Although such a policy probably would result in a better match between the legal system's needs and the expert's knowledge, that positive effect is not the primary reason for my advocacy of specialization in forensic mental health. Rather, my preference for specialists rests on (a) the possible adverse effects of forensic work on other aspects of mental health practice and (b) the need for a special system to maximize legal professionals' access to forensic expertise.

Adverse Effects of Forensic Work on General Mental Health Practice

Perhaps the strongest reason for reliance primarily on specialists to deliver forensic services is that forensic clinicians' proper emphasis on uncertainty is not fully compatible with either conventional or optimal clinical practice. Maximum assistance to the fact finder requires adoption of a scientist's mindset, with a skeptical view of the validity of inferences and careful scrutiny of the probabilities involved. Although there is no question that both the design and the delivery of clinical services should be informed by empirical research, continuous self-scrutiny—in effect, self-doubt—about the validity of one's impressions and plans is likely to undermine therapeutic efficacy (cf. Frank, 1973; White, Tursky, & Schwartz, 1985).

The techniques involved in forensic assessment also may be antitherapeutic. Forensic evaluations typically must be conducted in a relatively short period of time, are not for the subject's own benefit, often focus on highly emotionally charged events, and commonly involve matters about which there is a motivation to lie. As a result, forensic interviews often are confrontational and address traumatic memories faster than would be common in therapeutic assessment and intervention.

The facts that the ultimate client often is not the person being evaluated and that the primary goal in any event is not to assist him or her both raise the potential for confusion of roles (and corollary ethical dilemmas) if a clinician also becomes involved as a therapist. Accordingly, both Division 41's guidelines (Committee on Ethical Guidelines for Forensic Psychologists, 1991, Guideline IV[D]) and the APA (1992, Standard 7.03) Ethics Code discourage such dual involvement.

Similarly, because of the exercise of authority that may be involved (e.g., directly in evaluations for civil commitment and indirectly in evaluations for sentencing and competency to be executed), forensic practice may alter clinicians' perspective or reputation in ways that interfere with therapeutic evaluations and interventions with clients without legal-system involvement. Indeed, this effect may occur even when the clinician's opinions do not directly translate into loss of a defendant's liberty or life. Mere association with the justice system may be enough to compromise the clinician's current and potential therapeutic relationships. To use the most blatant example, the presence in a clinician's waiting room of defendants confined in leg irons and guarded by armed deputies does little to diminish the stigma associated with receipt of mental health services or to increase the trust that clients have in their therapist's benevolence.[23]

Development of a Community-Based Forensic Service System

Reliance on forensic specialists makes sense not only because of the potential adverse effects of forensic work on general mental health practice but also because of the effort needed to build a forensic service system. There are formidable obstacles to sustained relations between the mental health and justice systems; overcoming the obstacles requires a level of commitment that may be unrealistic for clinicians for whom forensic work is a secondary task.

In addition to philosophical issues and ordinary problems of interaction ("turf") between agencies, forensic mental health programs face practical problems of work in the legal system (e.g., uncertain scheduling, security problems, involvement with litigious people). As a result, leaders in law and mental health have begun to focus on the need to develop a *system* of forensic services (Keilitz, 1992).

The development by my colleagues and me of a system of forensic teams in community mental health centers in Virginia (Melton, Weithorn, & Slobogin, 1985) showed that community-based forensic services are both desirable and practical. Well-organized community-based systems preserve defendants' rights to bail, a speedy trial, and effective assistance of counsel. We also demonstrated a substantial reduction in costs to the state while achieving higher quality evaluations (in comparison with hospital-based evaluations) as assessed by prosecutors, defense attorneys, and judges. The implementation of a system of criminal forensic evaluations also resulted in dramatic increases in frequency of interaction between the mental health centers and the legal system, even in civil domains and in crisis intervention, consultation, and treatment services in jails.

Although the benefits of a community-based forensic service system are great, we also showed that its implementation requires careful planning and sustained diligent efforts. As we summarized,

---

[23] Of course, this particular problem can be avoided—albeit often with some loss of efficiency and privacy—by conducting jail-based evaluations of defendants currently in custody. Nonetheless, the broader point is still applicable. General clinicians' forays into the legal system—often with great publicity—may affect other clients' and potential clients' trust.

> Successful implementation of community-based forensic services requires much more than simply training community mental health clinicians in the techniques of forensic assessment. Notably, the system can fall apart without active involvement—or without co-optation—of all the relevant parties (e.g., state mental health and court administrators, judges, prosecutors, defense attorneys, sheriffs, directors of community mental health centers, guild organizations of the various mental health professions). (Melton et al., 1985, p. 113)

Implementation required not only correcting economic disincentives for community-based services[24] but also developing and disseminating model court orders, interagency agreements, and routine referral procedures and arranging transportation and security for defendants in custody. Most important, various legal constituencies had to be educated to overcome their intuition that brief community-based evaluations are inherently low-quality and defense-oriented.

Consensus also had to be reached about complex legal issues (e.g., whether clinicians could address problems of diminished capacity; whether prosecutors could obtain potentially incriminating evaluation information at will). It is unsurprising that judges, public defenders, and prosecutors often had differing views on such matters, and the legal academicians among us sometimes had still another opinion. The appearance of swaying in one direction or another was a continuous early threat to the project. Ultimately, lengthy amendments to the state code were needed to institutionalize the system and preserve defendants' rights (Va. Code, 1990/1993).

Our experience confirmed the conclusions of other observers of interaction between the mental health and justice systems (e.g., Ogloff & Roesch, 1992). If such interaction is to go smoothly, there must be *boundary spanners* (Steadman, 1992)—staff whose job is to provide the necessary coordination. Such positions are necessary at both state and local levels. An advisory board representing defense attorneys, prosecutors, and judges was crucial in resolving the interagency and legal issues and lobbying for, or at least minimizing opposition to, the complex legislative package that ultimately was adopted.

The complexity of a successful forensic mental health system implies a substantial economy of scale. Clinicians who plan to undertake a limited forensic practice are unlikely to have incentives to invest the time needed to create and sustain working relationships with authorities

---

[24]Payment for community-based evaluations came from court budgets while the much greater cost of state-financed hospital evaluations was not incurred by the referring agency.

in the justice system, master the legal issues raised by forensic mental health services, and negotiate solutions to such problems.

The Need for Specialized Knowledge

An economy of scale also may be applicable to expertise itself. The level of familiarity with the literature that is necessary for optimal education of the trier of fact (cf. Poythress, 1980) may be difficult to achieve amid the demands of full-time general clinical practice.

Forensic practice involves a specialized body of knowledge that typically is not possessed by either lawyers or general mental health professionals (Melton et al., 1985). Appropriately trained forensic clinicians have specialized knowledge about relevant legal standards and issues, the technology of various forms of forensic assessment (e.g., Grisso, 1986), and the effects of various dispositions. They also probably are better aware than general clinicians about potential threats to the rights of subjects of evaluations (e.g., use of the fruits of evaluations of competency to stand trial for the purpose of discovering incriminating information).

This body of knowledge can be learned at an acceptable level relatively quickly. A knowledge level commensurate with that of forensic diplomates can be attained by general mental health clinicians (regardless of specific discipline) in an 8-day training program (Melton et al., 1985). Thus, although I favor development of a specialty in forensic mental health, that position is not based on a belief that the skills involved are so difficult or the relevant knowledge so vast. Rather, my preference for specialty clinics in forensic psychology is derived from the conviction that the organizational and role demands of forensic assessment are incompatible with general clinical practice.[25]

It is common even for leaders in law and mental health to attribute the problems in interaction between the two systems to differences in training and jargon. If only we used the same vocabulary, so the argument goes, many of our problems would be eliminated (Casey, Keilitz, & Hafemeister, 1992). Undeniably, miscommunication—or perhaps more commonly, inapposite or unresponsive reports and testimony—does sometimes occur as a result of a lack of understanding by mental health professionals of legal standards or by jurists of social science methods

---

[25] Although most forensic assessments should be conducted by specialists in forensic mental health, such services should be integrated into the regular community mental health system to avoid establishing a de facto corrections program that is "the unwanted stepchild of the mental health system, chronically underfunded and understaffed" (Melton et al., 1985, p. 115). Such a community-based system can assure responsiveness to people in conflict with their relatives and neighbors and in periods of great personal crisis. Unnecessary court referrals may be reduced as a result.

and clinical jargon. An appalling number of clinicians give opinions, breach (or fail to breach) confidentiality, or directly deprive individuals of liberty on the basis of legal standards that they do not know or know but ignore (e.g., Kalichman, Craig, & Follingstad, 1989; Roesch & Golding, 1980).

It is a mistake, though, to identify interdisciplinary problems in communication as the primary root of issues in forensic mental health. The communication problems themselves may be overblown. In fact, there is substantial overlap among trial court judges, forensic psychologists, and forensic psychiatrists in their ratings of the meaningfulness of mental health jargon (Dietz, Cooke, Rappeport, & Silvergleit, 1983). To the degree that vocabulary problems do interfere, their remediation will illuminate much more difficult problems emanating from disciplinary differences in conceptualization of the nature of a fact, attributions of causality, application of group data to individual cases, responses to interpersonal conflict, and definition of roles (Melton, Petrila, Poythress, & Slobogin, 1987, chap. 1).

In short, specialization facilitates acquisition of knowledge that is particularly relevant to forensic work, and it may increase the appreciation of paradigmatic differences between law and psychology. The body of specialized forensic knowledge is not so large and technical, though, that its mastery necessitates specialization. Rather, such professional development can be seen as a positive by-product of the level of specialization that is needed to establish and manage the intersystem relations that a forensic practice requires.

Regardless, even if general clinicians could acquire expertise about forensic psychology with a modest investment of time, research suggests that such knowledge is not widely shared. Although lack of specialization should not be cause for barring admission of clinical opinions that are the product of general expertise in mental health, there is good reason for legal authorities to seek the assistance of forensic specialists.

Guidelines for Effective Diffusion of Psychological Research

Ensuring the Availability and Usefulness of Scientific Evidence

My preference for the development of a specialty practice in forensic mental health is based in large part on the desirability—and the difficulty—of systematizing legal authorities' access to psychological knowledge that would be useful in their decision making. As a matter of public policy, this problem may be even more acute in regard to research than it is to clinical expertise because judges' assumptions about human behavior often underlie decisions about issues affecting large numbers of people. By contrast, clinical opinions may have little application beyond the parties in a particular case.

With the ultimate task of guiding researchers in diffusing knowledge among potential users in the legal system, a study group that I chaired for the Society for Research in Child Development examined ways that various actors in the legal system learn about social science research and then use, misuse, or ignore it (Melton, 1987c). Besides applying our experience in law schools and courts, we synthesized existing research about knowledge dissemination and use (especially in the legal system), and we commissioned several studies of reading habits of judges and probation officers and citation practices of judges. Our work resulted in several broad recommendations (Melton, 1987b):

Report research where it is accessible to users. Research that we conducted on the reading habits of judges and probation officers (Grisso & Melton, 1987) and the citation practices of judges and law professors (Hafemeister & Melton, 1987) showed that for research to be discovered by judges and lawyers actively seeking it, it must be available in journals covered by the *Index to Legal Periodicals*. For incidental exposure, popular media and practitioner journals, such as state bar journals, are the best bet. The low hit rate for attempts to penetrate the national news media combined with the virtual certainty of nonpenetration if active efforts are not made (Weiss & Singer, 1988) means that substantial time must be invested if researchers want their policy-relevant findings to be used. The diversity of professional reading across various specialties has the same implication.

Use informal networks to diffuse information. News about the law, like other disciplines, travels primarily by word of mouth (see Wasby, 1976). Whether in the legislative or the judicial process, relatively small issue networks of opinion leaders not only shape policy and practice but also serve as the primary sources of information for their professional peers.

My colleagues at the Center on Children, Families, and the Law at the University of Nebraska (Olson & McKinlay, 1993) collaborated with the American Bar Association Center on Children and the Law to attempt to harness the informal process of knowledge diffusion among judges. A small group of judges, judicial educators, and staff of the National Center for State Courts identified judges in Iowa and Nebraska whom they believed were likely to be leaders of judicial views about child sexual abuse. The resulting list of 16 judges were contacted. All agreed to participate in conference-call seminars, read selected written materials, communicate the information to peers, and log such activities.

In brief, the low-cost process that we undertook proved to have significant impact. Judges appreciated the convenience of continuing education at their desks and having the opportunity for direct discussions with respected peers and experts. Most important, virtually all of the judges did spread the word, usually through multiple face-to-face interactions with other judges. About three fourths of these informal brief educational events occurred at the networker's initiation. The remainder involved "teachable moments" when peers sought information or opinions.

Look for opportunities to apply the research. Whether in amicus briefs or briefings of advocates or legislators and their staff, the most direct impact comes when researchers bring their information to fora in which decisions are to be made about matters to which particular social science findings are relevant. In this regard, integration into issue networks can do double duty. Not only can researchers use the networks as avenues for diffusion of knowledge but they also can learn about forthcoming opportunities for its application.

Use professional organizations. Professional associations play two important roles in the application of scientific information in the legal process. First, they are de facto arbiters of good science and practice. Courts are especially prone to use policy statements, practice guidelines, testimony, or briefs by professional associations or government commissions as authoritative statements of the state of knowledge or practical art.

Second, the professional associations—and APA is more active and influential than most—have active programs to bring knowledge into the policy arena through lobbying of legislative and administrative officials, contacts with representatives of other professional and advocacy groups, legislative testimony, and amicus briefs. Because of staff integration into issue networks, professional associations can be an efficient avenue for diffusion of policy-relevant knowledge.

Incidentally, given the fact that most legal policy issues are primarily matters of state law, the minimal involvement of most state psychological associations in issues other than those with direct guild implications (Melton, 1985) is tragic. The opportunities for assuring socially responsive policy are greatest in the state capitols and courtrooms. Positive by-products of systematic efforts to diffuse policy-relevant psychological knowledge in such venues would be likely to include heightened credibility of the state association and the profession as well as greater respect for the state universities and the psychology departments within them. Although money and power may help advocates to get through the door in state capitols, the significance of honest presentation of useful knowledge should not be underestimated (see Melton, 1983, chap. 7, on effective lobbying).

Meet legal professionals on their own terms. Psychological knowledge is most likely to be used when it is presented within the context of a legally sound policy analysis that identifies the important empirical issues and their policy significance. The quality of the legal scholarship is likely to be as important as the rigor of the science in determining whether research is used (and not misused). Although many psycholegal scholars themselves are capable of this disciplinary integration, there is a need at the very least for effective collaboration between psychological researchers and law professors. Such a collaboration requires psychologists to master the sociology of law schools, which is quite different from that of psychology and psychiatry departments (Melton, Monahan et al., 1987), and the publication practices of law reviews, which bear little resemblance to those of social science and health journals.

Psychologists also must appreciate the institutional constraints that their legal colleagues face and, when appropriate, work with them for change. In that regard, it is useful to note that by far the most powerful known correlate of trial judges' frequency of reading behavioral science literature was the level of secretarial services available to them ($r =$ .72 in one judicial sample; Melton et al., 1985).

The general message is clear. If researchers want their legally relevant findings to be used, they must invest substantial time in myriad activities outside the usual duties of professors, such as the following

- preparing reports for specific audiences of potential consumers of the information
- participating in, or at least obtaining the confidence of, networks of opinion leaders
- watching for relevant judicial cases or legislative bills and presenting briefs or testimony
- lobbying for support staff for judges.

Thus, as with issues about use of clinical opinions in the legal system, the questions that have dominated both legal and psychological discourse about the proper use of research evidence may pale in the face of the practical problems of ensuring decision makers' access to information in an easily usable form. The need for systemic development is clear. Not only should evidentiary standards be developed (as in Monahan and Walker's research) to guide judges in determining when use of scientific evidence is appropriate, but university standards for tenure, promotion, and merit pay also should be reformed. Without due recognition of scholars' investment of time in diffusion as well as creation of knowledge, timely application of relevant scientific findings is unlikely.

Presenting Psychological Evidence Clearly and Honestly

Suppose that one does get through the door of the courthouse. What can psychologists do to ensure that their opinions are given appropriate weight? Obviously, this problem applies to both clinicians and researchers who become involved in work in the legal system.

Numerous practical pointers for effective expert testimony have been presented by Brodsky (1991) and Melton, Petrila, Poythress, and Slobogin (1987, chap. 14). For now, let me indicate that, apart from the evidentiary framework that Monahan and Walker present, I hope that their encouragement of presentation of research evidence by briefs is heeded by the bench and the bar.

Notwithstanding the historic assumption in the law that cross-examination is an effective method for illuminating the weaknesses of evidence, it is a poor means of showing the deficiencies (and strengths) of expert opinions. Numerous factors make expert testimony difficult to test: jurors' lack of background knowledge, expert witnesses' apparent confidence, their frequent failure (like other people) to be able to identify the factors that actually influenced their opinions, and often their vagueness (e.g., reference to findings "in the literature"; see Smith, 1989).

In overturning a conviction based in part on victim syndrome evidence, the New Hampshire Supreme Court (*State v. Cressey*, 1993) noted the following problems:

> We are not convinced that a thorough cross-examination can effectively expose any unreliable elements or assumptions in [the psychologist's] testimony. The methodology used in the psychological evaluations makes her presentation of evidence effectively beyond reproach. [The psychologist's] conclusions do not rest on one particular indicator or symptom, but rather on her interpretation of all the factors and information before her. So even though the defendant may be able to discredit several of the indicators, symptoms, or test results, the expert's overall opinion is likely to emerge unscathed. An expert using this methodology may candidly acknowledge any inconsistencies or potential shortcomings in the individual pieces of evidence she presents, but can easily dismiss the critique by saying that her evaluation relies on no one symptom or indicator and that her conclusions still hold true in light of all the other available factors and her expertise in the field. In such a case, *the expert's conclusions are as impenetrable as they are unverifiable.* (*State v. Cressey*, 1993, p. 701; emphasis added)

Although cross-examination is often an ineffective method of exposing weaknesses in an expert's opinion, it can also undermine solidly grounded opinions. My experience is that the most effective cross-examination, especially of testimony about research findings, is that which obfuscates by deflecting attention away from methodology and central findings to witness credentials and irrelevant results.

Regardless, there are strong pressures in the adversary process toward unduly confident testimony (Champagne, Shuman, & Whitaker, 1992; Grisso, 1987). Little is required to secure an identification with "my" side (Otto, 1989; Zusman & Simon, 1983), especially when ideology—including, for example, relatively subtle beliefs about the politics of gender interaction (as in child custody disputes)—plays a role (Homant & Kennedy, 1986, 1987a, 1987b).

To be most useful, experts must bend over backwards—or be bent—to be fully honest. The cognitive debiasing literature may provide useful guidance in this regard (Arkes, 1989). For example, experts may be encouraged to develop reasons why each competing explanation for an event—not just the one that they view as most plausible—may be true and why their own answer may be incorrect.

It also may be helpful to move the focus away from *the* report and *the* testimony providing *the* opinion to view assistance to the legal system as a consultation process. The most common clinical forensic questions are well fitted to such an approach. For example, referral for evaluation of competency to stand trial often is an easy way of getting access to a mental health professional when the actual question or need is something else. In that context, a defendant's ability to assist counsel in his or her defense often is related as much to the attorney's ability to deal with a difficult client as the defendant's own cognitive and social skills.

Similarly, referrals for evaluation of parental fitness in long-lingering child-protection cases may mask the actual desire for identification of dispositional alternatives that both the parent and child welfare authorities can accept and for related mediation among the parties. There also may be a need for direct consultation about working with a parent who is not so disabled or unmotivated that termination of parental rights is possible or desirable but who also is not cooperative with authorities.

More generally, both scientific and clinical experts often can assist counsel in identifying potential theories of the case, interpreting opposing evidence, identifying weaknesses in it, and framing the evidence so that it is most comprehensible and persuasive. Such a consultive role in lawyering has been expressly approved by the Supreme Court in its holding that due process requires that indigent defendants have access to independent mental health consultation in defending charges in which the defendant's mental state at the time of the offense is potentially at issue (*Ake v. Oklahoma*, 1985). The challenge to experts then is to maintain their objectivity when they do shift to a role of assistance to the fact finder rather than the party.

Conclusion: Facilitating the Just "Resolution of Particularized Legal Disputes"

Although the problems involved in ensuring legal decision makers' access to reliable and valid expert opinions are formidable, there is little question that the overall level of mental health and social science involvement in the legal system has risen dramatically in recent decades (Melton, 1987a; Smith, 1989). There also is evidence that expert testimony does increase sensitivity to psychological issues related to eyewitnesses (Cutler, Dexter, & Penrod, 1989) and battered (Schuller, 1992; Schuller & Vidmar, 1992) and raped (Frazier & Borgida, 1992) women, and expert testimony and amicus briefs have been influential in many other areas.

In closing, though, it is useful to provide a reminder that psychologists' legal involvement often may be unimportant in practice. In many courts, mental health and social science evidence is rarely submitted even on questions in which such involvement is often viewed as standard (Melton et al., 1985), and state appellate courts still rarely have or use social science knowledge (Melton, 1987a).

At least to some extent, these omissions are by choice. For example, mental health testimony in child protection and divorce cases is rarely perceived by judges as helpful (Melton et al., 1985). Moreover, given the scant research on effects of family court dispositions and the conclusory testimony of many clinicians in such matters, the judges' skepticism is commonly warranted (Melton, Petrila, Poythress, & Slobogin, 1987, chaps. 12 & 13).

Even if the scientific foundation were stronger, however, there is good reason to desire a diminished role of purported psychological knowledge in many areas of legal decision making (Melton, 1987d). Too often, assumptions about social reality are used to obfuscate the real reasons for judicial decisions and to deflect attention from core issues of justice. Although there is a great need for psychological-mindedness in identifying central concerns in support for human dignity (Melton, 1992), that need does not necessarily translate into a need for psychological research. To the degree that it does, it is likely to be a need for a kind of research that psychologists have seldom undertaken.

Although it is a mistake to exaggerate the significance of psychologists' actual or potential involvement in the legal system, it also is a mistake to overestimate the risk that is derived from such involvement. Research does not support the public perception that there is a cottage industry of "hired guns" who earn most of their income from expert testimony and who obtain their work through expert referral sources and advertisements in legal newspapers (Champagne et al., 1992). Similarly, one of the most articulate and pointed critics of APA amicus briefs (Saks, 1993) conceded that they are "already very good, and perhaps among the best of this genre being written" (p. 236).

As I have argued here, the search for a platonic ideal of science is not required by the rules of evidence and indeed should not be. Justice is served by scientific evidence that improves or facilitates legal decision making, even when its probative value is low. (Such a conclusion is based on the assumption that presentation of opinions is done with honesty about their foundation so that the trier of fact can place appropriate weight on the expert evidence.)

Issues about the proper bounds of expert evidence thus involve no more and no less than the question of whether opinions will facilitate the just "resolution of particularized legal disputes." In debating such issues, psychologists need to go beyond defensive consideration of the state of the field (whether the attempt is to defend professional prerogatives or scientific standards) to respond to this practical, case-specific question.

References

Ake v. Oklahoma, 470 U.S. 68 (1985).

American Psychological Association. (1992). Ethical principles of psychologists and code of conduct. *American Psychologist, 47*, 1597–1611.

Areen, J., King, P. A., Goldberg, S., & Capron, A. M. (1984). *Law, science, and medicine*. Mineola, NY: Foundation Press.

Arkes, P. (1989). Principles in judgment/decision making research pertinent to legal proceedings. *Behavioral Sciences and the Law, 7*, 429–456.

Barefoot v. Estelle, 463 U.S. 880 (1983).

Barrett, G. V., & Morris, S. B. (1993). The American Psychological Association's amicus curiae brief in *Price Waterhouse v. Hopkins*: The values of science versus the values of the law. *Law and Human Behavior, 17*, 201–215.

Begley, S. (1993, March 22). The meaning of junk. *Newsweek*, pp. 62–63.

Bernstein, D. E. (1993, March 24). Junk science in the courtroom. *Wall Street Journal*, p. A15.

Bersoff, D. N. (1987). Social science data and the Supreme Court: *Lockhart* as a case in point. *American Psychologist, 42*, 52–58.

Black, H. C., Nolan, J. R., Nolan-Haley, J. M., Connolly, M. J., Hicks, S. C., & Alibrand, M. N. (1990). *Black's law dictionary: Definitions of the terms and phrases of American and English Jurisprudence, ancient and modern* (6th ed.). St. Paul, MN: West.

Bonnie, R. J., & Slobogin, C. (1980). The role of mental health professionals in the criminal process: The case for informed speculation. *Virginia Law Review, 66*, 427–522.

Brodsky, S. L. (1991). *Testifying in court: Guidelines and maxims for the expert witness*. Washington, DC: American Psychological Association.

Brown v. Board of Education, 347 U.S. 483 (1954).

Callahan, L. A., McGreevy, M. A., Cirincione, C., & Steadman, H. J. (1992). Measuring the effects of the guilty but mentally ill (GBMI) verdict: Georgia's 1982 GBMI reform. *Law and Human Behavior, 16*, 447–462.

Casey, P., Keilitz, I., & Hafemeister, T. L. (1992). Toward an agenda for reform of justice and mental health systems interactions. *Law and Human Behavior, 16*, 107–128.

Champagne, A., Shuman, D., & Whitaker, E. (1992). Expert witness in courts: An empirical examination. *Judicature, 76*(i), 5–10.

Charrow, R. P. (1992). Peer reviews and a jury of peers. *Journal of NIH Research, 4*(12), 79–81.

Christoffel, T., & Teret, S. P. (1991). Epidemiology and the law: Courts and confidence intervals. *American Journal of Public Health, 81*, 1661–1666.

Chubin, D. E., & Hackett, E. J. (1990). *Peerless science: Peer review and U.S. science policy.* Albany: State University of New York Press.

Cohen, M., McEwen, J., Williams, K., Silver, S., & Spodak, M. (1986). *A base expectancy model for forensic release decisions.* Alexandria: Research Management Associates. Cited in Monahan, J., & Steadman, H. J. (in press). Toward a rejuvenation of risk assessment research. In J. Monahan & H. J. Steadman (Eds.), *Violence and mental disorder: Developments in risk assessment* (pp. 1–17). Chicago: University of Chicago Press.

Committee on Ethical Guidelines for Forensic Psychologists. (1991). Specialty guidelines for forensic psychologists. *Law and Human Behavior, 15*, 655–665.

Conte, J. R., & Berliner, L. (1987). The impact of sexual abuse of children: Empirical findings. In L. Walker (Ed.), *Handbook of sexual abuse of children* (pp. 72–93). New York: Springer.

Cutler, B. L., Dexter, H. R., & Penrod, S. D. (1989). Expert testimony and jury decision making: An empirical analysis. *Behavioral Sciences and the Law, 7*, 215–225.

Daubert v. Merrell Dow Pharmaceuticals, 951 F.2d 1128 (9th Cir. 1991), *vacated*, 113 S.Ct. 2786 (1993).

Dietz, P. E., Cooke, G., Rappeport, J. R., & Silvergleit, I. T. (1983). Psychojargon in the psycholegal report: Ratings by judges, psychiatrists, and psychologists. *Behavioral Sciences and the Law, 1*, 77–84.

Elliott, R. (1991). Social science data and the APA: The *Lockhart* brief as a case in point. *Law and Human Behavior, 15*, 59–76.

Elliott, R. (1993). Expert testimony about eyewitness identification: A critique. *Law and Human Behavior, 17*, 423–437.

Ellsworth, P. C. (1991). To tell what we know or wait for Godot? *Law and Human Behavior, 15*, 77–90.

Expert testimony [Special issue]. (1989). *Behavioral Sciences and the Law, 7*(2).

Faust, D., & Ziskin, J. (1988a). The expert witness in psychology and psychiatry. *Science, 241*, 31–35.

Faust, D., & Ziskin, J. (1988b). Response to Fowler and Matarazzo. *Science, 241*, 1143–1144.

Fiske, S. T., Bersoff, D. N., Borgida, E., Deaux, K., & Heilman, M. E. (1993). What constitutes a scientific review? A majority retort to Barrett and Morris. *Law and Human Behavior, 17*, 217–233.

Fowler, R. D., & Matarazzo, J. D. (1988). Psychologists and psychiatrists as expert witnesses. *Science, 241*, 1143.

Frank, J. D. (1973). *Persuasion and healing* (rev. ed.). Baltimore: Johns Hopkins University Press.

Frazier, P. A., & Borgida, E. (1992). Rape trauma syndrome: A review of case law and psychological research. *Law and Human Behavior, 16*, 293–311.

Frye v. United States, 293 F. 1013 (D.C. Cir. 1923).

Gardner, W., Scherer, D., & Tester, M. (1989). Asserting scientific authority: Cognitive development and adolescent legal rights. *American Psychologist, 44*, 895–902.

Golding, S. L. (Ed.). (1992). Expert evidence [Special issue]. *Law and Human Behavior, 16*(3).

Goodman, G. S., Levine, M., & Melton, G. B. (1992). The best evidence produces the best law. *Law and Human Behavior, 16*, 244–251.

Goodman, J. (1993). Evaluating psychological expertise on questions of social fact: The case of *Price Waterhouse v. Hopkins. Law and Human Behavior, 17*, 249–255.

Grisso, T. (1986). *Evaluating competencies: Forensic assessments and instruments.* New York: Plenum.

Grisso, T. (1987). The economic and scientific future of forensic psychological assessment. *American Psychologist, 42*, 831–839.

Grisso, T., & Appelbaum, P. S. (1992). Is it unethical to offer predictions of future violence? *Law and Human Behavior, 16*, 621–633.

Grisso, T., & Appelbaum, P. S. (1993). Structuring the debate about ethical predictions of future violence. *Law and Human Behavior, 17*, 482–485.

Grisso, T., & Melton, G. B. (1987). Getting child development research to legal practitioners: Which way to the trenches. In G. B. Melton (Ed.), *Reforming the law: Impact of child development research* (pp. 146–176). New York: Guilford.

Grisso, T., & Saks, M. J. (1991). Psychology's influence on constitutional interpretation. *Law and Human Behavior, 15*, 205–211.

Hafemeister, T. L., & Melton, G. B. (1987). The impact of social science research in the judiciary. In G. B. Melton (Ed.), *Reforming the law: Impact of child development research* (pp. 27–59). New York: Guilford.

Hiday, V. A. (1977). Reformed commitment procedures: An empirical study in the courtroom. *Law and Society Review, 11*, 651–666.

Hiday, V. A. (1981). Court discretion: Application of the dangerousness standard in civil commitment. *Law and Human Behavior, 5*, 275–289.

Homant, R. J., & Kennedy, D. B. (1986). Judgment of legal insanity as a function of attitude toward the insanity defense. *International Journal of Law and Psychiatry, 8*, 67–81.

Homant, R. J., & Kennedy, D. B. (1987a). Subjective factors in clinicians' judgments of insanity: A comparison of a hypothetical and an actual case. *Professional Psychology: Research and Practice, 18*, 439–446.

Homant, R. J., & Kennedy, D. B. (1987b). Subjective factors in the judgment of insanity. *Criminal Justice and Behavior, 14*, 38–61.

Huber, P. (1991). *Galileo's revenge: Junk science in the courtroom.* New York: Basic Books.

Kalichman, S. C., Craig, M. E., & Follingstad, D. R. (1989). Factors influencing the reporting of father-child sexual abuse: Study of licensed practicing psychologists. *Professional Psychology Research and Practice, 20*, 84–89.

Keilitz, I. (1992). Justice and mental health systems interactions [Special issue]. *Law and Human Behavior, 16*(1).

Kahneman, D., & Tversky, A. (1973). On the psychology of prediction. *Psychological Review, 81*, 237–251.

Koshland, D. E., Jr. (1993). Get-rich-quick science. *Science, 259*, 1103.

Lidz, C., Mulvey, E., & Gardner, W. (1993). The accuracy of predictions of violence to others. *Journal of the American Medical Association, 269*, 1007–1011.

Litwack, T. R. (1993). On the ethics of dangerousness assessments. *Law and Human Behavior, 17*, 479–482.

Loftus, E. F. (1983). Silence is not golden. *American Psychologist, 38*, 564–572.

Marshall, E. (1993). Supreme Court to weigh science. *Science, 259*, 588–590.

Matarazzo, J. D. (1990). Psychological assessment versus psychological testing: Validation from Binet to the school, clinic, and courtroom. *American Psychologist, 45,* 999–1017.

Matarazzo, J. D. (1991). Psychological assessment is reliable and valid: Reply to Ziskin and Faust. *American Psychologist, 46,* 882–884.

McCloskey, M., & Egeth, H. E. (1983). Eyewitness identification: What can a psychologist tell a jury? *American Psychologist, 38,* 564–572.

McCloskey, M., Egeth, H. E., & McKenna, J. (Eds.). (1986). The ethics of expert testimony [Special issue]. *Law and Human Behavior, 10*(1).

McNiel, D. E., & Binder, R. L. (1991). Clinical assessment of the risk of violence among psychiatric inpatients. *American Journal of Psychiatry, 148,* 1317–1321.

Melton, G. B. (1983). *Child advocacy: Psychological issues and interventions.* New York: Plenum.

Melton, G. B. (1985). Organized psychology and legal policy-making: Involvement in the post-*Hinckley* debate. *Professional Psychology: Research and Practice, 16,* 810–822.

Melton, G. B. (1987a). Bringing psychology to the legal system: Opportunities, obstacles and efficacy. *American Psychologist, 42,* 488–495.

Melton, G. B. (1987b). Guidelines for effective diffusion of child development research into the legal system. In G. B. Melton (Ed.), *Reforming the law: Impact of child development research* (pp. 280–300). New York: Guilford.

Melton, G. B. (Ed.). (1987c). *Reforming the law: Impact of child development research.* New York: Guilford.

Melton, G. B. (1987d). The clashing of symbols: Prelude to child and family policy. *American Psychologist, 42,* 345–354.

Melton, G. B. (1990a). Knowing what we do know: APA and adolescent abortion. *American Psychologist, 45,* 1171–1173.

Melton, G. B. (1990b). Realism in psychology and humanism in law: Psycholegal studies at Nebraska. *Nebraska Law Review, 69,* 251–277.

Melton, G. B. (1992). The law is a good thing (Psychology is, too): Human rights in psychological jurisprudence. *Law and Human Behavior, 16,* 381–398.

Melton, G. B. (in press). Doing justice and doing good: Conflicts for mental health professionals. *Future of Children.*

Melton, G. B., & Limber, S. (1989). Psychologists' involvement in cases of child maltreatment: Limits of role and expertise. *American Psychologist, 44,* 1225–1233.

Melton, G. B., Monahan, J., & Saks, M. J. (1987). Psychologists as law professors. *American Psychologist, 42,* 502–509.

Melton, G. B., Petrila, J., Poythress, N. G., & Slobogin, C. (1987). *Psychological evaluations for the courts: A handbook for mental health professionals and lawyers.* New York: Guilford.

Melton, G. B., Weithorn, L. A., & Slobogin, C. (1985). *Community mental health centers and the courts: An evaluation of community-based forensic services.* Lincoln: University of Nebraska Press.

Monahan, J. (1981). *The clinical prediction of violent behavior.* Washington, DC: U.S. Government Printing Office.

Monahan, J., & Steadman, H. J. (in press-a). Toward a rejuvenation of risk assessment research. In J. Monahan & H. J. Steadman (Eds.), *Violence and mental disorder: Developments in risk assessment* (pp. 1–17). Chicago: University of Chicago Press.

Monahan, J., & Steadman, H. J. (Eds.). (in press-b). *Violence and mental disorder: Developments in risk assessment*. Chicago: University of Chicago Press.

Monahan, J., & Walker, L. (1985). Teaching social science in law: An alternative to "law and society." *Journal of Legal Education, 35*, 478–482.

Monahan, J., & Walker, L. (1986). Social authority: Obtaining, evaluating, and establishing social science in law. *University of Pennsylvania Law Review, 134*, 477–517.

Monahan, J., & Walker, L. (1988). Social science research in law: A new paradigm. *American Psychologist, 43*, 465–472.

Monahan, J., & Walker, L. (1990). *Social science in law: Cases and materials* (2nd ed.). Mineola, NY: Foundation Press.

Monahan, J., & Walker, L. (1991). Judicial use of social science research. *Law and Human Behavior, 15*, 571–584.

Monahan, J., & Wexler, D. (1978). A definite maybe: Proof and probability in civil commitment. *Law and Human Behavior, 2*, 37–42.

Muller v. Oregon, 208 U.S. 412 (1907).

Ogloff, J. R. P., & Roesch, R. (1992). Using community mental health centers to provide comprehensive mental health services in local jails. In J. R. P. Ogloff (Ed.), *Law and psychology: The broadening of the discipline* (pp. 241–260). Durham, NC: Carolina Academic Press.

Olson, K., & McKinlay, A. C. (1993). *Peer networking as a method of dissemination of information to judges on child sexual abuse*. Unpublished manuscript, University of Nebraska-Lincoln, Center on Children, Families, and the Law.

Otto, R. K. (1989). Bias and expert testimony of mental health professionals in adversarial proceedings: A preliminary investigation. *Behavioral Sciences and the Law, 7*, 267–273.

Perry, G. S., & Melton, G. B. (1984). Precedential value of judicial notice of social facts: *Parham* as an example. *Journal of Family Law, 22*, 633–676.

Petrila, J. (1982). The insanity defense and other mental health dispositions in Missouri. *International Journal of Law and Psychiatry, 5*, 81–101.

Pope, K. S., & Vettner, V. A. (1992). Ethical dilemmas encountered by members of the American Psychological Association: A national survey. *American Psychologist, 47*, 397–411.

Poythress, N. G., Jr. (1980). Coping on the witness stand: Learned responses to learned treatises. *Professional Psychology, 11*, 139–149.

Poythress, N. G., Jr. (1983). Psychological issues in criminal proceedings. *Criminal Justice and Behavior, 10*, 175–194.

Roesch, R., & Golding, S. L. (1980). *Competency to stand trial*. Urbana: University of Illinois Press.

Roesch, R., Golding, S. L., Hans, V., & Reppucci, N. D. (1991). Social science and the courts: The role of amicus curiae briefs. *Law and Human Behavior, 15*, 146–156.

Rogers, R., Bagby, R. M., & Chow, M.-M. K. (1992). Psychiatrists and the parameters of expert testimony. *International Journal of Law and Psychiatry, 15*, 387–396.

Rogers, R., Bagby, R. M., Crouch, M., & Cutler, B. (1990). Effects of ultimate opinions on juror perceptions of insanity. *International Journal of Law and Psychiatry, 13*, 225–232.

Rogers, R., & Ewing, C. P. (1989). Ultimate opinion proscriptions: A cosmetic fix and a plea for empiricism. *Law and Human Behavior, 13*, 357–374.

Rosen, D. (1984). Democracy and demographics: The inevitability of a class-based interpretation. *University of Dayton Law Review, 10*, 37–96.

Rothman, K. (1986). *Modern epidemiology.* New York: Little, Brown.

Saks, M. J. (1992). Do we really know anything about the behavior of the tort litigation system—and why not? *University of Pennsylvania Law Review, 140*, 1147–1292.

Saks, M. J. (1993). Improving APA science translation briefs. *Law and Human Behavior, 17*, 235–247.

Schlesinger, S. R., & Nesse, J. (1980). Justice Harry Blackmun and empirical jurisprudence. *American University Law Review, 29*, 405–437.

Schuller, R. A. (1992). The impact of battered woman syndrome evidence on jury decision processes. *Law and Human Behavior, 16*, 597–620.

Schuller, R. A., & Vidmar, N. (1992). Battered woman syndrome evidence in the courtroom. *Law and Human Behavior, 16*, 273–291.

Slater, D., & Hans, V. P. (1984). Public opinion of forensic psychiatry following the *Hinckley* verdict. *American Journal of Psychiatry, 141*, 675–679.

Slobogin, C. (1984). Dangerousness and expertise. *University of Pennsylvania Law Review, 133*, 97–174.

Slobogin, C. (1985). The guilty but mentally ill verdict: An idea whose time should not have come. *George Washington Law Review, 53*, 494–527.

Slobogin, C. (1989). The "ultimate issue" issue. *Behavioral Sciences and the Law, 7*, 259–266.

Smith, S. R. (1989). Mental health expert witnesses: Of science and crystal balls. *Behavioral Sciences and the Law, 7*, 145–180.

State v. Cressey, 137 N.H. 402, 628 A.2d 696 (1993).

State v. Saldana, 324 N.W.2d 227 (Minn. 1982).

Steadman, H. J. (1992). Boundary spanners: A key component for the effective interactions of the justice and mental health systems. *Law and Human Behavior, 16*, 75–87.

Stier, S. D., & Stoebe, K. J. (1979). Involuntary hospitalization of the mentally ill in Iowa: The failure of the 1975 legislation. *Iowa Law Review, 64*, 1284–1458.

Thibaut, J., & Walker, L. (1978). A theory of procedure. *California Law Review, 66*, 541–566.

Tremper, C. R. (1987). Organized psychology's efforts to influence judicial policy-making. *American Psychologist, 42*, 496–501.

Turkheimer, E., & Parry, C. D. (1992). Why the gap? Practice and policy in civil commitment proceedings. *American Psychologist, 47*, 646–655.

Underwager, R., & Wakefield, H. (1992). Poor psychology produces poor law. *Law and Human Behavior, 16*, 233–243.

U.S. Advisory Board on Child Abuse and Neglect. (1993). *Neighbors helping neighbors: A new national strategy for the protection of children.* Washington, DC: U.S. Government Printing Office.

Va. Code §§ 19.2–168.1 & 19.2–169.1 to 19.2–169.7 (1990 & Supp. 1993).

Wald, M. S., & Woolverton, M. (1990). Risk assessment: The emperor's new clothes. *Child Welfare, 69*, 483–511.

Walker, L., & Monahan, J. (1987). Social frameworks: A new use of social science in law. *Virginia Law Review, 73*, 559–598.

Walker, L., & Monahan, J. (1988). Social facts: Scientific methodology as legal precedent. *California Law Review, 76*, 877–896.

Wasby, S. (1976). *Small town police and the Supreme Court: Hearing the word.* Lexington, MA: Lexington Books.

Weinstein, J. B., & Berger, M. A. (1987). *Weinstein's evidence manual: A guide to the United States rules based on* Weinstein's evidence (Student ed.). New York: Matthew Bender.

Weiss, C. H., & Singer, E. (1988). *Reporting of social science in the national media.* New York: Russell Sage Foundation.

White, L., Tursky, B., & Schwartz, G. E. (Eds.). (1985). *Placebo: Theory, research, and mechanisms.* New York: Guilford.

Willging, T. (1986). *Court-appointed experts.* Washington, DC: Federal Judicial Center.

Wolfe, D. A. (1992). *The role of intervention and treatment services in the prevention of child abuse and neglect.* Paper prepared for the U.S. Advisory Board on Child Abuse and Neglect.

Ziskin, J., & Faust, D. (1988). *Coping with psychiatric and psychological testimony* (4th ed., 3 vols.). Venice, CA: Law and Psychology Press.

Ziskin, J., & Faust, D. (1991). A reply to Matarazzo. *American Psychologist, 46*, 881–882.

Zusman, J., & Simon, J. (1983). Differences in repeated psychiatric examinations of litigants to a lawsuit. *American Journal of Psychiatry, 140*, 1300–1304.

MICHAEL OWEN MILLER

THE PSYCHOLOGIST AS DEFENDANT

M ichael Owen Miller is a partner with the law firm of Lewis and Roca in their Tucson, Arizona, office. Miller received his BS and MA from Michigan State University and his PhD in educational psychology from the University of Michigan in 1980. After completing a National Institute of Mental Health–sponsored postdoctoral fellowship in forensic clinical psychology at Florida State University, he received his JD at the University of Arizona in 1984. He has served as a student editor of *Law and Human Behavior*.

Miller published in the juvenile justice area until attending law school. At that time, he began collaborating with Bruce D. Sales to create and edit a national series on law affecting mental health professionals. The first volume, *Law and Mental Health Professionals: Arizona* (Miller & Sales, 1986), is the prototype for a series that will report the law in individual volumes for every state, the District of Columbia, and federal jurisdictions; there will also be a volume on federal law. Approximately 12 volumes have been published or are in press, and many more are in progress.

Miller is active in state and national professional psychology organizations. He has served as chairperson for the American Psychological Association's (APA) Committee on Professional Practice and Standards as well as APA's Committee on Legal Issues. In those capacities, he had major involvement in the creation of APA's "Record Keeping Guidelines" (Committee on Professional Practice and Standards, 1993) and *Legal Risk Management* (APA, 1993). He chaired the Arizona State Psychological Association's Ethics Committee and helped draft the Arizona licensing law.

Miller's law practice focuses on health law, malpractice, and product liability. He represents psychologists and other mental health professionals in licensing, business, and malpractice matters. Conversely, he advises trial lawyers about psychology and psychological research through seminars and writings, such as a recent article (Miller, 1993) on memory in *Litigation*, the journal for the American Bar Association's Section of Litigation.

References

American Psychological Association. (1993). *Legal risk management*. Washington, DC: Author.

Committee on Professional Practice and Standards. (1993). Record keeping guidelines. *American Psychologist, 48*, 984–986.

Miller, M. O. (1993). Working with memory. *Litigation, 19*(4), 10–16.

Miller, M. O., & Sales, B. D. (Eds.). (1986). *Law and mental health professionals: Arizona*. Washington, DC: American Psychological Association.

MICHAEL OWEN MILLER

THE PSYCHOLOGIST AS DEFENDANT

J ust over 40 years ago, psychologist Calvin Hall (1952) wrote in the *American Psychologist* that the American Psychological Association (APA) should not adopt a code of ethics because it

> plays into the hands of crooks.... The crooked operator reads the code to see how much he can get away with, and since any code is bound to be filled with ambiguities and omissions, he can rationalize his unethical conduct by pointing to the code and saying, "See, it doesn't tell me I can't do this," or "I can interpret this to mean what I want it to mean." (p. 430)

Instead, Hall argued, each psychologist should agree

> to conduct myself professionally according to the common rules of decency, with the understanding that if a jury of my peers decides that I have violated these rules, I may be expelled from the association. (pp. 430–431)

The APA did not accept Hall's argument, instead adopting its first ethics code in 1953. The 1953 *Ethical Standards of Psychologists* had six major sections. The most frequently violated principle concerned the invalid presentation of professional qualifications, which accounted for 44 complaints over a period of about 12 years ("Cases and inquiries before the Committee on Scientific and Professional Ethics and Conduct," 1954).

Hall's perspective seems quaint in light of psychologists' concerns about malpractice, discriminatory psychological tests, violent patients, subpoenas, depositions, and the other legal hobgoblins of today's psychological practice. In addition, it seems that, at times, most psychologists have more to fear from unexpected or arbitrary legal rulings and from juries of their peers or citizens of the communities in which they practice (Brodsky, 1988; Bursztajn, Gutheil, Brodsky, & Swagerty, 1988) than they do from a group of psychologist–crooks who seek to dodge ethical prohibitions as if they were taken from the Internal Revenue Code.

I suggest, however, that despite Hall's failure to anticipate the complex web of legal and regulatory controls that affect psychologists, his principal point is well taken even today. Psychologists should strive to provide competent services, be adequately aware of their legal and ethical duties, and reasonably address the occasional complaint. If they do, they face a low risk of being cast as a defendant and an even lower risk of an adverse result in a legal or disciplinary proceeding. However, regardless of caution taken, it is wise to be prepared in the event that legal action occurs.

In this chapter, I discuss the activities and mistakes that are likely to place a psychologist in the role of defendant, the various forums in which a psychologist may be a defendant, how the psychologist can reduce the likelihood of becoming a defendant, and, finally, how the psychologist can best advance his or her interests if in the role of defendant.

Multiple Problems Across Multiple Forums

In the parlance of attorneys, I work both sides of the street. I represent mental health professionals in administrative and civil proceedings, and I chaired the ethics committee of my state's psychological association. On behalf of the state bar association, I also represent attorneys charged with negligent conduct and prosecute attorneys to seek suspension or disbarment for unethical conduct.

My experience with actual and alleged negligent or unethical conduct in two professions indicates that there are very few cases in which there is a single, isolated problem. Simple mistakes or single, less serious occurrences are addressed directly, without fanfare, and usually do not end in a formal, adverse determination. Contested, drawn-out cases almost inevitably entail an egregious breach of well-established practice, a constellation of practice problems, or a complex scenario that involves a number of questionable decisions by the psychologist.

I have also observed that charges of misconduct are frequently brought in multiple forums. It is not uncommon for a sophisticated or very angry client to file a disciplinary complaint with the licensing board, ethics complaints with professional associations, and a claim for damages in state court. This appears to be an emerging trend and may be stimulated by those attorneys who regularly initiate battles on several fronts to obtain evidence and to wear down their opponents. Unfortunately, it is only recently that the procedural rules of the various forums have recognized that there may be overlapping actions and that the sole reason for one prosecution may be to obtain an advantage in an entirely different proceeding.

Researchers have not addressed whether the existence and use of these multiple forums affects the frequency and seriousness of psychologist misconduct. In addition, there is no scholarly study that examines all of the elements together: the frequency and seriousness of various types of misconduct, the multiple forums in which the same misconduct is prosecuted, interactions among the forums, and whether proceedings are affected by multiple prosecutions. A case example provides the best mechanism to describe the operation and interaction of multiple forums.

A Case Example

Dr. D. is an established, health-care psychologist who practices with a small group. The bulk of his practice involves eclectic, outpatient therapy, but he also consults on an inpatient basis at several local hospitals where he has staff privileges. He has a good reputation in the community, among both his colleagues and other professionals.

Several months ago, he began treating a professional woman who initially presented with depression and anxiety relating to separation from her husband and increasing problems with her child, for whom she had primary responsibility. Additionally, not long after her separation, she was involved in an automobile accident that resulted in soft-tissue injuries and a constant sense of tension when she was driving. Dr. D.'s fees were mostly paid by the husband's health insurance policy.

Dr. D. met with this client weekly, including several meetings in restaurants, concerning her increasing anxiety over driving and being out in public. Although she reported decreasing levels of depression and better relations with her child, the therapeutic relationship became increasingly problematic when Dr. D. pressed her for payment of his fees that were not covered by the insurance. He also declined to provide a custody fitness report requested by her attorney because he had not met with the child and father. From a clinical perspective, he felt increasingly frustrated at her dependence on him, which she manifested by suggestions for romantic involvement, intermixed with periods of strong anger.

The client failed to pay the deductible over 4 months. She first stated that she had cash-flow problems and later complained that his fees were too high. Shortly thereafter, Dr. D. told her that therapy was becoming ineffective and sought to refer her to another therapist. The client reacted angrily and rejected the list of other psychologists that Dr. D. had prepared for her. He undertook no follow-up.

When the client had not paid her outstanding balance 1 month after termination, Dr. D. sent her a form letter indicating that he would forward her account to a collection agency if payment was not made within 2 weeks. Although he had never actually referred a delinquent account to a collection agency, he found that such a letter was more effective than a simple request for payment. Exhibit 1 summarizes the direct participants in this case, the indirect participants or affected parties, and events that raise red flags.

Several weeks later, Dr. D. received a letter from the attorney handling his client's divorce and her personal injury lawsuit arising from the automobile accident. The attorney alleged that Dr. D. had committed malpractice by initiating a personal relationship with the client. The attorney demanded immediate reimbursement of all fees the client had paid to Dr. D. and offered to settle her malpractice and emotional distress claim for $25,000. The attorney's letter was followed several days later by copies of complaints that the client had filed with the psychology licensing board and the state psychological association. In addition, Dr. D. was contacted by the client's health insurer concerning fees that he had charged for services that he had provided at the restaurant. He also learned that the client's estranged husband had notified his health insurance company when he learned about the events during the divorce proceedings.

Each fact, taken alone, would probably not constitute an independent ethical or legal violation. At least, no single fact would likely result in initiation of an action against Dr. D. Taken together, however, the facts could lead to a variety of actions. Table 1 illustrates the various entities that could investigate or bring a claim against Dr. D., the forums where the claim would be made, and the types of claims or investigations. Table 1 is a shorthand representation of Dr. D's worst nightmare. It is unlikely, but possible, that he would face all of the legal and disciplinary actions described here. The probability of each event could, in large part, depend on factors independent of Dr. D. and certainly beyond his control. For instance, the client, her husband, and the other party involved in the automobile accident could have lawsuits with each other that could benefit from or be harmed by Dr. D.'s testimony and his psychological records. The health insurance carrier would be interested in minimizing its costs; the prosecutor would want to appear

Exhibit 1
Hypothetical Case Example:
Summary of Participants and Events

Direct Participants:
Dr. D.
   Experienced, private practice health-care psychologist
   Good reputation; approved provider with hospital privileges
Ms. P.
   Professional; mother of young child
   Marital separation; recent automobile accident
   Presents anxiety/depression, child-rearing problems, and possible PTSD

Indirect Participants or Affected Parties:
Mr. P.
   Estranged spouse of patient
   Father of child
Health insurance company
   Payor of Dr. D.'s fees
Defendant automobile driver
   Person whom Ms. P. claims is partially responsible for her stress arising
   out of the automobile accident

Events:
   Eclectic weekly therapy; several meetings in restaurants to address possible
   agoraphobia and driving anxiety
   Majority of fees paid by husband's health insurance carrier
   Ms. P. falls behind in payment of deductible; she is angry at Dr. D.'s aloof
   manner and refusal to provide a custody fitness report requested by her
   attorney
   Dr. D. is discouraged by Ms. P.'s lack of recent progress, her increasing
   demands on him, and the fees problem
   Dr. D. terminates therapy, unsuccessfully attempts to refer her to another
   psychologist, and sends a collection letter for her outstanding balance

Note. PTSD = posttraumatic stress disorder.

vigilant against insurance fraud. Administrative bodies would respond to complaints from anyone who claims harm from Dr. D.'s psychological activities. Finally, the client, on the advice of her attorney, might pursue Dr. D. because of her dissatisfaction with his services and actions, in addition to as part of her generalized anger at her litigation-filled situation.

The point is that even small incidences, when multiplied or coupled with outside factors, can lead to serious, multiple legal and regulatory consequences for psychologists.

Table 1
Hypothetical Case Example: Claims, Forums, and
Originating Parties

Forum	Party	Claim or Event
State or federal court	Ms. P.	Breach of professional duties (e.g. negligence, abandonment, and dual relationship)
		Subpoena & deposition of Dr. D (re: accident or custody)
	Mr. P.	Breach of professional duties (e.g. foreseeable victim of a dual relationship)
		Subpoena and deposition Dr. D (re: custody)
	Health insurance carrier	Civil fraud
	Prosecutor	Criminal fraud
	Driver	Subpoena and deposition Dr. D (re. Ms. P's mental state)
Licensing board	Mr. and Ms. P. Health insurance carrier Prosecutor	Same allegations as above
Ethics committee	Mr. and Ms. P. Health insurance carrier Prosecutor	Same allegations as above
Hospital peer review committee	Mr. and Ms. P. Health insurance carrier Prosecutor	Same allegations as above

Problem Areas in Psychological Practice

What are the types of misconduct that will likely result in a psychologist becoming a defendant? Is a psychologist more likely to suffer an adverse legal result because of the frequency of the misconduct or because of the nature of it? What is the relation between adjudicated misconduct and unethical or illegal behavior that has not been the subject of investigation and adjudication by others? These questions frame the larger issue of what activities and circumstances can force psychologists into the role of a defendant.

The following section describes some of the problems that plague efforts to collect data concerning these questions. Four sources of data provide preliminary results and help estimate the likelihood of any complaint being filed against a psychologist.

Psychologist Misconduct Data: Methodological Problems and Limitations

Despite psychology's half century of professional service and even longer tenure as a scholarly field, there is not an abundance of empirical data concerning the types of misconduct that result in adverse legal and professional consequences for psychologists. Certainly, psychologists have long been subject to laws concerning their professional activities, and a national ethics code has been in place for more than 40 years. Nonetheless, until recently, there was little attempt to gather systematic data on legal or ethical violations. It has only been within the past 15 years that ethics committees, professional liability insurers, licensing boards, and researchers have started to examine in detail the frequency and seriousness of particular types of misconduct (e.g., APA Ethics Committee, 1986; Brownfain, 1971; "Cases and Inquiries," 1954; Cummings & Sobel, 1985; Pope & Vasquez, 1991). These data must be considered preliminary for the several reasons.

First, they have not been consistently collected or coded. For instance, the American Psychological Association Insurance Trust (APAIT) stated that it has "the single best collection of statistical information available on the subject of psychological malpractice"; however, it has never published a comprehensive report of these data because of varying data-collection problems (Bennett, Bryant, VandenBos, & Greenwood, 1990, p. 3). A second, and related, issue involves confusion between underlying conduct and procedural factors, such as the claim for relief and the context out of which the claim arose. For instance, APAIT malpractice claims have been categorized as "loss from evaluation" or "countersuit for fee collection" (Pope & Vasquez, 1991, p. 31). A loss of any sort can be a result of improper psychological activities; categorizing the claim on the basis of the services provided, however, does not tell anything about what the psychologist allegedly did that was wrong. Similarly, when a psychologist sues for unpaid fees and becomes the defendant in a retaliatory lawsuit, which is called a *counterclaim*, the lawsuit by the client must allege particular conduct that was wrongful. Simply reporting "countersuit" does not explain the type of improper conduct. Without this information, it is impossible to determine whether wrongful conduct alleged in a countersuit is in some manner different from the kind of conduct alleged in an original lawsuit.

This problem is not limited to APAIT data. The APA Ethics Committee reported "prior adjudication" and "child custody" as bases for many of the complaints it received (e.g., APA Ethics Committee, 1993). Such categories fail to identify the underlying conduct.

Finally, the time period for reported information is too brief. The great majority of the ethical and legal reports of psychologist misconduct were published after 1985. Even assuming high-quality data, one cannot assume that the statistics on the types and rates of misconduct would not change if one were to analyze a longer period of time (Pope, 1990). Nonetheless, these data show general trends or considerations that can be used to explore problem areas.

I discuss four sources of data concerning psychologists' misconduct: (a) ethics complaints filed with the APA's Ethics Committee, (b) claims reported to the APAIT, (c) complaints to psychology licensing boards, and (d) published cases involving claims against psychologists. The information from these sources is complementary and overlapping, but it is not equivalent. For instance, just because a claim is filed with a liability carrier or with a licensing board does not mean that a lawsuit has also been filed. However, there are remarkable similarities among the sources in the types, frequency, and seriousness of occurrences.

Ethics Complaints

The APA first formed an ethics committee in 1938 (Pope & Vasquez, 1991). That committee functioned without a formal code until 1953. There have been eight significant revisions of the ethics code, the most dramatic of which occurred in 1992 (APA, 1992). The newest code moves from aspirational principles only to a combination of six general principles and 102 ethical standards, the latter of which function as enforceable rules of conduct similar to statutory law. Although the Ethics Code is not intended to govern beyond association membership, the APA recognizes that state licensure boards, courts, and other public bodies frequently look to its Ethics Code when determining whether a psychologist has met standards of care (APA, 1992). In some jurisdictions, the Ethics Code is incorporated directly into the law governing the licensure of psychologists. In other jurisdictions, the general reference to national standards is interpreted to mean the APA Ethics Code. As a practical matter, the Ethics Code constitutes a national agreement concerning standards for recognizing appropriate and inappropriate behavior for many psychological activities; as such, it inevitably influences decisionmakers regardless of whether the code is referenced explicitly.

Although only the most recent Ethics Code contains specific references to conduct, complaints under the prior ethics codes usually referenced conduct that could be categorized. For the past 7 years, the Ethics Committee has issued increasingly sophisticated reports tracking these data (APA Ethics Committee, 1986, 1987, 1988, 1990, 1991, 1993). Although the most recent report did not reflect complaints filed after adoption of the current code, it analyzed all complaints from 1990 to 1992. If proven true, the misconduct alleged in a complaint may constitute a violation of the licensing laws and common-law professional duties in most jurisdictions, in addition to violating ethical norms.

Table 2 presents data on the primary issue in APA ethics complaints and the primary reasons for mandatory membership termination from the APA from 1990 to 1992. The largest percentage of complaints had as their primary issue legal and ethical violations adjudicated in the courts or by state psychology associations. These involved felony convictions, loss of licensure, state association expulsions, among other matters. Although the underlying misconduct that leads to these adjudications generally falls within one of the other categories in the table, the report does not provide this information.

Allegations of sexual misconduct, which usually involve a male therapist and an adult female client, constituted the next largest category of ethics complaints. Although not included in Table 2, sexual misconduct allegations—regardless of whether they constituted primary, secondary, or underlying conduct leading to a prior adjudication—accounted for 27% of ethics complaints.

The next two largest categories of primary allegations, when combined, accounted for approximately 25% of ethics complaints; they involve activities that are usually considered malpractice, which is defined as negligence in the course of a professional activity. Conspicuous by their absence or very low percentages are duty to protect, breach of

Table 2
**Complaints of Misconduct Reported by the APA Ethics Committee
1990–1992**

Category (nature or context of complaint)	Primary issue of ethics complaint	Primary reason for membership termination
Prior adjudications (e.g., criminal, state association, and licensure actions)	21	
Sexual misconduct	17	63
Practice beyond competence	14	
Other professional practice problem	12	
Dual relationship	8	6
Child custody evaluation	8	
Insurance/fee	7	16
Research/teaching	6	
Public statements	5	
Other	1	16
(N = 264)	100%	100%

Note. APA = American Psychological Association. From "Report of the Ethic Committee: 1991 and 1992" by American Psychological Association, Ethics Committee, 1993, *American Psychologist, 48*, pp. 813–819. Copyright 1993 by the American Psychological Association.

confidentiality, abandonment, and other activities that are frequently discussed as pitfalls for the unwary practitioner.

Sexual misconduct not only accounts for the greatest number of complaints but is also very serious. Sixty-three percent of the cases that resulted in loss of membership did so because of sexual misconduct. Unfortunately, the data are not present that would allow us to understand fully the implications of the range of sexual misconduct complaints. For instance, we do not know whether a sexual misconduct allegation is more or less likely to be true than other violations. I hope the Ethics Committee will present such data so that we can determine the likelihood of an incorrect decision of guilt as well as of sexual misconduct that results in discipline other than termination.

APA Insurance Trust

The second source of data comes from the APAIT. Although there are various malpractice carriers that provide coverage for psychologists, the APAIT-sponsored insurance program is among the largest and most well known. The most recent, publicly available data date from approximately 1987 and show trends that are very similar to those shown in the Ethics Committee data (Pope & Vasquez, 1991).

Table 3 shows that sexual misconduct constituted the most frequent type of claim. More important, however, is that sexual misconduct cases constituted more than half of the claims dollars paid out by the APAIT. As with the Ethics Committee data, sexual misconduct was the most frequent and the most serious or expensive type of claim. Again, the percentage of sexual misconduct claims that are without any basis or that are minor are not known.

Incorrect or improper treatment was the next largest category of ethics violations. This category includes negligent choice or implementation of treatment and poor results. Negligent diagnosis constituted 14% of these cases. As with the Ethics Committee data, the areas that often worry psychologists, such as failure to protect, constituted a very small percentage of the total claims.

The APAIT indicated that it has implemented new data collection and analysis procedures that will eventually provide a more complete, instructive view of the types and frequency of monetary claims made against psychologists. Until that time, however, it is difficult to say with any certainty whether claims for damages differ significantly from disciplinary, ethical, or peer-review complaints.

Licensing Boards

The third source of data is the American Association of State Psychology Boards. These data represent the reasons for disciplinary actions taken

Table 3
Complaints of Misconduct Reported by the APA Insurance Trust
1976–1988

Category (nature or context of allegations)	Claims	Losses (% of claims money paid)
Sexual misconduct	23	53
Negligent treatment	15	8
Negligent diagnosis	14	7
Wrongful death	11	13
Countersuit for fee collection	6	1
Breach of confidentiality	6	1
Defamation	4	1
Bodily injury	2	2
Violation of civil rights	2	1
Licensing	2	1
Child custody	2	1
Failure to protect	1	1
Miscellaneous/unknown	12	10
(N = 779)	100%	100%

Note. APA = American Psychological Association. From *Ethics in Psychotherapy and Counseling* (pp. 27–32) by K. S. Pope and M. J. Vasquez, 1991, San Francisco: Jossey-Bass. Copyright 1991 by Jossey-Bass. Adapted by permission.

by state psychology licensing and certification boards. However, like the Ethics Committee and APAIT claims data, these data are fraught with problems induced by inconsistent coding and vague descriptions.

Despite data interpretation problems, the data presented in Table 4 reveal general trends similar to those in the data from the other sources. Sexual misconduct accounted for the largest percentage of disciplinary complaints. Fraud or improper billing practices were reported but were much rarer than sexual misconduct. Finally, disciplinary actions for failure to protect and breach of confidentiality were relatively rare.

Case Law

The final source of data consists of published court decisions over the past 10 years that involved a criminal or civil action against a psychologist. Using literature reviews, specialized summaries, and computerized databases, I attempted to locate all cases in which a psychologist had been sued because of the performance of psychological

Table 4
Complaints of Misconduct Reported by the American Association of
State Psychology Boards 1986–1988

Category (nature or context of the allegations)	Primary issue in disciplinary complaint
Sexual misconduct and dual relationships	36
Unprofessional conduct and ethical violations	13
Improper actions involving the board	11
Fraud and billing problems	11
Conviction of a felony	10
Negligent treatment	6
Breach of confidentiality	1
Others	12
(N = unknown)	100%

Note. From *Ethics in Psychotherapy and Counseling* (pp. 26–27) by K. S. Pope and M. J. Vasquez, 1991, San Francisco: Jossey-Bass. Copyright 1991 by Jossey-Bass. Adapted by permission.

services. Before discussing the cases, however, it is important to understand the nature and limitations of this information.

Published decisions are the written opinions of courts that have the authority to publish their determinations. A published decision means that the court determined that the legal principles in the case were significant and should be available to lawyers and other courts. A published decision may be issued prior to a verdict by a trial court (e.g., a pre-trial evidentiary ruling), in a trial court verdict (e.g., a significant bench-trial verdict), or from one or more of the various appellate courts. Published decisions may be issued by either state and federal courts. Because not every court has the authority to publish, and even those courts with broad authority do not publish all of their cases, these cases do not represent the universe of complaints filed, jury verdicts rendered, or even decisions on final appeal. As with the other data, then, interpretation must be strictly limited to general trends and the formation of hypotheses.

I found 43 published decisions dating from 1982 to 1993. The citations are provided in Appendix A.

Who sues psychologists? The great majority of cases are brought by clients of psychologists, although other parties can be plaintiffs as well. For instance, in one case a psychologist who had not received insurance payments sued the psychologist retained by the insurance company to review the claims.

What allegations do plaintiffs make against psychologists? Psychologists are sued for the same reasons that clients and others bring disciplinary and ethics complaints. The general breakdown is shown in Table 5.

Again, sexual misconduct led the list. The great majority of the sexual misconduct cases involved a male psychologist and a female client. The allegations concerned both present and former clients.

The second largest category, negligent treatment, encompassed a variety of claims, not all of which were detailed. These claims included failure to refer, failure to recommend proper physical safeguards, and problems related to medication. Breach of confidentiality, which can be conceptualized as part of negligent treatment, is presented separately in this table to allow comparison with the other data sources.

The third largest category concerns negligent diagnosis. As with confidentiality, child custody suits are shown separately in this table even though negligent assessments to determine the appropriate cus-todial arrangement could be conceptualized as part of the negligent diagnosis category. The negligent diagnosis cases include workers' com-pensation, prisoner evaluation, and educational assessment suits.

Primary allegations, however, tell only part of the story. As is true of litigation in general, associated factors can explain much of what drives the decision to initiate or to continue litigation. Many of these 43 cases involved one or both of two significant associated factors: the presence of (a) collateral or underlying litigation and (b) codefendant health-care professionals.

In cases of alleging negligent diagnosis or child custody evaluation, all but 15% involved collateral or underlying litigation. Cases involving allegations of negligent treatment predominantly involved parties who were themselves defendants in a related civil or criminal lawsuit or who had sued the psychologist as well as other mental health professionals. Only 12% of the negligent treatment cases involved lawsuits against an

Table 5
Categories of Misconduct Involved in Published Federal and State
Court Decisions 1982–1993

Category	Primary issue of case
Sexual misconduct	35
Negligent treatment	18
Negligent diagnosis	16
Child custody	14
Failure to protect	5
Breach of confidentiality	5
Peer review	5
Fraud	2
(N = 43)	100%

individual psychologist by a client who did not have current or former litigation as a principal factor driving the need for psychological services.

Cases involving sexual misconduct stand in stark contrast because of the absence of these associated factors. In each case alleging sexual misconduct, the client sued only the psychologist. Furthermore, none of the clients was involved in pending or former litigation.

Likelihood of a Complaint

Whatever the problems with the data on the frequency and seriousness of various types of misconduct, the base-rate data on complaints generally is even less informative. We can make only very rough estimates concerning the frequency of any kind of complaint in any forum. Moreover, base rates based on periods more than 5 years back may not predict present rates.

In its most recent report, the APA Ethics Committee (1993) stated that the likelihood of a complaint against an APA member for the years 1990, 1991, and 1992 were 0.21%, 0.16%, and 0.18%, respectively. No information was provided concerning a breakdown by division membership, employment setting, or nature of the complaint. The APAIT reported that it receives 125 liability claims each year against the 36,000 practitioners insured under the professional liability program it sponsors (Bennett et al., 1990). Thus, a member insured under the APAIT faces a 0.38% likelihood of being sued in any given year. There does not appear to be data on the likelihood of a disciplinary complaint being filed with a psychology licensing board.

Self-report data provide a global measure for the likelihood of a complaint being filed in any forum. Pope and Tabachnick (1993) reported in a self-report survey of 285 therapists randomly selected from Divisions 12, 17, 29, and 42 of the APA that just over 1 in 10 therapists had an ethics, disciplinary, or malpractice complaint being filed against them by their clients. This survey group was evenly divided between therapists over and under 45 years of age. These data, which must be interpreted with great caution, suggest that the likelihood of a psychologist receiving any kind of complaint in any given year is very small, under 5%. After 15 years of practice, the likelihood increases to approximately 10% that sometime with his or her career, a psychologist will experience a complaint in some forum.

Forums in Which Allegations Are Made

As already noted, a person who claims misconduct by a psychologist can make the allegation in one or more forums. In this context, *forum* refers to a judicial body or assembly, which includes the courts (both civil and criminal), government administrative boards, and professional associations. The choice of forum depends on the nature of the misconduct, the remedy sought, the time elapsed since the alleged misconduct, and the complexity and expense of the proceeding. The jurisdiction of the forum, meaning the power of an entity to consider a claim and enter a particular order, determines whether it is the proper place to file a complaint. Of course, many uninformed people simply file a complaint in the most convenient or readily available forum, regardless of whether it is appropriate. Timing, complexity, and expenses generally involve strategic considerations about the most favorable forum into which to enter a complaint. This section describes the workings of the various forums and how the proceedings in one forum may affect those in another forum.

The first forum, and the one that most psychologists fear, is the civil court, where a civil lawsuit for monetary damages is filed. The complainant alleges that the psychologist violated a statute or common law. Statutory law is created by elected officials for the particular jurisdiction, usually the state legislature or Congress. Common law is judge-made law. Civil lawsuits are usually brought in state or federal court; however, as litigation becomes more expensive and the courts become more backlogged, such civil claims are increasingly adjudicated outside of the courtroom. These alternatives to court, which are generally referred to as *alternative dispute resolution* (e.g., mediation or arbitration), involve the same substantive matters but attempt to resolve them in a less adversarial and more streamlined fashion.

In a civil law claim, a claimant (called a *plaintiff* in a lawsuit) alleges that the psychologist breached a duty to him or her that resulted in an injury for which the plaintiff demands monetary recompense. The psychologist's duty to the plaintiff must be recognized by statute or common law. The lawsuit must be filed within a set period of time, usually 2 to 3 years after the alleged misconduct.

Plaintiffs usually fall into one of two categories: the direct recipient of psychological services or a person foreseeably injured by a psychologist's conduct with a client. An example of the former would be malpractice actions for sexual misconduct or incomplete evaluation. An example of the latter would be failure to protect another, which is commonly referred to as a *Tarasoff claim*. Both types of suits, however, involve allegations that the psychologist violated a legal duty and that monetary compensation is an appropriate remedy. A person cannot be imprisoned as the result of a malpractice action.

The next, and most serious, type of forum is the criminal court. A criminal prosecution occurs only in a criminal court, whether state or federal, because a criminal defendant's liberty, as well as his or her finances, are at stake. A criminal complaint or indictment alleges that the psychologist violated the state or federal criminal code. Clients or third parties may request that a psychologist face criminal charges, but the final decision to prosecute generally rests with government officials.

Psychologists can face criminal liability in a variety of ways. The most likely activities or omissions that may lead to this kind of liability include failure to report abuse and fraud in obtaining fees. Federal criminal law violations may involve misconduct in a federally funded program or on property under the exclusive jurisdiction of the federal government.

The third forum, an administrative tribunal, involves administrative law. The great majority of these complaints concern a psychologist's license to practice and almost always involve revocation or some limitation on the right to practice.

The jurisdiction of the licensing entity is defined by its enabling statute. Generally, the state legislature creates a governing body with authority to issue and administer licenses to practice in a particular area. Its jurisdiction may be limited to psychology, or it may encompass several related professions. A broad grant of authority usually includes authorization to promulgate specific rules or regulations that do not contradict or go beyond the general authority granted to the licensing board. These are known as *administrative rules and regulations*. They have the same force of law for most purposes as if they had been issued by the legislature itself. Many licensing boards function like traffic cops: Their primary concerns are egregious violations of good practice that endanger the public safety, but they have sufficient authority to cite even minor infractions if they choose to do so.

The fourth forum concerns professional organizations. The jurisdiction of this forum is limited to members of the organization. These groups generally have a code of ethics or a set of standards to which members must adhere. Violations of the ethics code or practice standards may result in a proceeding against the member. The purpose of the proceeding is to determine whether a violation occurred and, if so, the appropriate response. These proceedings range in degrees of formality. The law generally requires some sort of due process that assures the member an opportunity to know the alleged violation and to respond to it in a manner that ensures fair consideration.

Interaction Among the Forums

The four forums are designed to operate independently, each with its own jurisdiction and procedures. There are at least three ways, however, in which the proceedings may interact.

The first interaction begins with persons who file complaints in more than one forum alleging the same set of operative facts against the same psychologist. They do so simultaneously or in serial fashion. Their motivations range from anger to vindictiveness to a genuine wish that no other person be harmed by the particular psychologist.

Multiple filings can provide plaintiffs with a strategic advantage. Sophisticated attorneys representing plaintiffs frequently advise their clients to file multiple complaints to obtain evidence and legal admissions through the efforts of others. For instance, a statement provided by a psychologist to an ethics committee or a licensing board may later be used against that psychologist unless there is a specific court rule or statute that prohibits such evidence. Although most licensing, ethics, and practice association proceedings are considered by the participants to be confidential, there is little or no legal effect to self-imposed confidentiality unless it is specifically recognized by law. When limited confidentiality is provided by law, the extent of its application is strictly observed. For instance, the licensing statute may prohibit subpoenas to the psychology board by any person. On the other hand, a subpoena to the psychologist for his or her files, including correspondence with the psychology board, would not be prohibited unless specifically stated in the law. Thus, a plaintiff may obtain information directly from a psychologist that he or she could not get from a licensing board or peer-review committee. The particularly cunning attorney also realizes that it is exhausting to defend a position involving even the same facts when the battle must be fought on more than one front.

There may also be direct, legal consequences of an adverse finding in one forum that can be used against the psychologist in another forum. For instance, a felony conviction in most jurisdictions can result in disciplinary action against the psychologist. Similarly, a psychologist who has had disciplinary action taken against him or her, regardless of the forum, will likely face that fact in a malpractice action. At issue is whether the jury can weigh the evidence independently or whether it must take the prior adjudication as prima facie evidence that the psychologist's conduct fell beneath the standard of care.

The second form of interaction among the entities may be required as a matter of law. In some jurisdictions, the plaintiff or court must notify the psychology licensing board whenever a psychologist is sued for malpractice (e.g., A.R.S. § 12–570). Similarly, hospitals may be required by statute to notify the licensing board if they learn that one of their health-care providers has engaged in substantial misconduct such that it calls into question that person's ability or willingness to practice competently (e.g., A.R.S. § 32–2081).

Finally, informal communication among boards, attorneys, and even judges also occurs. Psychologists should not assume that because a particular entity has the right to keep information confidential that it also has the duty to do so. An entity with the right to keep something confidential may waive that right; only if it has the duty to keep matters confidential can one reasonably expect that there will be no communication without express consent. In my experience, many administrative bodies routinely share information about psychologists who have engaged in serious misconduct.

How to Avoid Becoming a Defendant

How does one avoid becoming a defendant? On the basis of the frequency and seriousness of the relatively few types of allegations made against psychologists, the simple rule encompassing more than half of the possibilities is quite simple: Restrict sexual activities to nonclients and decline evaluations that will likely be used in litigation. Although simplistic, following this prescription will reduce the likelihood of becoming a defendant by as much as two thirds. Such simplicity, however, is not satisfying because just saying "no" to sexual misconduct has not generally been effective, and psychologists should not be deterred from offering their services to the legal system because of fear of personal liability.

This section outlines prevention issues concerning sexual misconduct, offers basic precautions for those working in the forensic area, and briefly reviews general risk-management principles that are applicable to almost any problem that is likely to result in a psychologist being labeled as a defendant. This is by no means a complete treatment of these areas. There is an increasing number of texts and seminars on each of these topics. Because of time and space limitations, I highlight only major points.

Sexual Misconduct

Sexual misconduct must be addressed in graduate school. There is disturbing evidence that sexual involvement between therapists-in-training and their educators is related to students' subsequent misconduct as professionals. Pope, Levenson, and Schover (1979) found that 17% of the female respondents reported sexual contact with at least one of their educators. Of these female respondents, 23% reported having sexual contact with clients as professionals, compared with only 6% of those who had no sex with their educators. The survey left unanswered the issue of causation versus mere correlation. There can be little doubt, however, that student–educators sexual contact did not have a beneficial effect in reducing the likelihood of subsequent sexual misconduct.

Practicing psychologists, particularly those who were trained before graduate schools began to confront directly sexual misconduct issues, should make use of the emerging literature on therapists' sexual feelings and activities with clients (e.g., Gabbard, 1989; Pope, Sonne, & Holroyd, 1993). Sexual feelings cannot be denied or ignored. Pope and Tabachnick

(1993) reported that over half of the therapist respondents to a national survey had experienced sexual arousal while in the presence of a client. The clinical use of sexual feelings or responses, however, has not been extensively discussed outside of the psychodynamic literature. Unfortunately, denial appears to be a frequent, perhaps even primary, response to both therapist sexual feelings and activities with clients (e.g., Brownfain, 1971; Stone, 1990). Discussion of the clinical and professional issues involving therapist sexual feelings is well beyond the boundaries of this chapter, but several points developed by Pope et al. (1993) should be noted. First, sexual feelings must be addressed. This is best done with others in a safe, nonjudgmental, and supportive context. Second, contextual factors such as age, gender, race, and physical contact offer insight into sexual feelings versus sexual conduct. Finally, sexual feelings can and must be distinguished from sexual intimacy with clients.

Litigation-Related Evaluations

Litigation spawns litigation. Lawyers have always known this simple fact, and the more practical attorneys always advise against litigation if at all possible. Litigation, at its worst, involves a system wherein one or more parties must lose. Not surprisingly, the losers frequently look to another party to erase or lessen their loss. The psychologist–evaluator is an available target, particularly in matters concerning children wherein the psychologist's evaluation plays a very important role.

The courts' increasing recognition that psychologists are sued merely for participating in the judicial process has caused them to immunize court-related psychological services. The precise immunity lines, however, vary by jurisdiction. Additionally, although the immunity makes it easy to get a case dismissed, it does not prohibit the filing of suit. In most cases, it is still necessary to retain an attorney to file the appropriate pleadings to have the matter summarily dismissed. For this reason, it is much better to take preventative measures that discourage the filing of a suit in the first place.

If one agrees to undertake an evaluation that likely will be used in litigation, one's protection against suit will be the greatest if the evaluation is conducted pursuant to a court order. If at all possible, the order should specify the following information about the evaluation: purpose, evaluator, participants, deadlines, fees and method of payment, and recipients of written reports. A detailed court order provides the psychologist with the absolute immunity of a court and reduces the likelihood that someone will charge a violation of an implied agreement. The psychologist should still affirm and obtain the written consent of the parties at the time of the evaluation. Attorneys do not always explain what the court has ordered and sometimes even distort what the court has ordered. In either event, the psychologist wants to ensure that he or she is not part of any misunderstanding. Additionally, obtaining the participant's written consent adds an additional layer of legal and practical protection against suit. Clients who understand beforehand what is going to happen, how the evaluation will take place, and who will use it are much more likely to accept the psychologist's role in an adverse result. Finally, psychologists who regularly undertake forensic evaluations should know the *Specialty Guidelines for Forensic Psychologists* (Committee on Ethical Guidelines for Forensic Psychologists, 1991) and be familiar with the law governing the subject matter about which they are providing a report. It is also important to understand the role and risks that await expert witnesses (e.g., Blau, 1984; Melton, Petrila, Poythress, & Slobogin, 1987; Ziskin & Faust, 1988).

Duty-to-Protect Problems

Despite the very low incidence of disciplinary or legal cases against individual psychologists alleging failure to protect, the topic has garnered considerable discussion (e.g., Monahan, 1993; Schopp, 1991). Psychologists report that it is a tremendous concern for them (Brodsky, 1988; Monahan, 1993). Thus, if only for palliative reasons, I offer the following observations and advice concerning preventive measures.

Most failure-to-protect cases do not specify what the therapist should have done or the specific circumstances requiring action. For instance, in the seminal case of *Tarasoff v. Regents of the University of California* (1976), the California Supreme Court did not hold that the psychologist's actions in notifying the police of his patient's intent to kill his fiancé were negligent. The holding was limited to establishing the legal principle that the victim could bring suit. The parties to *Tarasoff* settled, so we do not know whether liability would have been attached to the psychologist.

There is a trend among jurisdictions to limit liability to those circumstances in which there is an identifiable victim. Furthermore, individual cases, as well as expert reports, suggest that liability rarely attaches if the psychologist has considered all or most of the relevant information and makes a considered judgment but when someone is nonetheless injured (Monahan, 1993). The exposure is much greater, however, if the psychologist does not even consider the issue of danger because he or she fails to obtain pertinent, recent information. This generally occurs in one or two circumstances: either the psychologist does not read or obtain readily available records from others or the psychologist fails to ask questions addressing the issue of danger when the situation warrants. Again, the critical issue is the consideration of information that is reasonably available. A second-guessed opinion is a rare event in a small universe of cases.

General Risk-Management Principles

In addition to the recommendations for specific problems already noted, there are a number of principles that will help create a practice that is effective and efficient and meets your financial goals. There are good texts on practice management that also cover this information (e.g., Bennett et al., 1990; Klein, Macbeth, & Onek, 1984; Sales, 1983; Stromberg et al., 1988; Woody, 1988). At the core of such a practice are satisfied clients. This is the best defense against miscellaneous varieties of malpractice: Satisfied clients rarely, if ever, sue.

As lawyers have learned, a good malpractice prevention program starts with an assessment of high-risk procedures or clients. Other than litigation-related evaluations, there is no evidence that one psychological service is more likely to result in litigation for the psychologist than another. The emphasis, therefore, should be on identifying the high-risk client.

As with clients who request an evaluation to be used in litigation, one should be equally cautious about clients who do not request an evaluation but are involved in litigation. Because of the litigation, it is more likely that one's records will be requested by one of the parties to the litigation. A client who receives an adverse result on the basis, at least in part, of information from a psychologist's records may be very dissatisfied. Additionally, a client in litigation may eventually request a report, which could place a psychologist in an awkward situation if the information is not helpful in most respects. Of course, one should not turn away a client simply because the person is involved in litigation, but one's records and procedures should be such that one would not be concerned about having them discussed in open court.

The second factor in assessing a new client is his or her willingness to accept the terms under which you offer psychological services. Fees are probably the most important (Kovacs, 1987). If a new client indicates that your fees will pose great difficulties, you should beware of the risk that if a problem occurs with collecting fees, you may have to write off an account or may risk a malpractice suit filed as a counterclaim to your collections action. In addition to a satisfactory fee agreement, the new client should receive and agree to your general policies in a written statement (e.g., charges for missed appointments, review of records by consultants or supervisors).

Written records not only assist you in measuring the course of psychological services, they are the principal evidence that you observed what you observed and that you provided the services in the manner and form described. The maxim from medicine applies: If it is not recorded, it did not happen. Your goal should be to have complete, consistent records that contain sufficient detail for their purpose. The psychology licensing laws in many states specify the minimum information that must be recorded each time a psychologist meets with a client. Records should never be destroyed or altered in response to a lawsuit or complaint. If the records contain mistakes, correct them with additions that show the date of the corrections. In other words, do not attempt to remake the record such that a reader would be mislead as to when and how the records were made. Finally, if a lawsuit has been filed, you should consult your attorney before making any record changes at all.

The APA-endorsed "Record Keeping Guidelines" (Committee on Professional Practice and Standards, 1993) should be consulted when assessing record-keeping procedures. If more than one psychologist maintains records on a certain client, it is advisable to have a written policy concerning record-keeping procedures. This does not mean, however, that the procedures should be complex or even detailed. The goal should be to create a system that is simple to use, allows for additional detail when necessary, and always meets the minimum requirements in your jurisdiction.

Risk management necessarily implies appreciating and understanding legal risks (Miller & Sales, 1991). Of course, it is impossible for anyone, lawyers included, to predict every problem area. The law, like science, is a moving target. Fortunately, most of the law that is likely to affect psychologists changes relatively slowly. These laws can be assembled in a notebook or folder for easy reference and occasional review. This notebook should contain the current licensing statute and any administrative rules or regulations issued by the licensing board. Although such reading is dry, it should be updated and reviewed on a regular basis. It should also include professional codes and guidelines that may have the force of law in your jurisdiction or specialty. The APA's Ethics Code (APA Ethics Committee, 1992) is the core of these documents and includes the "General Guidelines for Providers of Psychological Services" (APA, Committee on Professional Standards, 1987), "Specialty Guidelines for the Delivery of Services" (APA, Committee on Professional Standards, 1981) and *Standards for Educational and Psychological Testing* (1985). Psychologists who further specialize, such as in treating sex offenders, should be familiar with guidelines or ethics codes for their specialty groups.

These core materials will provide the law, regulations, and standards covering most of a psychologist's practice. Inevitably, it will be necessary, or at least useful, to become familiar with the law in your jurisdiction that is not covered in these core materials. There is no encyclopedia compendium addressing mental health law in every jurisdiction. However, the APA is addressing this gap by publishing a series of books that comprehensively review and integrate all of the law that affects mental health professionals in each state, the District of Columbia, and the federal jurisdictions. The first five volumes of the *Law and Mental Health Professionals* series (Sales & Miller, 1986–1993) have been published. If your jurisdiction does not have a published volume yet, more traditional and laborious methods will have to suffice for the present. Your state psychological association is a good place to begin seeking information. Many associations have compiled a list of laws that go beyond the licensure law for psychologists, or they are aware of private efforts to do so. If such a collection does not exist or is inadequate, the library of any law school, a government library, or a county court library will generally have collections of most primary legal materials. Recognize, however, that you may reach the point where you will need an attorney's services.

The last element of a good malpractice prevention program is a consultant. Because malpractice revolves around a deviation from what other practitioners in your field would do in like circumstances, the opinion of a consultant can help assure that you are following accepted practices. Choose a person whose opinion you respect, whose credentials are at or above your level, and who has a good reputation in your professional community. Even better would be a network of colleagues who consult with each other when particularly difficult situations arise. The relation should be sufficiently formal that you will not hesitate to record consultations with the person or persons, including any suggestions made. You and your consultants should be aware, however, that formal consultations of this sort may lead to legal liability if a consultant provides advice that a jury determines is beneath accepted practice. For this reason, and to remind the participants that consultation involves responsibilities the same as other psychological service, the consultant should be compensated or other arrangements made involving an equitable trade.

What to Do if You Must Defend a Lawsuit or Complaint

Although the likelihood of a lawsuit, disciplinary action, or ethics complaint in any given year is small, it must be acknowledged and analyzed and at least an initial response must be filed. Unfortunately, the successful defense and resolution of complaints relating to psychological services require more time and effort than most psychologists initially expect.

Notification that you are under investigation or that formal allegations have been made against you is, at best, very unpleasant. Most professionals immediately recognize the significance of a complaint; however, there is the occasional individual who ignores or denies its significance. Any investigation by a reputable entity and any lawsuit must be addressed. Ignoring or responding inappropriately to such a matter, even if the underlying complaint is trivial or without merit, virtually ensures that a legitimate, substantial complaint will be brought by the investigating or prosecuting body itself. For instance, the APA Ethics Code provides that it is a violation of the standards of conduct to ignore an inquiry by the Ethics Committee (APA Ethics Committee, 1992, Ethical Standard 8.06).

A measured analysis of the lawsuit or complaint must be the first order of business after learning that you are a defendant or may become one. If formal, legal allegations have been filed, a psychologist should at least consult an attorney. Handling a legal matter where the opposition has an attorney is fraught with difficulties and dangers, regardless of the merits of the complaint. The complexity of the substantive law and procedural rules mandates at least a consultation with an attorney.

How does one find an attorney? Preferably, you will have established a relationship with an attorney prior to legal action. In addition, your professional liability insurer may retain an attorney to defend you. This topic is covered in a separate section because of the unique and some-times complex issues involved. If you do not know a reputable attorney, colleagues or the local psychology associations can usually provide you with several names. Do not retain an attorney without conducting at least a telephone interview to assure yourself that this person possesses the requisite knowledge and that you will be able to work with him or her.

Your interview of an attorney candidate should cover at least the following areas. Determine whether and to what extent this person has represented psychologists or other mental health professionals, the person's litigation experience, and his or her specific knowledge about the exact proceeding you are facing, including firsthand knowledge of the professional people involved. Unless there are compelling circumstances, avoid attorneys with less than five years of experience. Instinct, persuasiveness, and judgment usually require at least that period of time to develop.

Understand the exact fee arrangement. Do not hesitate to negotiate the fees, terms, and conditions. For instance, you may wish to be advised if the overall fees exceed a certain limit or if any single item costs more than $1,000. Similarly, you should request a detailed accounting of the attorney's fees. Except for naive clients, the time is long past when a lawyer hands the client a single page statement with the words "For Professional Services Rendered," followed by a very large number.

Coverage and Defense Under Your Malpractice Policy

Whether your malpractice carrier will retain an attorney to defend you in a civil or criminal lawsuit, before the licensing board, or in an ethics complaint depends on the terms of your policy and whether you have complied with its procedural requirements. You must be familiar with your policy to determine your rights to defense, as well as any obligations that you must satisfy. Policies differ greatly in their terms and conditions of coverage; however, several general points can be made.

First, almost every policy requires that you notify the insurance carrier when you have been sued or know of a matter that likely will result in a claim for damages or a lawsuit. Failure to notify the carrier, even if the carrier would have done nothing at that point, may be grounds for subsequent denial of coverage. Refusal by the malpractice carrier to retain an attorney occasionally results in serious mistakes if the psychologist proceeds alone to licensing, criminal, or ethics proceedings. The psychologist may take an unnecessary or inappropriate position that adversely affects subsequent civil litigation. To avoid such a result, when providing initial notice of a lawsuit or complaint, be candid with the carrier about the nature of the claim, the forums in which you are being investigated, and whether your accuser has retained an attorney.

After notice has been given, the determination of whether an attorney will be appointed often depends on the nature and forum of the complaint and the terms of the policy. Most policies provide protection against law-related complaints only. For instance, defense of complaints filed with an ethics or peer-review committee are rarely covered, regardless of the nature of the complaints. Even if the complaint is filed in a court, the nature of it may result in limitations in coverage.

The insurance carrier generally has separate duties to defend and to indemnify. The duty to defend generally requires the carrier to retain an attorney to defend you at its cost, including related expenses. Whether the insurance carrier can extinguish its duty to defend by paying a certain amount of money, typically determined by policy limits, depends on the particular policy. The duty to indemnify means that the insurance carrier will pay money damages against you, subject to policy limits, deductibles, and the basis for the judgment. The latter exclusion can be complex. For instance, most, if not all, malpractice policies for mental health professionals exclude or place a low limit on judgments that arise out of sexual misconduct. Intentional infliction of harm is also excluded. Most lawsuits, however, frequently allege at least a half dozen violations of professional duties, one or more of which may be excluded under the malpractice policy. Therefore, the malpractice carrier may inform you, through a notification called a *reservation of rights,* that all or part of any judgment against you may not be covered under the policy. This creates the possibility for implied or explicit conflicts between you and the insurance company. This may also create conflicts with the attorney retained by the insurance carrier to defend you.

Although the insurance carrier retains and exercises general control over the attorney, the psychologist is the attorney's client. The attorney cannot undertake any action or work with an insurance carrier to the psychologist's detriment. For instance, if the attorney learns about information that he or she believes could adversely effect coverage, such information cannot be provided to the company with the advice that the carrier should deny coverage. Certainly, the attorney cannot represent you and then turn around and represent the carrier against you in a subsequent action.

There should be a comfortable, working relationship between you and the attorney retained by the carrier. Presumably, the carrier has selected the particular law firm for its expertise in handling the particular kind of case. Nonetheless, an attorney and a psychologist may have antagonistic styles, or the case may be passed to a junior attorney who does not have sufficient knowledge or ability. You should feel free to ask questions and expect answers the same as if you were paying the legal bills directly.

If a problem exists between you and the retained attorney that cannot be resolved through reasonable efforts between the two of you, you should notify the carrier of the situation. In general, responsible carriers listen to such concerns and attempt to provide reasonable accommodations. This does not include, however, hiring your local version of Clarence Darrow. A malpractice policy usually states that the carrier will provide a competent defense, not necessarily the best defense available.

If a problem continues between you and the attorney despite efforts to resolve it with the attorney and the malpractice carrier, and if you believe that your interests have been or will be adversely affected, you should contact a personal attorney to discuss the matter. In many jurisdictions, it is possible to enter into an agreement with the plaintiff that protects one's legal interests in exchange for the right of the plaintiff to obtain a default judgment and to proceed directly against the insurance carrier. Although the carrier is never pleased with such a result, the possibility of such an arrangement usually encourages the carrier to consider carefully your demand that the problems be resolved. This is a very technical area of insurance law that cannot be negotiated without the advice of a knowledgeable attorney.

Responding to Minor or Spurious Complaints

What if you are the subject of an insignificant or totally groundless complaint? In the course of a long, active career, it is almost inevitable that some person associated with your practice will be unhappy about some aspect of it and will be motivated or told to file a complaint, even on a trivial point. It is understandable that many psychologists do not want to incur the cost of an attorney to represent or even advise them on what they consider to be minor or unjustified complaints. Fortunately, malpractice policies do not exclude coverage based on the significance or merits of the complaint.

If the complaint is filed only with the licensing board or an ethics committee and if the malpractice policy does not provide a defense, there is a great temptation to handle the matter on one's own. I suggest, however, that some sort of consultation with an experienced colleague or attorney is necessary any time a complaint is filed against you or some aspect of your practice is under investigation. In fact, regardless of whether you consult with an attorney, as a matter of good professional practice, you should consult with a trusted, experienced colleague about the merits of the complaint, potentially weak or troublesome areas of practice, remediation, and your personal response to the entire situation. Neither your clients, your practice, nor you can afford to have blind spots.

The consultation should be sufficiently formal such that the consultant would feel comfortable charging you for the time or for testifying on your behalf. It should include a complete review of the case, the complaint and attendant procedures, and recommendations on how to proceed. A thorough review will address any real problems, avoid careless mistakes, and turn what is otherwise a very negative experience into a positive, strengthening exercise. Additionally, in many jurisdictions, the law will treat your consultation with another psychologist as privileged. If there is any question about whether the privilege applies, you may wish to have the consultation arranged by an attorney, which will protect it under the attorney–client privilege.

Dealing With a Client Who Has Filed a Complaint

How should you respond to a past or present client who has brought a complaint against you? Once a client has made a decision to bring a complaint, the relationship is altered, both legally and psychologically. Your response depends on several factors.

If the client is represented by an attorney, then you are well advised, and possibly mandated, to speak only with the attorney. Of course, you may speak with your client to the extent that is necessary to explain that because he or she has retained counsel, it is preferable for communications to go through the attorney unless alternative arrangements are made. If you communicate with a represented client on substantive matters and the client withdraws the complaint, the attorney may claim that you exerted undue influence or control over the client against his or her best interest. You must avoid even the appearance of impropriety if you are the subject of a complaint or investigation.

If the complainant is not represented by an attorney, there is generally no reason why you cannot contact the person yourself. Nonetheless, the same considerations apply concerning allegations of undue influence. For this reason, it is generally better to refrain from unnecessary contact with the client unless you are certain there is a simple misunderstanding or that the problem can be resolved with a minimum of intervention. If you believe that the problem can be resolved through your direct involvement but that it will take more than minimal effort or time, you should make the offer of assistance through the entity that received the complaint. In that manner, you will protect yourself against additional allegations while at the same time impressing those people charged with handling the complaint of your sincerity and position.

If the complainant is your active client, regardless of whether he or she is represented, you face a substantial problem. In almost all circumstances, the professional relationship will be fractured by a complaint. Regardless of what action you take, it may be viewed as a conflict of interest. Legally and psychologically, it will be difficult to separate the client's problems from those that you share with him or her. Make no mistake, the filing of a complaint means that you now share a problem on an individual, personal basis.

That you should not continue a professional relationship with a client who has filed a complaint does not mean that you can abruptly terminate the relationship. Abandonment would only compound the problem. As with any other client who requires continued psychological services, or at least an independent evaluation of such need, you must arrange for an appropriate transfer to another mental health professional or agency.

How to Be a Good Defendant

What can you do to increase the likelihood of the best possible result? For a variety of reasons, it is tempting to allow or encourage your attorney to handle everything. Do not fall into this trap. Although most attorneys are very comfortable in handling all aspects of their cases, I believe that the defense is enhanced in direct proportion to the involvement of the client. Only you can provide firsthand detail. Unless you were practicing far outside your area of expertise, you know the substantive material better than your attorney. You must work together at each step of the process. Do not worry about micromanaging the case; there is much more danger from disinterest or a misguided grant of authority to the attorney. If the attorney is not comfortable with your interest and participation, especially after an attempt to resolve any problems, it is time to start looking for a new attorney. As with other professions, paternalism and rigid control are no long acceptable modes of practice.

Although personal, substantial involvement ultimately benefits the result, the effort is very stressful. The stress of being a defendant is directly correlated with the length of time and seriousness of the psychologist's involvement. Even if there is nothing that can be done, this itself may cause stress. Expect that you will be easily distracted during this period. Similarly, your friends and family may notice that you are not quite the same. Because your profession requires high acuity of emotion and concentration, you should consider seriously entering into an ongoing consultation with a colleague, analogous to personal, clinical supervision. Many psychologists ignore the obvious benefits of clinical consultation as a way of denying the seriousness of what occurred or as a way of inadequately coping with their own fears about their conduct and what will result. The effective psychologist, however, recognizes that the process itself, regardless of what finally occurs, is stressful and that he or she will cope better when assisted by a colleague.

Conclusion

Psychology began its formal response to misconduct 40 years ago with an empirically developed ethics code. It focused inward to the extent that the research involved collection of events that psychologists perceived to be ethical dilemmas. The means and goals have changed since that time. The most recent ethics code reflects legal concerns as much as aspirational principles. Despite this trend toward the legalization of psychological practice, the available data indicate that common sense and observance of clear strictures reduce the likelihood that a psychologist will be named as a defendant by almost two thirds.

Psychologists who become defendants must take seriously the allegations and process. There should be a dual perspective: psychological substance and legal or administrative procedure. To obtain this bifocal perspective, it is usually necessary to obtain the assistance of a colleague and an attorney, both of whom are knowledgeable about the subject matter and proceeding. The initial evaluation should provide you with objective information about the merits of the allegations, the course and possible outcomes of the proceedings, and what you should or can do. Whether you handle it yourself or seek formal representation, such an evaluation will allow you to make an informed decision. From that point, you will be in a much better position to take a stressful experience and make it a positive one.

References

American Psychological Association. (1992). Ethical principles of psychologists and code of conduct. *American Psychologist, 47*, 1597–1611.
American Psychological Association, Ethics Committee. (1986). Report of the Ethics Committee: 1985. *American Psychologist, 41*, 694–697.
American Psychological Association, Ethics Committee. (1987). Report of the Ethics Committee: 1986. *American Psychologist, 42*, 730–734.

American Psychological Association, Ethics Committee. (1988). Report of the Ethics Committee: 1987. *American Psychologist, 43*, 654–672.

American Psychological Association, Ethics Committee. (1990). Report of the Ethics Committee: 1988. *American Psychologist, 45*, 873–874.

American Psychological Association, Ethics Committee. (1991). Report of the Ethics Committee: 1989 and 1990. *American Psychologist, 46*, 750–757.

American Psychological Association, Ethics Committee. (1992). Rules and procedures of the Ethics Committee of the American Psychological Association. *American Psychologist, 47*, 1612–1628.

American Psychological Association, Ethics Committee. (1993). Report of the Ethics Committee: 1991 and 1992. *American Psychologist, 48*, 811–820.

Bennett, B. E., Bryant, B. K., VandenBos, G. R., & Greenwood, A. (1990). *Professional liability and risk management*. Washington, DC: American Psychological Association.

Blau, T. H. (1984). *The psychologist as expert witness*. New York: Wiley.

Brodsky, S. (1988). Fear of litigation in mental health professionals. *Criminal Justice and Behavior, 15*, 492–500.

Brownfain, J. J. (1971). The APA professional liability insurance program. *American Psychologist, 26*, 648–652.

Bursztajn, H., Gutheil, T. A., Brodsky, A., & Swagerty, E. L. (1988). "Magical thinking," suicide, and malpractice litigation. *Bulletin of the American Academy of Psychiatry and Law, 16*, 369–375.

Cases and inquiries before the Committee on Scientific and Professional Ethics and Conduct. (1954). *American Psychologist, 9*, 806–807.

Committee on Ethical Guidelines for Forensic Psychologists. (1991). Specialty guidelines for forensic psychologists. *Law and Human Behavior, 15*, 655–665.

Committee on Professional Practice and Standards. (1993). Record keeping guidelines. *American Psychologist, 48*, 984–986.

Cummings, N. A., & Sobel, S. B. (1985). Malpractice insurance: Update on sex claims. *Psychotherapy, 22*, 186–188.

Gabbard, G. O. (1989). *Sexual exploitation in professional relationships*. Washington, DC: American Psychiatric Press.

Hall, C. S. (1952). Crooks, codes, and cant. *American Psychologist, 7*, 430–431.

Klein, J. I., Macbeth, J. E., & Onek, J. N. (1984). *Legal issues in the private practice of psychology*. Washington, DC: American Psychiatric Press.

Kovacs, A. L. (1987). Insurance billing: The growing risk of lawsuits against psychologists. *Independent Practitioner, 7*, 21–24.

Melton, G. B., Petrila, J., Poythress, N., & Slobogin, C. (1987). *Psychological evaluations for the courts: A handbook for mental health professionals and lawyers*. New York: Guilford Press.

Miller, M. O., & Sales, M. O. (1991). The importance of law in psychological careers. In R. R. Kilburg (Ed.), *How to manage your career in psychology* (pp. 197–204). Washington, DC: American Psychological Association.

Monahan, J. (1993). Limiting therapist exposure to *Tarasoff* liability: Guidelines for risk containment. *American Psychologist, 48*, 242–250.

Pope, K. S. (1990). Therapist–patient sexual involvement: A review of the research. *Clinical Psychology Review, 10*, 477–490.

Pope, K. S., Levenson, H., & Schover, L. R. (1979). Sexual intimacy in psychology training: Results and implications of a national survey. *American Psychologist, 34*, 682–689.

Pope, K. S., Sonne, J. L., & Holroyd, J. (1993). *Sexual feelings in psychotherapy.* Washington, DC: American Psychological Association.

Pope, K. S., & Tabachnick, B. G. (1993). Therapists' anger, hate, fear, and sexual feelings: National survey of therapist responses, client characteristics, critical events, formal complaints, and training. *Professional Psychology: Research and Practice, 24,* 142–152.

Pope, K. S., & Vasquez, M. J. (1991). *Ethics in psychotherapy and counseling.* San Francisco: Jossey-Bass.

Sales, B. D. (Ed.). (1983). *The professional psychologist's handbook.* New York: Plenum.

Sales, B. D., & Miller, M. O. (Series Eds.). (1986–1993). *Law and mental health professionals series.* Washington, DC: American Psychological Association.

Schopp, R. (1991). The psychotherapist's duty to protect the public: The appropriate standard and the foundation in legal theory and empirical research. *Nebraska Law Review, 70,* 327–360.

Stone, A. (1990, March). No good deed goes unpunished. *Psychiatric Times,* pp. 24–27.

Stromberg, C. D., Haggarty, D. J., Leibluft, R. F., McMillian, M. H., Mishkin, B., Rubin, B. L., & Trilling, H. R. (1988). *The psychologist's legal handbook.* Washington, DC: Council for the National Register of Health Service Providers in Psychology.

Tarasoff v. Regents of the University of California, 131 Cal.Rptr. 14, 551 P.2d 334 (1976).

Woody, R. H. (1988). *Fifty ways to avoid malpractice: A guidebook for mental health professionals.* Sarasota, FL: Professional Resource Exchange.

Ziskin, J., & Faust, D. (1988). *Coping with psychiatric and psychological testimony* (4th ed., 3 vols.). Venice, CA: Law and Psychology Press.

Appendix A

Accounts Adjustment Bureau v. Cooperman, 158 Cal.App.3d 844, 204 Cal.Rptr. 881 (1984).

Bankston v. Alexandria Neurosurgical Cl., 583 So.2d 1148 (La.App. 1991).

Batoff v. State Farm Ins. Co., 977 F.2d 848 (3rd Cir. 1992).

Brandon v. The Wisconsin Department of Public Instruction, 595 F.Supp. 740 (E.D. Wis. 1984).

Carmichael v. Carmichael, 597 A.2d 1326 (D.C.App. 1991).

Chambers v. Ingram, 858 F.2d 351 (7th Cir. 1988).

Coddington v. Robertson, 407 N.W.2d 666 (Mich.App. 1987).

Corgan v. Muehling, 522 N.E.2d 153 (Ill.App. 1 Dist. 1988).

Deed v. Condrell, 568 N.Y.S.2d 679 (Sup. Ct. 1991).

Dockweiler v. Wentzell, 425 N.W.2d 468 (Mich.App. 1988).

Doe v. Board of Educ. of Montgomery County, 453 A.2d 814 (Md. 1982).

Doe v. Douglas County School Dist. RE-1, 775 F.Supp. 1414 (D.Colo. 1991).

Dunkle v. Food Service East, 400 P.Super. 58, 582 A.2d 1342 (1990).

Figueiredo-Torres v. Nickel, 321 Md. 642, 584 A.2d 69 (1991).

Glazier v. Lee, 429 N.W.2d 857 (Mich.App. 1988).

Gootee v. Lightner, 274 Cal.Rptr. 697 (Cal.App. 1990).

Govar v. Chicago v. Chicago Ins. Co., 879 F.2d 1581 (8th Cir. 1989).

Grote v. J.S. Mayer & Co., Inc., 570 N.E.2d 1146 (Ohio App. 1990).

Groth v. Weinstock, 610 So.2d 477 (Fla.App. 5 Dist. 1992).

Hedlund v. Superior Court, 34 Cal.3d 695, 194 Cal.Rptr. 805, 669 P.2d 41 (1983).

Howard v. Drapkin, 271 Cal.Rptr. 893 (Cal.App. 1990).

Howes v. U.S., 887 F.2d 729 (6th Cir. 1989).

Jackson v. U.S., 789 F.Supp. 1109 (D.Colo. 1992).

Jacobsen v. Muller, 352 S.E.2d 604 (Ga.App. 1986).

Jarallah v. Schwartz, 413 S.E.2d 210 (Ga.App. 1991).

Landstrom v. Illinois Department of Children and Family Services, 699 F.Supp. 1270 (E.D. Ill. 1988).

Lather v. Beadle County, 879 F.2d 365 (8th Cir. 1989).

Lavit v. Superior Ct., 173 Ariz. 96, 839 P.2d 1141 (App. 1992).

Lenhard v. Butler, 745 S.W.2d 101 (Tex.App. 1988).

MacClements v. Lafone, 104 N.C.App. 179, 408 S.E.2d 878 (1991).

Myers Through Myers v. Price, 463 N.W.2d 773 (Minn.App. 1990).

Patricia C. v. Mark D., 16 Cal.Rptr.2d 71 (Cal.App. 1 Dist. 1993).

Pomilee v. City of Detroit, 121 Mich.App. 121, 328 N.W.2d 595 (1982).

Riley v. Collins, 828 F.2d 306 (5th Cir. 1987).

Snow v. Koeppl, 464 N.W.2d 215 (Wis.App. 1990).

St. Paul Fire and Marine Ins. Co. v. Love, 447 N.W.2d 5 (Minn.App. 1989).

Stamy v. Packer, 138 F.R.D. 412 (D.N.J. 1990).

State v. Sword, 713 P.2d 432 (Hawaii 1986).

Susan A. v. County of Sonoma, 3 Ca.Rptr.2d 27 (Cal.App. 1991).

Taylor v. Best, 746 F.2d 220 (4th Cir. 1984).

Turney v. O'Toole, 898 F.2d 1470 (10th Cir. 1990).

Whinston v. Kaiser Foundation Hospital, 763 P.2d 177 (Or.App. 1988).

Zar v. S.D. Bd. of Examiners of Psychologists, 976 F.2d 459 (8th Cir. 1992).

JULIE BLACKMAN

AT THE FRONTIER: IN PURSUIT OF JUSTICE FOR WOMEN

J ulie Blackman received her BA from Cornell University in 1974 with an independent major in "Contemporary American Personality." She then applied to law school and to graduate school to study social psychology. She chose to attend graduate school, but her continuing interest in law has greatly influenced the nature of her work. She studied with R. Gary Bridge, Morton Deutsch, and Harvey Hornstein and received her PhD in social psychology from Teachers College, Columbia University, in 1978.

From 1978 to 1987, Blackman was assistant professor at Barnard College, where she taught courses on the psychology of women, psychology and the law, and social psychology. Between 1986 and 1990, she taught part-time at Sarah Lawrence College and at Eugene Lang College of the New School.

Blackman is a member of Divisions 1, 9, 35, and 41 of the American Psychological Association (APA). She served as a member of the Council for the Society for the Psychological Study of Social Issues (SPSSI— Division 9) for 1 year and chaired the Courtwatch Committee of SPSSI for 4 years (1988–1992). This committee prepares the "Judicial Notebook" columns that appear in the APA *Monitor*.

Blackman has maintained a long-standing interest in reactions to human acts of injustice. This interest led her to explore the psychology of victims of family violence, with an early focus on battered women. This work soon attracted the attention of attorneys, and in 1979, she testified for the first time as an expert witness in a criminal case that involved a battered woman. Since then, Blackman has appeared as an expert witness at more than 40 criminal trials of battered women or abused children who have struck back and killed their abusers.

In 1981, Blackman extended her forensic work into the area of jury selection and began her career as a trial-strategy consultant. She has been involved with criminal and civil cases, in both federal and state courts around the United States. Since 1991, she has worked exclusively as a forensic social psychologist, working both as an expert on lethal family violence and as a trial consultant in cases involving a wide range of other issues—from patent infringement and antitrust violations to homicide cases and acts of terrorism.

In 1989, her book *Intimate Violence: A Study of Injustice* (Blackman, 1989) was published by Columbia University Press. Her journal publications include articles in *Women's Rights Law Reporter* and *Behavioral Science and the Law*. She also authored a chapter in *Violence Against Women: A Critique of the Sociobiology of Rape* (Sunday & Tobach, 1985). She is currently at work on a new book about children who die as a result of abuse and neglect. Titled *Buried Treasures*, this book will combine social and psychological theories on abusive parents with the criminal justice system's treatment of mothers and fathers whose actions have resulted in the deaths of their children.

Presently, Blackman lives in Montclair, New Jersey, with her husband, Mitchell Dinnerstein, and their two children, Jed and Molly.

References

Blackman, J. (1989). *Intimate violence: A study of injustice*. New York: Columbia University Press.

Sunday, S. R., & Tobach, E. (Eds.). (1985). *Violence against women: A critique of the sociobiology of rape*. New York: Gordian Press. (A Genes and Gender Mongraph)

AT THE FRONTIER: IN PURSUIT OF JUSTICE FOR WOMEN

Prelude

H e stood nose pressed to the rough wood of the door. Too small to reach a window, he leaned into the door as if to open it. Too young to speak, his mind raced wordlessly. He gulped, swallowing air and more air. He felt his belly rumble, and a sound traveled up through him and out into the room. The sound came unbidden. No words shaped his cry. He wailed, hollow, steady, and high. Some small comfort came to him from the very sound of his voice. His sound was outside him. It accompanied him now, and now he was himself the wailer and himself the listener. He had become two, twinning himself, mothering himself. His mother was gone.

She had left while he was asleep or awake. It did not matter. She was a sound in his mind—the one who cried a different cry from his own. Small comfort came to him from her cry. Sometimes he heard her, and his heart beat a different pace.

Once when she was there, he had cried, and she had held his small hand to the stove flame to make him stop. He had not understood. She had said, "This will shut you up, you motherfucker." He had not understood. The pain was bright and sharp and everywhere. He was enveloped by sensation. She held his hand, watched his skin blister. His skin became translucent. Could she see into him now? His pain passed, but his fear of her and his urge to feel something made him yearn for her again and again.

She was back, wild-eyed, strung out. She burst in when he was nosed up to the door. She swept him across the floor and his head banged hard against the wall. No sound came from him. She closed the door behind her, careful to double bolt it. The neighborhood was dangerous, and she feared the men in the hallways. She was impressed by her son's silence and congratulated herself that no one had heard that high sound he made sometimes and had called the cops. She'd done time herself in foster care and group homes, and she knew what happened when the cops came. She'd lived with her mother until she was nine. Then, her mother's boyfriend blew her mother's brains out with a rifle. Used to be that she could still see the splatter, still smell the blood. No more.

He rose slowly. His diaper dragged low, and his skin looked raw around the edges as he pushed himself up, baby-style, with his little legs straight, his hands on the floor and his butt high in the air. He walked toward her and then veered off toward the radiator.

"Phew. You stink." She lay him down and pulled his diaper off. Steam rose from him as the ammonia from his urine-filled diaper met with the air. He lay still, legs stiff, arms stiff, eyes unmoving. "You dead, you little bastard?" she joked. She pulled a wet wipe from the dispenser and began to clean him. His chest rose and sucked in as he felt the sting of the cold, wet wipe against his raw bottom. She re-diapered him and offered him some water from a cup. He sipped greedily, and this she noticed. "Always hungry. Always thirsty. Can never get enough." He eyed her. She pulled the water to her and put the glass high out of his reach.

She handed him a box of Cheerios, clicked on the TV, and went to bed. She was so tired. She wondered if she was HIV positive, if that was why the doctors had given her a hysterectomy after he was born. They told her she had an infection so they had to take out her female parts. "Why didn't they know I had the infection before the baby was born?" She felt dry and bony inside, carved out and hollow.

I thank Cessie Alfonso, Frances Blackman, Leonard Blackman, Ellen Brickman, Mitchell Dinnerstein, Michael Dowd, Roberta Faulk, Michelle Fine, Susan Jacobs, Daniel Hill, Jeanne Kwartler, Pamela Reid, Barbara Reisman, Mun Wong, and Joan Zorza for reading and commenting on earlier versions of this chapter and/or for participating in a meeting I called to discuss issues contained in this chapter. I thank Holly Maguigan and Elizabeth Schneider for guiding me through the feminist legal literature and thank Holly for making the resources of the New York University Law School Library available to me. I thank Janet Gochman and Lauren Shedletsky for their research assistance. I thank Gary VandenBos and four anonymous reviewers for their suggestions about this material at the lecture stage. I thank Barbara Hammonds for her guidance throughout the process of preparing this master lecture. I thank Peggy Schlegel, development editor at the American Psychological Association, and Bruce Sales and Gary VandenBos, editors of this book, for their help in transforming the lecture into a chapter.

He ate the Cheerios, pushing his arm deep into the box and pulling up the Cheerios one by one. They were round and dry and reminded him of nothing besides themselves. He was hungry and he ate and ate.

She woke up later. He was sleeping on the floor next to her bed. She left. Today was the day she picked up her check. She was gone when he woke up. There was a burning feeling in him that was stronger than usual. He made his way to the door and nosed himself into the wood again. The sound came from him louder than usual, longer than usual. He wanted her.

This time her luck had run out. A neighbor heard the child and called the cops. The cops came to the apartment. The child was alone, dirty, filthy, starving. They could barely look at him. He never looked at them either. Nor did he approach them. He ran for the radiator the moment they broke down the door and burst into the room.

When she came in it was late, dark. The door swung open, unlocked, nearly unhinged. She turned the light on to search for her son. She looked everywhere that made sense and a few places that didn't. She stood completely still and listened for the sound of his breathing. Nothing. "Oh, God. My baby. My baby. I am so lonely. I need my baby. I wonder which one of my motherfucking neighbors called the cops. Nobody helps you when you need help but everybody's ready to put their nose in your business. Why did that little bastard have to cry so loud? Now what am I going to do with all these Cheerios?"

■

At the frontier are women without privilege. By *privilege*, I refer to a range of resources: the goods and services that money can buy, social support, and individual sources of privilege, such as self-esteem and good judgment.

Many, perhaps most, women without privilege are also very poor. My objective in this chapter is to illuminate the plight of these women so that we, as psychologists, can see them, get to know them, and act to help them. So far, we have mostly excluded them or have made them tangential to our scholarship, our teaching, and our treatment strategies (Fine, 1985; Fine & Gordon, 1989; Yoder & Kahn, 1993).

To understand the exclusion of these women and ultimately to facilitate their inclusion, it is vital first to understand the influence of values both in the science of psychology and in the law that affects them. In this chapter, I explore the ways in which values function like lenses, which, although they can clarify problems, can also blur or obscure completely the ability to see and therefore to know the problems that threaten women's well-being and survival.

I first consider the work of feminist psychologists. Their thinking has reground the lens and widened the aperture of psychology. They have changed and clarified psychology's view of women, although the problems of lower status women have been generally excluded (Fine, 1994, in press; Yoder & Kahn, 1993).

I next explore the concept of legal rights as the formalized expression of what we as a society value. I consider the great disagreement about what society values by focusing on *value tensions*. The most significant of these is the tension between a woman's individual liberty and society's interest in and duty to protect women and children from harm. In this context, I discuss reason and justice as related concepts drawn from the law and psychology, respectively.

Finally, I consider three major problem areas as they affect women without privilege: (a) women and their relationship to childbearing (specifically abortion, the implications of drug use and/or HIV positivity during pregnancy, and prenatal care); (b) women and their relationship to children (specifically mothering; abused, neglected, and murdered children; foster care; the termination of parental rights; and adoption decisions); and (c) battered women and rape victims.

Throughout this discussion, I use a metaphor about a room representing our scholarship on these issues in psychology. Too often, this room does not include women whose problems it is our responsibility to address. So far, few psychologists have written about the problems of women without privilege (exceptions include Blackman, 1990a, 1990b; Fine, 1992; Garbarino, 1976, 1977, 1981; Reid, 1992a, 1992b; Shinn & Weitzman, 1990; Zuravin, 1989). It is time for us to enter the room from which the abandoned child was taken and in which his mother was left alone.

Feminist Transformations: Values Revealed in Scientific Psychology and the Law of Reason

In the pursuit of justice in psychology and for women, feminist psychologists in the 1970s and 1980s made major contributions to both theoretical psychology and the scientific method. They did this in part by identifying the role of subjectivity in science, in general, and in psychology, in particular. This early, critical attention to bias in psychology and the cogency of the attacks against those who claimed objectivity "reground the lens" and transformed psychology. Such feminist psychologists as Carol Gilligan (1982), Mary Brown Parlee (1979), Stephanie Shields (1975), Rhoda Unger (1979), and Naomi Weisstein (1971)— to name only a few—made transformational, revolutionary contributions in the early years of feminist psychology.

These feminist psychologists addressed theory, method, and the previously unanalyzed, unacknowledged assumptions that had influenced the data-gathering work of psychologists (Crawford & Marecek,

1989; Fine, 1985, 1986; Fine & Gordon, 1989; Riger, 1992; Tavris, 1991). Spurred by such lens-altering views as Weisstein's (1971) statement that much of psychology reflected the "fantasy life of the male psychologist," feminist psychologists sought to redefine the representation of women in psychology. In essence, feminists argued that the lens of psychology illuminated too small a field of vision. The insights of feminist psychologists opened the angle of vision. The accusations that fostered this widening were fueled by attention to previously unseen distortions in psychology's self-definition. Feminists led the way to a redefining of psychology.

Feminism and Women Without Privilege

Although these inclusionary efforts are clearly relevant to the problems of women without privilege, feminist psychology has generally not yet achieved its goals for these women. Women without privilege continue to be generally excluded from psychological scholarship, even in the area of women's studies in the postfeminist era. As psychologist Fine (1985) wrote,

> The experiences of diverse groups of women ... need to gain further recognition in psychology of women. This literature currently mirrors traditional psychology with studies of white, middle-class, other professional women ... The experiences and relationships of most women, those on the bottom of the proverbial ladder of success, are overlooked. (p. 171)

Some of the solutions that feminist scholars proposed for fixing what was wrong with male-centered psychology are relevant to fixing what is wrong with a psychology that suffers from what psychologists Yoder and Kahn (1993) called "the fallacy of a normative woman." This fallacy follows from the idea that only certain women—such as White, middle-class women—provide the right standard for comparison and that all other women are "less." What are some of the problems that have contributed to the exclusion of women without privilege, and how can we begin to solve them?

First, the narrow scope of prefeminist psychology overemphasized the individual, who was separated from his or her relationships and responsibilities (Broughton, 1983; Gilligan, 1982; Hare-Mustin & Marecek, 1985; Sherif, 1982). Furthermore, laboratory research was seen as context-stripping (Crawford & Marecek, 1989; Fine, 1986), in response to which feminist psychology advocated attending to the social context within which individuals, especially women, acted. Crawford and Marecek (1989) proposed an increased reliance on nonexperimental methods to capture the real complexity of human beings in relation to others.

A second problem that has contributed to the exclusion of women without privilege is the psychology of gender and gender differences that has flourished in the past 20 years. Psychologists who were critical of this trend, from Maccoby and Jacklin (1974) to Tavris (1991), explored the learning and the limitations that followed from defining women by comparing them to men (i.e., as superior, inferior, or essentially the same). Tavris, who delivered a master lecture on this topic in 1990, advised that a study of gender differences can promote knowledge and appreciation of both diversity and commonality as long as the questions about the future unite us. That is, we should not ask what is to be done about *them*, the "other," but rather, "What shall we do about *us*, so that our relationships, our work, our children and our planet will flourish?" (Tavris, 1991, p. 128; see the reference section for a full listing of Tavris's work on the exploration of gender differences).

Yoder and Kahn's (1993) suggestions were less moderate. Whereas Tavris (1991) recommended a continued reliance on comparison followed by a dedication to solutions that would unify rather than divide us, Yoder and Kahn (1993) advised that the best way to avoid negative comparisons was to avoid comparisons altogether. They wrote that psychologists should

> value descriptive studies of social groupings independent of how they compare with other social categories of people. In comparative studies, care must be taken in the interpretation of comparisons so that no group is held up as the baseline from which other groups deviate.... Researchers must avoid the tendency to describe "women in general" with tangential asides about how Latinas, working-class women, and other subgroups of women differ on certain points. (p. 848)

A third problem is that, since the awakening began by feminist psychologists, many in the scientific community have seen the extraordinary but unacknowledged power that resides in the experimenter who not only frames the questions but then records only certain answers as relevant. To help resolve this problem, collaborative research models have been proposed wherein the experimenter and the participant are seen as equal partners in the pursuit of knowledge. At least at the time of data collection, the experimenters cede much of their expertise to the participants, who are considered experts at presenting and interpreting their own life experiences (Fine, 1992, in press; Riger, 1992).

Each of these suggestions—(a) attention to context in both theory and methodology, (b) avoidance of comparison as a way to refine knowledge, and (c) advocacy for experimenter–participant collaboration in the selection of research questions and answers—represents action implications that will enable us to see and to know women without privilege.

Science and Values

When theory, method, and data are seen as influenced by the research-ers' status, history, and attendant assumptions, then the nature of sci-ence as the way to know truth is challenged. The problems and potential solutions I have discussed reflect real limitations in the capacity of scientists to know truth. Ruth Bleier (1984), a physician and professor of neurophysiology, and Anne Fausto-Sterling (1985), a professor of med-ical sciences, noted that science must reflect not only the values of the scientists but also the values of the culture in which they work. Philos-opher Zillah Eisenstein (1988) in *The Female Body and the Law* extended the influence of values beyond scientific theory to the realm of seemingly hard facts or what is real. She wrote, "All facts involve theory, all theories involve values and all values reflect a history" (p. 25). Thus, even facts are the products of interpretation. They do not exist meaningfully apart from their context.

Psychology can be said to be a science that can not be separated from values. Therefore, even science-driven knowledge can not be neu-tral. Because science is valued as good, it can serve ideological ends and justify power (Eisenstein, 1988; Foucault, 1980). Science and the values that infiltrate it can be applied in ways that change people's lives.

Sometimes, the courts turn to psychologists for our science on women's issues and, thus, for our values. Before considering what hap-pens in this interaction of psychology and the law, I want to discuss the law as an entity unto itself.

Legal Rights and Values

The law, in theory, consists of rules intended to regulate human behavior without sacrificing individual rights. The work of judges and legislatures in making law transforms values into rights. Rights, like our most fun-damental rights to life, liberty, and the pursuit of happiness, are legalized values. Thus, ideally, as the law preserves our rights, it should also promote human welfare (Melton, 1992a).

However, just as the word *science* can obscure the real role of values and bias in the pursuit of truth, the word *rights* can obscure the role of the value conflicts that gave rise to them. For example, any discourse on responsibility, the natural partner to rights, is lost when there is an emphasis on rights alone. It is easier to guarantee abstract rights than to provide the real, concrete resources that are required to fulfill responsibilities There is, of course, no governmental agency charged with the responsibility for ensuring that supposed rights are real. Individuals must first find the wherewithal to tell of their own deprivation. Unfortunately, for those who have never experienced their entitlement, it may be hard to know just what is missing or how much of it is gone.

Those without the resources to ensure that their rights are protected are the most likely to be held individually responsible when they act in anger—destructively or self-destructively. The fact that society promised them goods, taught them in school that they had rights, but did not deliver real opportunities does not matter when that individual with no real rights and no good choices behaves irresponsibly.

Liberty and the Duty to Protect. A right—like the right to individual liberty that permits a pregnant woman to act self-destructively by not getting enough rest, by not eating a balanced diet, or even by taking drugs—is countered by society's interest in and perhaps responsibility for seeing healthy babies born (Fineman, 1991; Wilkins, 1990). However, the much-touted right to individual liberty appears to obscure the missing right to prenatal care that could promote more responsible behavior on the part of pregnant women. Thus, rights that pit a woman's individual liberty against society's duty to protect even her unborn children could be reframed at less cost to her individual liberty if women truly had the right to those services that are the real signs of society's responsibility, interest, and duty—the right to prenatal care, the right to general health care, the right to decent housing.

The tension between a woman's individual liberty and society's duty to protect the unborn is magnified further when a woman chooses not to have an abortion but does not adequately protect herself during her pregnancy. For the purposes of this chapter, *inadequate care* is defined as using drugs and not obtaining prenatal care during pregnancy. Even more difficult issues are raised by women who know themselves to be HIV positive but choose to bear children. One can question the reasonableness of those who make such choices, although I hesitate to make such a judgment knowing that this could be costly to the personal liberty of women and therefore dangerous to women without privilege. Nonetheless, it is important to strive for reason, just as it is important to strive for justice. When the medical model is applied, the striving is toward health, and drug addiction is clearly identified as a disease to be cured (Jessup, 1990). Psychological interventions, too, can fit within a nonpunitive model in which the goals reflect the pursuit of justice, attained by advancing the psychological health of individuals and by strengthening the family and the community as sources of support.

Justice and Reason. Lawyers define justice in terms of what is reasonable. For example, if it is reasonable to use violence against another person, then this is called *self-defense*, and it is legal and just to use it. Although psychologists have not explored reasonableness in this way (Crocker, 1985; Maguigan, 1991; Schneider, 1980, 1986), they have explored its analog, justice. I deal very briefly here with social psychologists' attention to justice and injustice. Kurt Lewin, a Jewish psychologist who fled Nazi Germany in the 1930s, set in motion in the United States theoretical and empirical explorations of the social conditions that promote or prevent justice. One of his students, Morton Deutsch (1973, 1974, 1985), advanced what he called a "crude law of social relations" about the way to achieve social justice. Deutsch (1973) wrote that "the characteristic processes and effects elicited by a given type of social relationship tend also to elicit that type of social relationship" (p. 365). Thus, Deutsch revealed the importance of treating those without privilege attentively and with dignity to create the consequences of justice and thereby foster its presence.

However, it is clear that the consequences and processes of just social relations are often absent, particularly when those with privilege relate to those without. Susan Opotow (1990) named the concept of *moral exclusion*, which

> occurs when individuals or groups are perceived as outside the boundary in which moral values, rules and considerations of fairness apply. Those who are morally excluded are perceived as ... undeserving. (p. 1)

They are the victims of social injustice (see also Cook, 1990; Crosby, 1982; Crosby & Lubin, 1990).

To be morally inclusive, psychologists must go to women without privilege and see them as they are, in their everyday lives (Melton, 1992a). This is an especially important next step because it is only when we take this next step that we will discover the hatred and the anger that can prevent society's victims from knowing justice. Audre Lorde (1981), a renowned Black lesbian feminist writer and poet reflected on this in an essay in *Sister Outsider*:

> We are Black women born into a society of entrenched loathing and contempt for whatever is Black and female. We are strong and enduring. We are also deeply scarred.... Racism and sexism are grown-up words. Black children in america cannot avoid these distortions in their living and, too often, do not have the words for naming them. But both are correctly perceived as hatred. (pp. 151–152)

In such a context, the capacities to know justice, to engage in fair social relations, to know reason, and to act reasonably are damaged by the presence of pain and by the absence of valued "goods." Justice is unfamiliar. One can not be expected to know justice as if such knowledge were innate and could not be scarred beyond recognition. To return to the language of the law, women raised in pain, filled with anger and hatred, can not be expected to act reasonably. Even so, the law will impose this requirement on them and will prosecute them and imprison them if they fail to meet the standard of reasonableness and break the law.

The point I am making is that it is important to unearth and examine values in psychology and in the law that affect decisions and actions and to attempt to illuminate the tensions between competing values. It is also important to attend to individuals as they are, to apply detailed, contextual, descriptive methods that are not founded in comparison. It is essential both to acknowledge the values that underlie legal decisions and to spend the time and effort needed to truly understand the lives of women without privilege. Truly, these are critical pursuits given that these values and decisions affect and control those with less power than the decisionmakers. Through the consideration of value tensions, set in the context of survival issues that affect women in relation to themselves and others, I hope to present these women clearly, as they are and as they should be represented at the intersection of psychology and the law.

The Goal: Good Lives for All of Us

Consider this passage from the work of Mari Matsuda (1990), a legal scholar:

> If our goal as scholars and ethical beings is to know as much as we can about the human condition so as to improve the prospects of good lives for all of us, our task ... is monumental and continual. Asking " *Who is not in this room and why are they not here?"* [emphasis added] whenever we gather to form theory is part of this. (pp. 1764–1765)

I apply the metaphor of the "room" to our texts—our writings about those we study and treat—and ask: Who is not represented in our scholarship, why are they not here, and how does their absence distort our vision of the landscape of problems that women face? I also discuss who is in the room, those women whose life experiences have been the subjects of psychological studies and whose voices have been heard more clearly in courtrooms throughout the country.

Who Is Not in This Room?

Women who use drugs during their pregnancies, whose babies are born drug-exposed, are not here (see Roberts, 1991, for an accounting of the legal treatise literature; see also Center for Reproductive Law and Policy, 1992). Also absent are women who do not get adequate prenatal care (Chavkin, 1990; Chavkin, Kristal, Seabron, & Guigli, 1987; Hewlett, 1991), women with HIV and AIDS (Arnold, 1992; Besharov, 1989; Chasnoff, 1989; Hunter, 1992; Hunter & Rubenstein, 1992), homeless women (DeParle, 1993; Molnar, Rath, & Klein, 1990; Oskamp, 1990; Reid, 1992a, 1992b; Shinn & Weitzman, 1990; Sonenstein & Wolf, 1991), women whose children are in foster care (Besharov, 1988; Melton, 1992b), women whose parental rights have been terminated, and women whose children are abused, neglected, or killed (Staff, 1993). Some of these women are in prison, serving sentences for what they did to themselves or for what they did or allowed to be done to their children. These women have been largely excluded from the room of our scholarship, teaching, and treatment. I want to bring them in.

For us, as psychologists, it is common knowledge that one can produce more positive and longer lasting behavioral change with reinforcement through treatment than with punishment. We need to make our voices heard on this point on behalf of those who are not here.

Why Are They Not Here?

I believe that we have averted our gaze from these women because it has been personally wrenching and politically dangerous for us to see them. Many of the women not in our room are women who have endangered not only themselves but their children as well. We have reason to worry that if we champion their causes, we will be pained as individuals and divided as a social movement. We, middle-class Whites mostly, have not simply failed to see and to know these women. We have deliberately turned away so as not to see these taboo acts that we might imagine at desperate moments but would never enact. We have kept our distance affirmatively, defensively, and perhaps even self-righteously.

What will happen if we acknowledge that women's agency—women's capacity to act affirmatively and to instigate change—can do harm? This is no linguistic transformation of "victims" into "survivors" to provide the appearance and the hope of agency (Roiphe, 1993). This is agency that hurts, even if we factor in the contributions of sexism, racism, poverty, and deprivation. And, in the ultimate value battles that comprise the pursuit of justice for all, we have to find a place to stand when victims use whatever agency they have to make more victims. At the end, when I discuss that place to stand, when you recall the room with the missing child and the desperate mother, I hope that you will not avert your psychological gaze but will as a first step commit yourself to looking, even if it hurts.

It is also important to realize that these women in unquestionable need have not come knocking on our door. Catherine MacKinnon (1987) saw the fundamental, essential dedication to staying alive that dogs poor women, keeps them from help, and functions to preserve the status quo: "One genius of the system we live under is that the strategies it requires to survive it from day to day are exactly the opposite of what is required to change it" (p. 16).

In addition, more than those of us here, these women are affected by the law. And, strangely or not, "the law offers least to those who need it most" (Rhode, 1991, p. 1734). That is, the law offers them the least by way of entitlement and protection of rights, although it maintains high expectations for them. For example, these women must not break the rules of good parenting, regardless of how limited their resources. Thus, we expect the greatest show of personal resourcefulness from those with the fewest resources. If these women do break the rules, the law has a great deal to "offer" in the form of prosecution and punishment. One of the saddest, most revealing reflections of this situation of low entitlement and high responsibility is that for some of these women, prison is the best place they have ever lived.

There are also reasons that reside in psychology, even in postfeminist psychology, that explain why they are not here. As Yoder and Kahn (1993) noted, psychologists have explored difference, a process that fosters the "normative" fallacy that middle-class White women are the standard and that all others are less.

What Difference Does Difference Make?

Attention to difference tends to make difference seem important. Thus, some who have rejected the idea that differences are inherent in individuals, or in racial or gender groups, have still retained this dedication to difference as important. The only distinction here is that the differences are seen as fluid and situational. Unfortunately, this difference is no difference for people too poor to be fluid, too deprived of options to pursue situational shifts (Deaux & Major, 1990; Thorne, 1990).

A variation of this position—that difference does not count and that, therefore, sameness should be asserted—is not the solution. It is alienating for those who are not here. There is no universal woman's voice. There is no unitary, essential, transcendent, normative woman's experience. Yet another variation on the difference theme transforms questions of difference into statements of respect for diversity. But even this offers no affirmative welcome, no real acknowledgment to those who are not here. Ironically, respect for diversity can coopt the pursuit of universal justice. Respect for cultural diversity is no comfort if everyone you know knows someone who's been shot, someone who's in prison, someone who's died young for no good reason.

Joan Williams (1991), a feminist legal theorist, echoed the advocacy put forward by such psychologists as Fine (1985, 1992) and Yoder and Kahn (1993). Williams advised that this difference/sameness/diversity debate be dissolved. She remarked that the controversies that surrounded these pursuits were diversionary and sidetracked scholars from an emphasis on discrimination. Fine (1985, 1986, in press) and Yoder and Kahn (1993) made this advocacy explicit: Let us attend to description within categories rather than comparison among categories, let us champion complexity over simplicity, and let us actively foster inclusion of historically excluded women.

At this time, women without privilege are not here. I know because, like some among you, I have gone to them. I have come to know women too poor to know home, too hurt to know family, too old when they are young to know hope, too imprisoned to know freedom or entitlement. I focus on women without privilege, not on difference, sameness, or diversity. And I consider the values that do battle when change—particularly change in women's roles—is afoot.

Who Has Come Recently to This Room?

Before I continue describing excluded women and their families, I would like to remind you that I also write of the women who are here, finally, in the room of psychology—the victims of battering (American Medical Association Council on Scientific Affairs, 1991; Browne, 1987; Gelles & Straus, 1988; Straus & Gelles, 1986; Straus, Steinmetz, & Gelles, 1980; Walker, 1979, 1984) and rape (Bart & Moran, 1993; Berger, 1977; Blackman, 1981, 1989; Brownmiller, 1975; Burgess & Holmstrom, 1974; Johnson, 1980; Russell, 1982; Scully & Marolla, 1993) and the women who fought back and killed their abusers (Blackman, 1986, 1987, 1989, 1990a; Blackman & Brickman, 1984; Bochnak, 1981; Browne, 1987; Crocker, 1985; Ewing, 1987; Gillespie, 1989; Jones, 1980; Maguigan, 1991; Schneider, 1980, 1986; Schneider & Jordan, 1978; Walker, 1990).

Women who have been harmed by patriarchy and men's bad acts are here. Women's problems as victims/survivors are far better explored in our research studies and are more affirmatively, if imperfectly, addressed under the law. We have been able to see ourselves as victims of men's violence and of patriarchy. In these areas, the connection between psychology and the law has been established. Still, there are problems in this connection, and the women in the room of our texts continue to deserve our attention (Blackman, 1990a, 1990b; Blackman & Brickman, 1984; Faigman, 1986; Schneider, 1986; Walker, 1990). I explore these problems as well.

I turn now to a psycholegal examination of the major problems that threaten women who lack privilege and who come to the attention of the courts. My overriding goal remains to illuminate the lives of women without privilege and to suggest insights and actions that will facilitate their inclusion by scientists and psychologists.

Three Problem Areas: Childbearing, Child Rearing, and Violence Against Women

I have divided the remaining discussion of the legal issues affecting women into three areas: (a) women and their relationship to child-bearing, (b) women and their relationship to children, and (c) women who have been battered or raped, with an emphasis on battered women who have fought back and gone to trial.

Beyond educating us about the relation between psychology and the law with respect to these women's issues, attention to these issues provides two additional opportunities. First, this attention enables a shift in emphasis from the difference/sameness/diversity triumvirate to a de-tailed focus on the problems of women without privilege. Second, within these issues, the "good fights" are fought—the fights that are value laden, that would unearth what justice requires and what protections the law will afford. Thus, value tensions are explored as they shape the work of psychologists and lawmakers.

Imagine an old, threadbare tapestry spread before us: The images are women, the warp is psychology, and the weft is the law. I hope to show to you not only what women have experienced and how the legal system has responded but also how you might apply your time and your training in psychology to the reparative art of reweaving our social fabric.

Women and Their Relationship to Childbearing

The value tensions that attend childbearing are the argumentative mid-wives of the competing values of individual liberty and society's duty to protect its citizens. The right to abortion—available in the United States since 1973, although with restrictive conditions in many states— frees women to choose not to bear children for whom they feel they can not adequately care (Petchesky, 1980, 1984). And, in the context of abortion decisions, the unborn are not entitled to right-to-life protec-tions before viability. *Burns, Commissioner, Department of Social Ser-vices of Iowa, et al. v. Alcala et al.* (1975) held that the term *dependent child* does not include unborn children. Aid to Families With Dependent Children, therefore, need not offer welfare benefits to pregnant women for their unborn children (see also *Planned Parenthood of Southeastern Pennsylvania et al. v. Robert P. Casey et al.*, 1992).

Justice O'Connor described this tension in her opinion in *Planned Parenthood v. Casey* (1992), the most recent case at the time of this writing to keep abortion legal:

> With abortion, reasonable people will have differences of opinion about these matters. One view is based on such reverence for the wonder of creation that any pregnancy ought to be welcomed and carried to full term no matter how difficult it will be to provide for the child and ensure its well-being. Another is that the inability to provide for the nurture and care of the infant is a cruelty to the child and an anguish to the parent. (pp. 2807–2808)

It is important to note that even in this value tension, certain presumptions unite the values. First, reasonable people can have reasonable differences of opinion. Second, both sides value the importance of protecting and caring for children's lives. One side would protect these lives without exception; the other would protect them by ensuring that those children who can not be truly and adequately protected are not born. (For a review of psychological research on abortion, see Adler et al., 1992; see also Wilmoth, 1992.)

However, reality is not so reasonable. Although perhaps unreasonable, poor women are correct to expect nothing. There is no legal right to prenatal care, and poor women are the least likely to receive adequate prenatal care (Pinnock, 1993; Roberts, 1991). Women who deliver drug-exposed babies are being prosecuted: By mid-1992, 160 women in 24 states had been prosecuted for the delivery of drugs to minors via the umbilical cord (Center for Reproductive Law and Policy, 1992). Although convictions in such cases have, in general, been reversed (*Overview of Opinions and Orders in Criminal Cases Based on Prenatal Conduct and Sentencing Based on Pregnancy Status*, 1993), they nonetheless reveal a societal vigor and willingness to dedicate public resources to the punishment of these women to whom we offer precious little help (Feinman, 1992).

Certainly, drug-addicted women who are virtually prevented from receiving prenatal care have reason to question the motivation behind these prosecutions. A study in New York showed that of all drug-treatment programs offered, 54% denied treatment to pregnant women and 67% denied treatment to pregnant addicts on Medicaid. If the drug involved was crack, and the woman was on Medicaid, then 87% were denied treatment (Chavkin et al., 1987). Thus, the ostensibly reasonable among us help least those who need help most.

Dorothy Roberts (1991) noted that the vast majority of women prosecuted in such cases are African Americans: "The government has chosen to punish poor Black women rather than provide the means for them to have healthy children" (p. 1447). Thus, the message is mixed.

The Supreme Court allows women their bodily integrity, including the right to choose whether to bear children, but with conditions. Women who choose to have children and then act without regard for the unborn child's developmental needs (i.e., act unreasonably) are subject to penalties. The law requires these women not to mistreat themselves while pregnant and to provide for the children growing inside them, in spite of the absence of the right to prenatal care, the right to drug treatment, or the right to general health care. The less privilege a woman has, the less access to justice and entitlement she has, the more unreasonably demanding are the conditions, especially given her likely inability to understand the requirements of this sort of reason.

Opportunities for intervention are ripe during pregnancy. Currently, standard practice avoids—and at some treatment facilities, explicitly forbids—the provision of care to pregnant, troubled women. Even women without privilege may see pregnancy as a transition time. Treatment models that emphasize and build from the opportunities for change created by pregnancy should be developed.

Women and Child Rearing

There is a three-way value tension that exists in the relationship between women and their children: (a) the woman's needs as an individual that persist, and probably even increase, after she becomes a mother; (b) the child's needs; and (c) society's role in helping to meet these needs. A corollary of this three-way tension is that the child's entitlement to getting his or her needs met is a subset of the mother's resources. Only if the child's virtual survival is endangered will society act to provide the child with more than the mother herself and her family can provide.

When one surveys the psychological literature on the concerns of women and men and child rearing, books like John Bowlby's (1969) *Attachment and Loss*, Nancy Chodorow's (1978) *The Reproduction of Mothering*, Mary Ainsworth and her colleagues' (Ainsworth, Blehar, Waters, & Wall, 1978) *Patterns of Attachment*, and Daniel Stern's (1985) *The Interpersonal World of the Infant* stand out as stellar examples of research in psychology that are oriented toward the care of children, especially infants.

In these books, mothers are presumed to be financially secure, personally fulfilled, and thus able to devote their primary attention to their children's emotional needs. Survival issues are absent from these considerations, and the issues of societal support for nurturant parent–child interactions are largely unaddressed. Maxine Baca Zinn (1989, 1990), on the other hand, has written about the real, negative effects of social structure and societal responsibility on child rearing and the extent to which the lack of societal support for impoverished families (especially those of color) has fostered the dissolution of traditional family structures, leaving no wholly effective substitute available to promote the sustenance of children.

Even those in psychology who have turned their attention to the role of society in sustaining families have tended to focus on middle-class families. Sandra Scarr (1985) in her *Mother Care/Other Care* dealt primarily with the complexity of the choices that caring, working parents must face. Edward Zigler and Meryl Frank's (1988) *The Parental Leave Crisis* and Sandra Hofferth and Deborah Phillips's (1991) issue of the *Journal of Social Issues* on "Child Care Policy Research" are both compendia of articles underscoring society's neglect of the needs of working parents in their pursuit of good and financially secure lives for themselves and their children. Although these works are commendable for their focus on women, children, and societal policy, they are largely exclusionary. Women without privilege are given less attention than they deserve.

The research addressing the issues faced by essentially reasonable, middle-class parents trying to bond with their infants and optimize their infants' current and future prospects is far afield from the realities of the lives of the women I see: single mothers, teenage mothers, women with four children under the age of 5, victims of abuse, women raising their children with no place to live.

When Developmental Psychology Becomes Science Fiction. As things stand now, when one brings to mind the kind of lives that poor, HIV-positive, drug-addicted women live and the sorts of environments into which their children are born and raised, the science of developmental psychology with its truths about how to nurture children seems like science fiction. Brazelton (1988) wrote,

> The powerful ambivalence of pregnancy forces parents to reshape their lives and even their adjustment to each other. The self-questioning that leads to worry about having an impaired baby is common to women during this time and represents the depth of their anxious ambivalence as they attempt to "make it" to the new level of nurturing and caring for the coming baby. Yet these forces can also serve to strengthen relations with other members of the family. But this can not be left to chance: supportive, sensitive interventions during pregnancy must be offered to stressed parents. (p. 37)

What world does Brazelton live in? He lives in the world of our room, of our scholarship, where the necessary personal and financial resources, although diminished and taxed by the birth of a baby, are essentially intact and available. Children in this world are tended to and nurtured with the sort of responsive give and take that enables people to develop empathy, the necessary precursor to insight into others and to the capacity to engage in the sort of reciprocal, egalitarian exchanges that promote justice and caring (Deutsch, 1973, 1974, 1985).

Help With Child Rearing: The Family and Medical Leave Act. Clearly, mothers could use help. President Clinton campaigned on his support of the Family and Medical Leave Act, which had been passed by both houses of Congress during Bush's presidency but had been vetoed twice by Bush. Clinton has already signed into law a Family and Medical Leave Act, which for the first time in the history of the United States protects the right to reemployment following a work lapse caused by the birth of a child. Even so, this is protection without pay and is available only for a period of 12 weeks. This act applies to all governmental employees but only to those private-sector employers who employ more than 50 people, a provision that exempts 95% of employers and 40% of all employees (J. Bills, personal communication, June 24, 1993; B. Reisman, personal communication, June 24, 1993).

The obviously limited quality of this protection lags far behind what citizens in other countries have come to expect as their just entitlement (Zigler, Frank, & Emmel, 1988). For example, in Sweden either parent may take a 9-month leave at 90% salary reimbursement plus $150 per month for the next 3 months. In France, paid leave is available only to women, but they receive 90% salary reimbursement for the first 4 months (Allen, 1988). In the United States, we have just begun to act at the federal level on issues of child care (Hofferth & Phillips, 1991), and one cannot help but hear the note of equivocation in our voice.

Thus, we find ourselves in a situation in which there has been and is little support beyond the individual woman and her own resources for raising and nurturing children. This situation exists in spite of the facts that raising children is very hard work and that children are of value not only in and of themselves but also because they are our hope for the future. If we raise children with a disregard for other people by failing to safeguard their own development, then we fuel the alternative: dangerous people who will risk our future as well as their own.

As Zinn (1989) suggested in her work on family, race, and poverty, the implications for action in this area reside with the sustaining of effective alternatives to traditional family structures. The increasing isolation of women without privilege from the middle class not only drains economic opportunities from inner-city neighborhoods but also reduces chances for supportive networking that could ease the burdens of child rearing and reduce the dangers posed to children raised by isolated, stressed parents. Societal responsibilities must also be more thoroughly and thoughtfully addressed. Educational and job-training programs must include child-care components. Child care, itself, is entitled to a heightened status with attendant increase in income for caregivers.

Foster Care and the Termination of Parental Rights. When mothers fail to do what mothers are supposed to do and their children suffer, the state becomes involved. There is, however, no responsive, reciprocal model of treatment for mothers whose children suffer at their hands or as a result of their inaction when action was needed. The foster-care system and decisions that lead to the termination of parental rights are responses not of constructive engagement but of disengagement and punishment of the parents. The hope that the damage done from tearing families apart will be less than and will remediate the damage done while they were together is not supported by research. Yet, these decisions proceed, with a sense of urgency, on a hope and a prayer. The legal standard is one of "reasonable effort," which means that, under federal law, state child-welfare agencies must make "reasonable efforts" to prevent a child's placement in foster care as well as to reunite the family if the child is removed (Grimm, 1990). But, how does one recognize reason, the right course, in the midst of the turmoil of these tragic, torturous families?

There is a need for research on these issues, especially longitudinal research detailing the experiences of children removed from and returned to biological parents versus the experiences of those children who are not removed or who are not returned. And, we need research on what happens to mothers who do and do not lose their parental rights. Such research will help us to address the very hard questions about the best interests of the worst families.

Adoption and Racial Matching. Other conditions beyond "reasonable effort" apply to decisions about children's placement, especially if children are to be made adoptable, particularly with regard to issues of racial matching. The adoption of African-American children has been besieged by the dilemmas created by the willingness of White families to adopt African-American children, the shortage of African-American families willing to adopt, and the opposition to transracial adoption by the National Association of Black Social Workers. This association has taken the position that "the placement of black children in white homes is a hostile act against our community" and a "blatant form of racial and cultural genocide" (in Simon, 1993, p. 95).

Simon (1987, 1993), who conducted longitudinal research on the effects of transracial adoption, documented few detrimental effects of transracial adoption. Even so, she credited the position taken by the National Association of Black Social Workers by advocating the view that "the best interests of the child" dictated that "transracial adoptions should be pursued when no appropriate permanent same race placements are available" (Simon, 1993, p. 95). Simon (1993) wrote that when no same race placements can be found, African-American children should be adoptable by White families because families can and do transcend racial barriers (see also Bartholet, 1993; Doe, 1993; Minow, 1993).

The Impact of AIDS on Child Rearing. Susan Jacobs, an attorney at the Legal Action Center in New York City, spoke with me about her experiences representing HIV-positive parents involved in custody proceedings (personal communication, June 16, 1993). Her descriptions of her cases were the unbearably tragic descriptions of physically ill, drug-dependent people simultaneously hoping for and undermining their entitlement to their own children. As court dates approached, drug users relapsed, and lied about their drug use, making their positions impossible to represent. Jacobs said, "The enormity of the evisceration of already decimated families is paralyzing." She went on to observe that HIV, associated with certain groups like gay men and drug users, has lulled people into a false complacency. She reflected on the fact that risks follow not from group membership but from behavior. It is essential to our collective future that we shake the paralysis that has inhibited attention to the problems associated with HIV, drug abuse, and pregnancy and make these issues priorities for research and treatment.

The Federal Context: The Case of Joshua DeShaney. Most of the actions that legally separate women from their children, either temporarily or permanently, happen in local contexts with states and cities exercising their authority within the home. However, when the issues are legal, the ultimate context is federal, and it is important to know that the Supreme Court has ruled on the relation between families and the state in a case in which a child was known to be at risk by the Department of Social Services and was then severely and permanently injured by his father. Here, the three-way tension between parent, child, and the state was stretched nearly to the breaking point, but the reality that children's entitlements are limited to what their parents can provide held firm.

In 1989, the Supreme Court decided the case of *DeShaney v. Winnebago County Department of Social Services.* Joshua DeShaney was a child who had been

> subjected to a series of beatings by his father, with whom he lived. Respondents, a county department of social services and several of its social workers, received complaints that petitioner was being abused by his father and took various steps to protect him; they did not, however, act to remove petitioner from his father's custody. [Joshua's] father finally beat him so severely that he suffered permanent brain damage and was rendered profoundly retarded. (109 *Supreme Court Reporter*, pp. 999–1000)

In the wake of his devastating injuries, Joshua and his mother brought action against the Department of Social Services, contending that Joshua's rights to due process under the 14th Amendment had been violated. That is, they argued that Joshua had been deprived of his right to life, liberty, or property without due process of law because the state failed to provide him with adequate protection against his father's violence.

The Supreme Court, in a 6-to-3 decision, ruled against Joshua and his mother. The majority opinion, written by Chief Justice Rehnquist, held that there is nothing in the language of the due process clause that requires the state to protect the life, liberty, and property of its citizens against invasion by private actors—such as Joshua's father. The court continued in its opinion to note that had Joshua been taken from his home, placed in foster care, and then grievously injured, then perhaps, the state would have had a duty to protect him as it must protect others over whom it exercises control (e.g., prisoners). However, because the state failed to act more affirmatively on its knowledge that Joshua was being abused, it incurred no special liability or duty to protect him. And, as the court noted, no one suggested that Joshua was injured by the state. He was injured by his father. Thus, Justice Rehnquist wrote, "While the State may have been aware of the dangers that Joshua faced in the free world, it played no part in their creation, nor did it do anything to render him any more vulnerable to them" (*DeShaney v. Winnebago County*, 109 S.Ct. 998, 1989, p. 1006).

The value tension that underlies this decision and the Supreme Court verdict reflects the extent of societal dedication to the idea that children belong to their parents, almost no matter what. The alternative view, that children—especially children known to be at risk—should be protected by the state is one that we come to with great trepidation and angst.

The *DeShaney* (1989) case notwithstanding, children are moved— if ambivalently, inconsistently, and inadequately—in and out of foster care placements, group homes, and larger institutional settings. The mothers of these children react in various ways. Some fight with great ardor to be reunited with their children; others disappear. Children whose mothers do not appear for appointments in court to discuss the placement of their children may find their parental rights terminated as a result (Tamilia, 1992).

In any case, the problems do not end with placement. Women and their families who make themselves available as foster-care providers may be turning to these children as sources of income in forbidding economic times. The responsibility of caring for foster children has been assumed, for the most part, not by middle-class families but by families that resemble quite closely, in terms of social status, the biological families of foster children.

Perhaps for those who imagine they would bond with these children, the thought of their relationships being ended by a court's decision to return children to their biological parent or to move them to another foster family is simply too painful (Doe, 1993). To save ourselves and our children the pain of connecting to and disconnecting from foster children, we turn away. We do not bring these problems home. There is no comfort in this reality, any more than one can derive comfort from the Supreme Court's legalistic denial of responsibility for the harm done to Joshua DeShaney. When one examines the role of reason and the place of justice in relation to the problems of women and child rearing—

especially child rearing that goes on under the worst of circumstances—it is not only the abusive parents who leave us confused and angry.

Affirmative outreach, treatment, follow-up, and a commitment to long-term, consistent intervention must become the hallmarks of our dedication to enhancing opportunities for women without privilege to raise their children in families and with care (Bronfenbrenner, 1988; Bronfenbrenner, Moen, & Garbarino, 1984).

Battered Women and Rape Victims

Now, I turn to a consideration of battered women and rape victims. The early research on battered women (Dobash & Dobash, 1980; Pagelow, 1981; Walker, 1979) and the early research on rape victims (Burgess & Holmstrom, 1974; Kilpatrick, Veronen, & Resick, 1979) accomplished for these women what remains to be accomplished for women without privilege. Lenore Walker (1979), Irene Frieze (1979), Mildred Daly Pagelow (1981), Rebecca and Russell Dobash (1980), and Susan Schechter (1983) ushered battered women into the room of our scholarship in the late 1970s and early 1980s. The values that were represented in their scholarship advocated for women's entitlement to safety at home and on the streets. The alternative, an historically high level of acceptance of violence against women, was effectively countered by this new scholarship.

It was as if the criminal justice system were waiting for us. The first use of expert testimony in a case of a battered woman who had killed her husband came in 1979. More than 200 battered women have been tried in the United States by juries or judges who have heard expert testimony on the psychology of battered women, most often called *battered woman syndrome testimony*.

I have testified as an expert on rape-trauma syndrome, a description of rape victims first proposed by Burgess and Holmstrom (1974). These researchers described a two-stage model of recovery from rape—an early acute stage that was hypothesized to endure for only a few days and a longer, reorganization–recovery phase that could last for years. Experts on rape-trauma syndrome were quickly employed by prosecutors to educate jurors about the behaviors that were characteristic of rape victims at these two stages. Thus, a woman's apparent calm on the first day after a rape would not be misinterpreted as a sign of her consent but would be correctly seen as a kind of traumatic shock response. Unfortunately, rape trauma-syndrome has struggled to maintain its initial image against the pressure brought by the wide range of behaviors that may be produced by trauma and the extent to which individual victims experience reactions shaped by the particular circumstances of their rape (Frazier & Borgida, 1992).

Battered-woman syndrome, with its emphasis on the "cycle" theory of violence—during which tension builds, explodes, and dissipates—and on learned helplessness—defined as a battered woman's belief that she could not make the violence stop—has also received only limited support from subsequent research (Rosewater, 1987, 1988; Schuller & Vidmar, 1992; Walker, 1984; Yllo, 1988; Yllo & Bograd, 1988).

In my opinion, the single greatest reason for the limited support of this model is that it was developed based on the experiences of middle-class women for whom the battering was a singular problem in otherwise better lives. For very poor women, whose lives are plagued by problems, their psychological responses to battering are different (Blackman, 1990a, 1990b). It is truly harder to make direct links among their fear, their depression, their valiance, their desperation, and the battering. They deserve a model of their own, one drawn from their life experiences.

Science Misperceived. The court's eagerness for us, for psychology, led judges and attorneys to treat the early publications like Lenore Walker's (1979) *The Battered Woman* and Anne Burgess and Lynda Holmstrom's (1974) *Rape: Victims of Crisis* as not only the first word but the last word, thereby fostering a disturbing reluctance to rely on subsequent work on these issues. The work that has naturally followed and that has conclusively demonstrated the heuristic value of the early formulations and the evolution of science-based ideas has been misperceived and construed as heresy. As a result, the courts fear that justice will be subverted. In this vision, juries and judges will become the victims of psychologists' willingness to say anything to further their value-based positions. Particularly when the individuals involved are victims of battering and rape and when the scientists are feminists, these concerns can function to undermine the likelihood that expert testimony will be permitted or, if it is permitted, that it will carry much weight (Frazier & Borgida, 1992).

In courtrooms, during cross-examination by ardent prosecutors, I have been accused of tailoring my testimony to fit the case. I no longer talk about "battered-woman syndrome" but about the "psychology of battered women" because I am aware of the limitations of the term *battered-woman syndrome*. I know that it can function prescriptively and restrictively for battered women who kill their abusers. I have learned that very poor women, who are trying very hard to survive, who live through endless episodes of violence with no discernible cyclicity, who do not present the signs of learned helplessness must be included in our work and in our models. If we can not extend our theories to encompass homeless, drug-addicted battered women and rape victims, then our involvement in the criminal justice system will help only the privileged and will deny equal, attentive treatment to those who need it most.

Specifically, for both battered-woman syndrome and rape-trauma syndrome, the concerns about change from original work by Walker

(1979) and Burgess and Holmstrom (1974) have challenged their reliability and validity in two ways: (a) There is nothing unique enough about these syndromes to separate them from reactions to other troubling events, so there is no basis for asserting that the syndromes exist, and (b) there are so many individual-difference variables to account for that the syndromes have no true coherence. The syndromes or the theories must constantly be modified and qualified to explain the behavior of particular individuals. If one does enough of that, it may appear as if the theory is being fit to the data, instead of the data fitting the theory.

However, it is in the nature of good science for evolution and increasing precision to occur in the description of any phenomenon. Thus, descriptions of the characteristics of reactions to battering and rape should progress to include specifying the influence of social class, for example, or of multiple experiences of victimization. Early models did not adequately account for dire poverty or for the likely multiplicity of problems in women's lives. Documenting real change is our strength and should not be misconstrued as our weakness.

The Court's Imposition of Stare Decisis *on Psychology*. Without question, the benefits that have resulted from heightened societal awareness of these problems far outweigh the price that is being paid now for the court's imposition of the principle of *stare decisis* on psychological research. This Latin phrase names the court's dedication to precedent and connotes a strong reluctance to allow change from a model that has worked—even if it now works only some of the time and could be made to work more of the time. The courts are loathe to change even as our theories legitimately do. Nor are they necessarily skilled at interpreting the results of our work. For example, at the time of this writing, the most recent court decision on the reliability of rape-trauma syndrome testimony was *State v. Black* (1987). According to Frazier and Borgida (1992), the court's review of the recent research on rape was quite thorough. Nonetheless, the court concluded that rape-trauma syndrome was not reliable. Their decision rested on a 1979 article by psychologists who claimed that the studies they surveyed "provide[d] little, if any, scientifically valid data regarding the effect of a rape experience" (Kilpatrick et al., 1979, pp. 658–659), thus discounting any advances made in the research concerning rape-trauma syndrome. For our future work to be meaningful, we must educate the courts about the nature of our work and the significance of legitimate theoretical revisions.

Cinderella: A Judicial Fantasy. In the courtroom of judicial fantasy, our data should be Cinderella's foot to the glass slipper of theory. If we appear to be slicing heel and toes away to get Cinderella's foot into the glass slipper, then the whole story changes. It looks as if Cinderella is not really cinderella at all, as if she is trying to trick the prince to get the good life to which she is not really entitled, because her foot is the wrong size. However, individual experiences are real, not fantasy, and one should not expect Cinderella to have the right size foot. It is more important for us to know how she felt while she danced with the prince, if she fully understood the implications of not leaving by midnight, and how she really felt about her fairy godmother—that is, how she thought and felt about her life. It is here where variation must exist within some knowable range. We may ultimately learn that all battered women do wear glass slippers but of different sizes and kinds of glass.

Unfortunately and impossibly, the courts want to know what size shoe battered women or rape victims wear. They ask for more simplicity than we can or should deliver. Perhaps, like Cinderella, we were seduced by the prince, by our chance to charm and to influence the court. And sometimes we have allowed ourselves to become the scientists of shoes of only one size. We can not be this precise or this simple, and such efforts are destined to fail. We must resist the lure of simplicity for the accuracy of complexity. We must educate the justice system to know that complexity, not simplicity, is our business. We must advocate for a psychological mindedness that will provide the right context for listening to the individual where she is and for granting her the dignity that all individuals deserve when they appear before the court (Melton, 1992b).

Conclusion

The survival problems that confront women without privilege are enormous. I urge you not to be paralyzed by this. Sensitive, nurturing attention to women in need can make a positive difference in their lives. The courts are designed to resolve disputes. As psychologists, we can aid in the process of dispute resolution. We can provide information, insight, and a discipline-informed advocacy for the usefulness of treatment and the futility of punishment in solving the problems of seriously deprived women and their children. We can educate the courts about the nature of science and its capacity to shed increasing circles of light in the darkness (Monahan & Walker, 1991).

As psychologists, we should seek opportunities to meet with lawyers and judges outside the courtroom to educate them in a less constraining forum about the nature of psychology. If you go to court to testify about the problems that beset women without privilege, testify about the real complexity of their lives, even if the shoe is not a perfect fit.

Know that the courts will need to be educated about the value of a descriptive, non-comparison-based approach. This will be especially important when these women are accused of crimes, given that they will be held accountable for the standards of behavior that are prescribed by law, regardless of their personal histories or their social category. If their behavior is sufficiently unacceptable as to receive legal attention, the value of Yoder and Kahn's (1993) advocacy for "separate and not tangential" may fade. Women without privilege who commit crimes may not be permitted to answer to a different God. Therefore, in courtrooms, before judges and juries, the importance of context as an influence on behavior will be put to the test of legal reasonableness. Only when context creates a *reasonable* change in a person's sense of what is reasonable can there be any shift in standards of justice—a shift that mirrors the legally acknowledged and important role of subjectivity in reasonableness.

Let us extend our moral community beyond its usual boundaries and bring the problems that attend childbearing and child rearing for women without privilege into the room of our scholarship. Let us work for inclusion and use research strategies that emphasize description, context, and the knowledge of the participants. Let us be sensitive to the bias inherent in psychology, in the law, and in ourselves.

We must acknowledge the kind of self-destructive agency that flows from life at the frontier and work to bring meaningful resources there by teaching, treating, and studying these problems. Let us offer ourselves as professionals and as people to those in dire need of social support and human attention. In these ways, we can work to enhance the psychological health of women without privilege, to strengthen families—however they are constituted—and to keep impoverished communities from becoming isolated ghettos. See that without real help, without a genuine entitlement to the rights we purport to value, the devastation in women's lives brought about by the dissolution of families, violence, drug use, and AIDS will continue.

In the United States, 30,000–50,000 babies are born drug-exposed each year (Besharov, 1989; Chasnoff, 1989). The Center for Disease Control reported 180,000 people over the age of 13 with HIV or AIDS (Arnold, 1992). HIV is spreading at a faster rate in women than in men, so that by the year 2000 more women than men will be affected worldwide (Hunter, 1992).

Seven million people in our country are "precariously housed," a category that includes the homeless as well as those who live in condemned buildings, cars, or airports (Oskamp, 1990). Eleven percent of children in the United States have mothers living on the income from Aid to Families With Dependent Children (Sonenstein & Wolf, 1991). Half a million children are living in the foster-care system (Melton, 1992b).

Reported cases of child abuse and neglect reached 2.69 million in 1991 (Staff, 1993). That year, 1,400 children died as a result of abuse or neglect (Staff, 1993). Family-violence researchers have estimated that approximately two million women are battered by their husbands or partners each year (Straus & Gelles, 1986; Straus et al., 1980). Two thousand interspousal homicides occur each year, approximately two thirds of which result in the deaths of women (Browne, 1987). In 1990, the number of reported rapes in the United States exceeded 100,000 for the first time (Judiciary Committee Majority Staff Report, 1990).

Far too many women without privilege and their children are already sick and dying. They will die. But, first, they may kill. And, knowing as we do, what their lives have been like, who can be surprised?

Let us see these women without privilege, get to know them, and share with them the benefits of privilege. As psychologists, we are uniquely positioned to help. Let us travel to the frontier. Although there are dangers there, the moral and practical dangers of not going are far greater. As we strive to be inclusive in the psychology of women and the law, as we open the door and bring new women into our room, we move forward in the pursuit of justice.

References

Adler, N. E., David, H. P., Major, B. N., Roth, S. H., Russo, N. F., & Wyatt, G. E. (1992). Psychological factors in abortion. *American Psychologist, 47*, 1194–1204.

Ainsworth, M., Blehar, M., Waters, E., & Wall, S. (1978). *Patterns of attachment: A psychology study of the strange situation*. Hillsdale, NJ: Erlbaum.

Allen, J. P. (1988). European infant care leaves: Foreign perspectives on the integration of work and family roles. In E. Zigler & M. Frank (Eds.), *The parental leave crisis* (pp. 245–274). New Haven, CT: Yale University Press.

American Medical Association Council on Scientific Affairs. (1991). *Violence against women* (Vol. 7). Chicago: Author.

Arnold, P. (1992). Betwixt and between: Adolescents and HIV. In N. D. Hunter & W. R. Rubenstein (Eds.), *AIDS agenda: Emerging issues in civil rights* (pp. 41–68). New York: New Press.

Bart, P. G., & Moran, E. G. (1993). *Violence against women: The bloody footprints*. Newbury Park, CA: Sage.

Bartholet, E. (1993). Where do black children belong?: The politics of race-matching in adoption. In M. Minow (Ed.), *Family matters: Readings on family lives and the law* (pp. 66–93). New York: New Press.

Berger, V. (1977). Man's trial, woman's tribulation: Rape cases in the courtroom. *Columbia Law Review, 77*, 1–103.

Besharov, D. J. (1988). *Protecting children from abuse and neglect: Policy and practice*. Springfield, IL: Charles C Thomas.

Besharov, D. J. (1989, Fall). The children of crack: Will we protect them? *Public Welfare*, pp. 7–11, 42–43.

Blackman, J. (1981, July). *Multiple victimizations: Those who suffer more than once*. Paper presented at the National Family Violence Researchers' Conference, University of New Hampshire, Durham, NH.

Blackman, J. (1986). Potential uses for expert testimony: Ideas toward the representation of battered women who kill. *Women's Rights Law Reporter, 9*, 227–238.

Blackman, J. (1987, March). *Battered women who kill and the Passover question: Why is this night different from all other nights? Or Is It?* Paper presented at the meeting of the Association for Women in Psychology, Denver, CO.

Blackman, J. (1989). *Intimate violence: A study of injustice.* New York: Columbia University Press.

Blackman, J. (1990a). Emerging images of severely battered women and the criminal justice system. *Behavioral Sciences and the Law, 9,* 121–130.

Blackman, J. (1990b, August). *Severely violent families: Values, data, activism and policy.* Paper presented at the 98th annual convention of the American Psychological Association, Boston, MA.

Blackman, J., & Brickman, E. (1984). The impact of expert testimony on trials of battered women who kill their husbands, *Behavioral Sciences and the Law, 2,* 413–422.

Bleier, R. (1984). *Science and gender: A critique of biology and its theories on women.* New York: Pergamon Press.

Bochnak, E. (Ed.). (1981). *Women's self-defense cases.* Charlottesville, VA: Michie.

Bowlby, J. (1969). *Attachment and loss.* New York: Basic Books.

Brazelton, T. B. (1988). Issues for working parents. In E. Zigler & M. Frank (Eds.), *The parental leave crisis* (pp. 36–51). New Haven, CT: Yale University Press.

Bronfenbrenner, U. (1988). Strengthening family systems. In E. Zigler & M. Frank (Eds.), *The parental leave crisis* (pp. 143–160). New Haven, CT: Yale University Press.

Bronfenbrenner, U., Moen, P., & Garbarino, J. (1984). Child, family and community. In R. Parke (Ed.), *Review of child development research* (pp. 283–328). Chicago: University of Chicago Press.

Broughton, J. (1983). Women's rationality and men's virtues: A critique of gender dualism in Gilligan's theory of moral development. *Social Research, 50,* 597–642.

Browne, A. (1987). *When battered women kill.* New York: Free Press.

Brownmiller, S. (1975). *Against our will: Men, women and rape.* New York: Simon & Schuster.

Burgess, A. W., & Holmstrom, L. L. (1974). *Rape: Victims of crisis.* Bowie, MD: Robert J. Brady.

Burns, Commissioner, Department of Social Services of Iowa, et al. v. Alcala et al., 95 S. Ct. 1180 (1975).

Center for Reproductive Law and Policy. (1992). *Newsletter.* Available from the Legal Action Center, 153 Waverly Place, New York, NY.

Chasnoff, I. (1989, June). *Advance Report of Final Natality Statistics, 1987* (Vol. 38 suppl., p. 1). Washington, DC: U.S. National Center for Health Statistics, U.S. Department of Health and Human Services.

Chavkin, W. (1990). Drug addiction and pregnancy crossroads. *American Journal of Public Health, 80,* 483–485.

Chavkin, W., Kristal, A., Seabron, C., & Guigli, P. E. (1987). The reproductive experiences of women living in hotels for the homeless in New York City. *New York State Journal of Medicine, 87,* 10–13.

Chodorow, N. (1978). *The reproduction of mothering: Psychoanalysis and the sociology of gender.* Berkeley: University of California Press.

Cook, S. W. (1990). Toward a psychology of improving justice: Research on extending the equality principle of victims of social injustice. *Journal of Social Issues, 46,* 147–162.

Crawford, M., & Marecek, J. (1989). Psychology reconstructs the female, 1968–1988. *Psychology of Women Quarterly, 13,* 147–166.

Crocker, P. (1985). The meaning of equality for battered women who kill men in self-defense. *Harvard Women's Law Journal, 8*, 121–153.

Crosby, F. (1982). *Relative deprivation and working women*. New York: Oxford University Press.

Crosby, F., & Lubin, E. P. (1990). Extending the moral community: Logical and psychological dilemmas. *Journal of Social Issues, 46*, 163–172.

Deaux, K., & Major, B. (1990). A social–psychological model of gender. In D. L. Rhode (Ed.), *Theoretical perspectives on sexual difference* (pp. 89–99). New Haven, CT: Yale University Press.

DeParle, J. (1993, June 21). Clinton aides see problem with vow to limit welfare. *New York Times*, pp. A1, A14.

DeShaney v. Winnebago County Department of Social Services, 109 S.Ct. No. 87–154, 998–1013 (1989).

Deutsch, M. (1973). *The resolution of conflict: Constructive and destructive processes*. New Haven, CT: Yale University Press.

Deutsch, M. (1974). Awakening the sense of injustice. In M. Ross & M. Lerner (Eds.), *The quest for justice* (pp. 19–42). New York: Holt, Rinehart & Winston.

Deutsch, M. (1985). *Distributive justice: A social psychological perspective*. New Haven, CT: Yale University Press.

Dobash, R. P., & Dobash, R. E. (1980). *Violence against wives*. New York: Free Press.

Doe, J. (1993). Why should I give my baby back? In M. Minow (Ed.), *Family matters: Readings on family lives and the law* (pp. 115–117). New York: New Press.

Eisenstein, Z. R. (1988). *The female body and the law*. Berkeley: University of California Press.

Ewing, C. (1987). *Battered women who kill*. Lexington, MA: D. C. Heath.

Faigman, P. C. (1986). The battered woman syndrome and self-defense: A legal and empirical dissent. *Virginia Law Review, 72*, 619–647.

Fausto-Sterling, A. (1985). *Myths of gender: Biological theories about women and men*. New York: Basic Books.

Feinman, C. (1992). *The criminalization of a woman's body*. New York: Harrington Park Press/Haworth Press.

Fine, M. (1985). Reflections on a feminist psychology of women: Paradoxes and prospects. *Psychology of Women Quarterly, 9*, 167–183.

Fine, M. (1986). Contextualizing the study of social injustice. In M. Saks & L. Saxe (Eds.), *Advances in applied social psychology* (Vol. 3, pp. 103–126). Hillsdale, NJ: Erlbaum.

Fine, M. (1992). *Disruptive voices: The transgressive possibilities of feminist research*. Ann Arbor: University of Michigan Press.

Fine, M. (1994). Working the hyphen: "Self" and "other" in qualitative research. In N. Denzin & Y. Lincoln (Eds.), *Handbook of qualitative research* (pp. 70–82). Newbury Park, CA: Sage.

Fine, M. (in press). Dis-stance and other stances for feminist researchers. In A. Gitlin (Ed.), *Power and method*. New York: Routledge.

Fine, M., & Gordon, S. M. (1989). Feminist transformations of/despite psychology. In M. Crawford & M. Gentry (Eds.), *Gender and thought: Psychological perspectives* (pp. 147–174). New York: Springer-Verlag.

Fineman, M. L. (1991). Images of mothers in poverty discourses. *Duke Law Journal, 2*, 274–297.

Foucault, M. (1980). Truth and power. In C. Gordon (Ed.), *Power/knowledge: Selected interviews and other writings, 1972–1977*. New York: Pantheon.

Frazier, P. A., & Borgida, E. (1992). Rape trauma syndrome: A review of case law and psychological research. *Law and Human Behavior, 16*, 293–312.

Frieze, I. H. (1979). Perceptions of battered wives. In I. H. Frieze, D. Bar-Tal, & J. Carroll (Eds.), *New approaches to social problems* (pp. 79–108). New York: Jossey-Bass.

Garbarino, J. (1976). A preliminary study of some ecological correlates of child abuse: The impact of socioeconomic stress on mothers. *Child Development, 47*, 178–185.

Garbarino, J. (1977). The human ecology of child maltreatment: A conceptual model for research. *Journal of Marriage and the Family, 39*, 721–735.

Garbarino, J. (1981). An ecological approach to child maltreatment. In L. Pelton (Ed.), *The social context of child abuse and neglect* (pp. 228–267). New York: Human Sciences Press.

Gelles, R. S., & Straus, M. A. (1988). *Intimate violence*. New York: Simon & Schuster.

Gillespie, C. K. (1989). *Justifiable homicide*. Columbus: Ohio State University Press.

Gilligan, C. (1982). *In a different voice*. Cambridge, MA: Harvard University Press.

Grimm, B. (1990). Drug-exposed infants pose new problems for juvenile courts. *Youth Law News, 11*(1), 9–14.

Hare-Mustin, R., & Marecek, J. (1985). Autonomy and gender: Some questions for therapists. *Psychotherapy, 23*, 205–212.

Hewlett, S. A. (1991). *When the bough breaks: The cost of neglecting our children*. New York: Basic Books.

Hofferth, S. L., & Phillips, D. A. (1991). Child care policy research [Special issue]. *Journal of Social Issues, 47*(2).

Hunter, N. D. (1992). Complications of gender: Women and HIV disease. In N. D. Hunter & W. R. Rubenstein (Eds.), *AIDS agenda: Emerging issues in civil rights* (pp. 5–40). New York: New Press.

Hunter, N. D., & Rubenstein, W. R. (1992). *AIDS agenda: Emerging issues in civil rights*. New York: New Press.

Jessup, M. (1990). The treatment of perinatal addiction: Identification, intervention and advocacy. *Addiction Medicine and the Primary Care Physician, 152*, 553–558.

Johnson, A. G. (1980). On the prevalence of rape in the United States. *Signs, 6*, 136–146.

Jones, A. (1980). *Women who kill*. New York: Holt.

Judiciary Committee Majority Staff Report. (1990). *Violence against women: The increase of rape in America: 1990*. Washington, DC: U.S. Government Printing Office.

Kilpatrick, D., Veronen, L., & Resick, P. (1979). The aftermath of rape: Recent empirical findings. *American Journal of Orthopsychiatry, 49*, 658–669.

Lorde, A. (1981). *Sister outsider*. Freedom, CA: Crossing Press.

Maccoby, E. E., & Jacklin, C. N. (1974). *The psychology of sex differences*. Stanford, CA: Stanford University Press.

MacKinnon, C. A. (1987). *Feminism unmodified: Discourses on life and law*. Cambridge, MA: Harvard University Press.

Maguigan, H. (1991). Battered women and self defense: Myths and misconceptions in current reform proposals. *University of Pennsylvania Law Review, 140*, 379–486.

Matsuda, M. J. (1990). Pragmatism modified and the false consciousness problem. *Southern California Law Review, 63*, 1763–1782.

Melton, G. B. (1992a, August). *Can caring and coercion coexist? Child protection and the law.* Paper presented at the 100th annual meeting of the American Psychological Association, Washington, DC.

Melton, G. B. (1992b). The law is a good thing (psychology is, too): Human rights in psychological jurisprudence. *Law and Human Behavior, 16*, 381–398.

Minow, M. (1993). *Family matters: Readings on family lives and the law.* New York: New Press.

Molnar, J. M., Rath, W. R., & Klein, T. P. (1990). Constantly compromised: The impact of homelessness on children. *Journal of Social Issues, 46*, 109–124.

Monahan, J., & Walker, L. (1991). Judicial use of social science research. *Law and Human Behavior, 15*, 571–584.

National Center for Youth Law. (1990). *Special issues on drug-exposed infants.* San Francisco: Youth Law News (114 Samsone Street).

Opotow, S. (1990). Moral exclusion and injustice: An introduction. *Journal of Social Issues, 46*, 1–20.

Oskamp, S. (1990). The editor's page. *Journal of Social Issues, 46* i–ii.

Overview of opinions and orders in criminal cases based on prenatal conduct and sentencing based on pregnancy status. (1993, February 2). (Available from the Legal Action Center, 153 Waverly Place, New York, NY)

Pagelow, M. D. (1981). *Woman battering: Women and their experiences.* Beverly Hills, CA: Sage.

Parlee, M. B. (1979). Psychology and women. *Signs: Journal of Women in Culture and Society, 5*, 121–133.

Petchesky, R. P. (1980). Reproductive freedom: Beyond "a woman's right to choose." *Signs: Journal of Women in Culture and Society, 5*, 661–683.

Petchesky, R. P. (1984). *Abortion and women's choice: The state, sexuality and reproductive freedom.* Boston: Northeastern University Press.

Pinnock, T. (1993). *Race and legal scholarship: The reproductive rights of black women.* Unpublished manuscript available through the New York University Law Clinic on Battered Women.

Planned Parenthood of Southeastern Pennsylvania et al. v. Robert P. Casey et al., 112 S. Ct. 2791–2885 (1992).

Reid, P. T. (1992a, December). *How do we separate and measure the contributions of culture and class?* Paper presented at National Institutes of Health Workshop on Violence Against Ethnic Women of Color: Research issues, Bethesda, MD.

Reid, P. T. (1992b, August). *Poor women in psychological research: Shut up and shut out.* Paper presented as the Presidential Address for the Division of Psychology of Women at the 100th annual meeting of the American Psychological Association, Washington, DC.

Rhode, D. L. (1991). The "no-problem" problem: Feminist challenges and cultural change. *Yale Law Journal, 100*, 1731–1793.

Riger, S. (1992). Epistemological debates, feminist voice: Science, social values, and the study of women. *American Psychologist, 47*, 730–740.

Roberts, D. (1991). Punishing drug addicts who have babies: Women of color, equality and the right of privacy. *Harvard Law Review, 104*, 1419–1482.

Roiphe, K. (1993, June 13). Rape hype betrays feminism. *New York Times Magazine*, pp. 26–30, 40, 68.

Rosewater, L. B. (1987). The clinical and courtroom application of battered women's personality assessments. In D. J. Sonkin (Ed.), *Domestic violence on trial: Psychological and legal dimensions of family violence* (pp. 86–94). New York: Springer.

Rosewater, L. B. (1988). Battered or schizophrenic? Psychological tests can't tell. In K. Yllo & M. Bograd (Eds.), *Feminist perspectives on wife abuse* (pp. 200–216). Newbury Park, CA: Sage.

Russell, D. E. H. (1982). *Rape in marriage*. New York: Macmillian.

Scarr, S. (1985). *Mother care/other care*. New York: Basic Books.

Schechter, S. (1983). *Women and male violence*. Boston, MA: South End.

Schneider, E. M. (1980). Equal rights to trial for women: Sex bias and the law of self-defense. *Harvard Civil Rights Law Review, 15*, 623–647.

Schneider, E. M. (1986). Describing and changing women's self-defense work and the problem of expert testimony on battering. *Women's Rights Law Reporter, 9*, 195–222.

Schneider, E. M., & Jordan, S. B. (1978). *Representation of women who defend themselves in response to physical and sexual assault*. New York: Center for Constitutional Rights.

Schuller, R. A., & Vidmar, N. (1992). Battered woman syndrome evidence in the courtroom: A review of the literature. *Law and Human Behavior, 16*, 273–292.

Scully, D., & Marolla, J. (1993). "Riding the bull at Gilley's": Convicted rapists describe the rewards of rape. In P. B. Bart & E. G. Moran (Eds.), *Violence against women: The bloody footprints* (pp. 26–46). Newbury Park, CA: Sage.

Sherif, C. (1982). Needed concepts in the study of gender identity. *Psychology of Women Quarterly, 6*, 375–398.

Shields, S. (1975). Functionalism, Darwinism, and the psychology of women: A study in social myth. *American Psychologist, 30*, 739–754.

Shinn, M., & Weitzman, B. C. (Eds.). (1990). Urban homelessness [Special issue]. *Journal of Social Issues, 46*(4).

Simon, R. J. (1987). *Trans-racial adoptees and their families*. New York: Praeger.

Simon, R. J. (1993). Comment on "Where do black children belong?" In M. Minow (Ed.), *Family matters: Readings on family lives and the law* (pp. 94–95). New York: New Press.

Sonenstein, F. L., & Wolf, D. A. (1991). Satisfaction with child care: Perspectives on welfare mothers. *Journal of Social Issues, 47*, 15–31.

Staff. (1993). Child abuse cases rise nationwide. *Family Violence and Sexual Assault Bulletin, 9*, 28.

State v. Black, 745 P.2d 12 (1987).

Stern, D. (1985). *The interpersonal world of the infant*. New York: Basic Books.

Straus, M. A., & Gelles, R. J. (1986). Societal change and change in family violence from 1975 to 1985. *Journal of Marriage and the Family, 48*, 465–479.

Straus, M. A., Steinmetz, S., & Gelles, R. J. (1980). *Behind closed doors: Violence in the American family*. New York: Doubleday.

Tamilia, P. R. (1992). Symposium: A response to elimination of the reasonable effort required prior to termination of parental rights status. *University of Pittsburgh Law Review, 54*, 211–227.

Tavris, C. (1991). The mismeasure of woman: Paradoxes and perspectives in the study of gender. In J. Goodchilds (Ed.), *Psychological perspectives on human diversity in America* (pp. 87–136). Washington, DC: American Psychological Association.

Thorne, B. (1990). Children and gender: Constructions of difference. In D. L. Rhode (Ed.), *Theoretical perspectives on sexual difference* (pp. 100–113). New Haven, CT: Yale University Press.

Unger, R. K. (1979). Toward a redefinition of sex and gender. *American Psychologist, 34*, 1085–1094.

Walker, L. (1979). *The battered woman*. New York: Harper & Row.

Walker, L. (1984). *The battered woman syndrome*. New York: Springer.

Walker, L. (1990). *Terrifying love: Why battered women kill and how society responds*. New York: Harper & Row.

Weisstein, N. (1971). *Psychologist constructs the female: Or, the fantasy life of the male psychologist*. Boston: New England Free Press.

Wilkins, M. D. (1990). Solving the problem of prenatal substance abuse: An analysis of punitive and rehabilitative approaches. *Emory Law Journal, 39*, 1401–1432.

Williams, J. C. (1991). Dissolving the sameness/difference debate: A post-modern path beyond essentialism in feminist and critical race theory. *Duke Law Journal, 1991*, 296–323.

Wilmoth, G. (Ed.). (1992). Psychological perspectives on abortion and it alternatives [Special issue]. *Journal of Social Issues, 48*(3).

Yllo, K. (1988). Political and methodological debates in wife abuse research. In K. Yllo & M. Bograd (Eds.), *Feminist perspectives on wife abuse* (pp. 28–50). Newbury Park, CA: Sage.

Yllo, K., & Bograd, M. (1988). *Feminist perspectives on wife abuse*. Newbury Park, CA: Sage.

Yoder, J. D., & Kahn, A. S. (1993). Working toward an inclusive psychology of women. *American Psychologist, 48*, 846–850.

Zigler, E., & Frank, M. (Eds.). (1988). *The parental leave crisis: Toward a national policy*. New Haven, CT: Yale University Press.

Zigler, E., Frank, M., & Emmel, B. (1988). Introduction. In E. Zigler & M. Frank (Eds.), *The parental leave crisis: Toward a national policy* (pp. xv–xxv). New Haven, CT: Yale University Press.

Zinn, M. B. (1989). Family, race and poverty in the eighties. *Signs: Journal of Women, Culture and Society, 11*, 856–874.

Zinn, M. B. (1990). Family, feminism and race in America. *Gender and Society, 4*, 68–82.

Zuravin, S. J. (1989). The ecology of child abuse and neglect: Review of the literature and presentation of data. *Violence and Victims, 4*, 101–120.

WAYNE F. CASCIO

THE AMERICANS WITH DISABILITIES ACT OF 1990 AND THE 1991 CIVIL RIGHTS ACT

REQUIREMENTS FOR PSYCHOLOGICAL PRACTICE IN THE WORKPLACE

W ayne F. Cascio received his PhD in industrial and organizational psychology from the University of Rochester in 1973. He is professor of management and director of international programs at the University of Colorado at Denver. He has taught at Florida International University; the University of California, Berkeley; the University of Hawaii; the University of St. Gallen, Switzerland; and the University of Geneva. During the academic year 1987–1988, he was a visiting scholar at the Wharton School of the University of Pennsylvania, and in 1988, he received the Distinguished Faculty Award from the Human Resources Division of the Academy of Management.

Cascio is a past president of both the Human Resources Division of the Academy of Management and the Society for Industrial and Organizational Psychology. He has served as a member of the American Psychological Association's (APA) Committee on Psychological Tests and Assessment, is a member of the APA Council of Representatives, and has testified on behalf of APA before Congress.

Cascio has authored six books in human resource management, including *Applied Psychology in Personnel Management* (Cascio, 1990); *Costing Human Resources: The Financial Impact of Behavior in Organizations* (Cascio, 1991); and *Managing Human Resources: Productivity, Quality of Work Life, Profits* (Cascio, 1992). He has published more than 40 journal articles and 20 book chapters.

Cascio has consulted with firms in North America, Asia, Africa, Europe, New Zealand, and Australia. His research on personnel selection, training, performance appraisal, and the economic impact of human resource management activities has appeared in a number of scholarly journals. Current and past editorial board memberships include *Journal of Applied Psychology*, *Academy of Management Review*, *Human Performance*, *Asia-Pacific HRM*, and *Organizational Dynamics*.

References

Cascio, W. F. (1990). *Applied psychology in personnel management* (4th ed.). Englewood Cliffs, NJ: Prentice Hall.

Cascio, W. F. (1991). *Costing human resources: The financial impact of behavior in organizations* (3rd ed.). Belmont, CA: Wadsworth.

Cascio, W. F. (1992). *Managing human resources: Productivity, quality of work life, profits* (3rd ed.). New York: McGraw-Hill.

WAYNE F. CASCIO

THE AMERICANS WITH DISABILITIES ACT OF 1990 AND THE 1991 CIVIL RIGHTS ACT

REQUIREMENTS FOR PSYCHOLOGICAL PRACTICE IN THE WORKPLACE

A s a society, we espouse equality of opportunity, rather than equality of outcomes. As applied to employment, the broad goal is to provide for all Americans an equal opportunity to compete for jobs for which they are qualified, regardless of race, age, gender, religion, national origin, or disability. The objective, therefore, is equal employment opportunity, not equal employment or equal numbers of employees from various subgroups.

For Americans with disabilities, the nation's goals are to assure equality of opportunity, full participation, independent living, and economic self-sufficiency. Perhaps Senator Ted Kennedy put it best when he said, "Civil rights has always been the unfinished business of America, and it will continue to be our unfinished business for many years to come" (Kennedy cited in Clymer, 1991, p. A10). But these goals are ones that have been brought closer to our grasp because of the enactment of two federal laws: the Americans With Disabilities Act of 1990 (ADA) and the 1991 Civil Rights Act (CRA).

These laws are now viewed, and will continue to be viewed, as cornerstones of civil rights legislation in the 20th century. They also directly affect employment practices. Because of their importance to society and to many practicing psychologists, this chapter considers them in some depth. I begin with a discussion of alternative forms of unfair discrimination in employment. I then examine the legal requirements of the ADA and the CRA. Following this, I consider provisions in both laws, together with the research base in psychology, that affect five areas of special relevance to psychological practice in the workplace. Finally, I examine an alternative method for achieving workforce diversity goals in light of the CRA prohibition against subgroup norming.

Unfair Discrimination: What Is It?

In the employment context, it is important to note that whenever there are more candidates than available positions, it is necessary to select some candidates in preference to others. Selection implies choice, and choice means exclusion. As long as the exclusion is based on job-related criteria (e.g., relevant training, experience, or licensure), then there is no unlawful discrimination. However, when exclusion is based on factors that are not job-related (e.g., age, race, or gender), then that constitutes unlawful and unfair discrimination.

Although no law has ever attempted to define precisely the term *discrimination*, in the employment context it can be viewed broadly as the giving of an unfair advantage (or disadvantage) to members of a particular group. The disadvantage (sometimes known as an *adverse impact*) usually results in denial or restriction of employment opportunities or in inequality in the extension of employment terms or benefits. Discrimination is a subtle and complex phenomenon that usually assumes the broad form of either unequal (disparate) treatment or adverse impact (unintentional) discrimination.

Unequal (Disparate) Treatment Discrimination

In this form of discrimination, one set of standards or procedures is used with respect to one group, and a different set of standards or procedures is used for all other groups. An example would be the use of a specific test or cutoff score for the members of a particular race, sex, or age group.

Included in this category are three approaches to proving unequal treatment. The first is direct evidence of the intention to discriminate. Such cases are proven with direct evidence of pure bias on the basis of direct and palpable hatred, stereotypes, or disrespect or of blanket exclusionary policies. An example would be the exclusion of women from jobs on the basis of reproductive hazards that affect both sexes.

The second type of proof is circumstantial evidence of the intention to discriminate unfairly. The standard for proof is a four-part test that was first articulated by the Supreme Court in *McDonnell Douglas v. Green* (1973). A plaintiff must be able to demonstrate that

- He or she is a member of a class of people protected by civil rights law (e.g., on the basis of age, race, religion, gender, or national origin).
- He or she applied for and qualified for a job for which an employer was seeking applicants.
- Despite having the qualifications, he or she was rejected.
- After rejection, the position remained open, and the employer continued to seek applications from people with the plaintiff's qualifications.

Statistical evidence may also be presented in an effort to prove circumstantially the existence of an intention to discriminate systematically against classes of individuals. This method of proof has been upheld by the Supreme Court in several landmark cases, such as *International Brotherhood of Teamsters v. U.S.* (1979) and *Hazelwood School District v. U.S.* (1977).

The third type of proof is a hybrid of the first two. Mixed-motive cases rely on both direct evidence of an impermissible basis for unlawful discrimination (e.g., gender) and proof that the basis for the employment decision that the defendant has presented as legitimate is merely a pretext. It is important to note that, in practice, these approaches are not mutually exclusive. The presence of evidence bearing on one may actually enhance the strength of the other.

Adverse Impact (Unintentional) Discrimination

This type of discrimination occurs when identical standards or procedures are applied to everyone, despite the fact that they lead to substantial differences in employment outcomes (e.g., selection, promotion, layoffs) for the members of a particular group and that they are unrelated to success on a job. An example would be the use of a minimum height requirement of 5 feet 8 inches for firefighters given that this would have an adverse impact on the eligibility of Asian Americans, Hispanic Americans, and women. The policy is neutral on its face because identical standards are applied to all job candidates. However, to use the standard legally, the employer must be able to demonstrate that candidates who do not meet the height requirement would be incapable of performing the job. One argument presented by fire department management to support the height requirement is that a person must be at least 5 feet 8 inches to lift a ladder from the top of a fire truck. However, in one case several women who had been appointed to a city fire department by a federal judge in the course of settling a lawsuit were rated by their supervisors as satisfactory on each dimension of firefighter performance over a period of six months. When a 5-feet, 4-inch female firefighter was asked how she removed a ladder from the top of the fire truck she said, "It's no problem; I just stand on the running board of the truck and lift it off!" Her approach was unorthodox but satisfactory in the opinion of her supervisor. As a result, the height requirement of 5 feet 8 inches was not a defensible standard.

Having considered the forms of unfair discrimination, I now examine the major provisions of the ADA and the CRA, with particular reference to how they respond to allegations of discriminatory practices.

Legal Requirements of the ADA

Passed to protect the estimated 43 million Americans with disabilities, this law became effective on July 26, 1992, for employers with 25 or more employees. On July 26, 1994, it becomes effective for employers with 15 or more employees. The term *employers* includes private employers, state and local governments, employment agencies, and joint labor–management committees. As an employer, the federal government is not covered under this law, although it is covered under the Rehabilitation Act of 1973.

Under the ADA, people with disabilities are protected from discrimination in employment, public services and transportation, and public accommodations. Title I of the law addresses discrimination in employment; it draws heavily on two prior pieces of legislation: Section 504 of the Rehabilitation Act of 1973 and Title VII of the Civil Rights Act of 1964. As a general rule, the ADA prohibits an employer from discriminating against a "qualified individual with a disability." Later, I discuss what *qualified* means for purposes of this law. The act also requires that employers make reasonable accommodation to a person's known physical and mental limitations, unless doing so would impose an undue hardship on the employer. The ADA applies to all aspects of employment: hiring, promotions and transfers, training, compensation, employee benefits, layoffs, and terminations.

Several of the terms in the law that have been described are ambiguous, although the Equal Employment Opportunity Commission's (EEOC) publication of final regulations and interpretive guidance on the ADA has provided some clarification. Some of the terms that I shall discuss are *disability, qualified individual with a disability, reasonable accommodation,* and *undue hardship.*

Who Is Considered a Person With a Disability?

The ADA defines the term *disability* very broadly. In fact, an individual is protected under this act if he or she

- currently has a physical or mental impairment that substantially limits one or more major life activities. Major life activities include functions such as caring for oneself, performing manual tasks, walking, seeing, hearing, speaking, breathing, learning, and working;
- has a record of such an impairment; or
- is regarded as having such an impairment. This would include, for example, an individual who is perceived as having a "disability" because of major scarring from a burn, even though the condition does not limit the person in any way.

Who Is Not Protected?

The ADA does not state explicitly what physical or mental impairments constitute disabilities. However, it does contain a number of exclusions. Perhaps the most important is that users of illegal drugs are not considered disabled, nor are those whose mental condition was brought on by the current use of illegal drugs. However, individuals who are engaged in or who have completed drug treatment and rehabilitation and who are no longer using drugs are protected under the act (Bruyere, 1992), as are people who have tested positive for the AIDS virus (Carey, 1990). Homosexuality, bisexuality, transsexualism, compulsive gambling, and pyromania are not considered disabilities and are not protected.

Who Is a "Qualified Individual With a Disability?"

The ADA protects an employee or applicant with a disability only if he or she is *qualified*, namely, able to perform the essential functions of a job with or without accommodation. *Essential functions* are primary job duties that are fundamental, not marginal. According to the EEOC, essential functions are generally determined on the basis of one or more of the following criteria:

1. Whether the reason a position exists is to perform a specific function (e.g., proofreading documents). By definition, therefore, that specific function is essential. Inability to perform the function with or without accommodation is grounds for not hiring a person.

2. Whether the other employees can perform a particular job function or whether that job function can be distributed among them.
3. Whether a certain degree of expertise or skill is required to perform a particular function. For example, if the main reason a person was hired was because of his or her special expertise or ability to perform a particular function, then the function itself would be considered essential.

The following may serve as bases for determining whether these criteria are met:

- the employer's judgment
- written job descriptions prepared before advertising for or interviewing applicants
- amount of time required to perform the function
- consequences of not requiring the candidate to perform the function
- terms of a collective bargaining agreement
- work experience of past candidates for the job
- current work experience of candidates for similar jobs.

As an example, a certified public accountant in a wheelchair would be considered qualified for a position in a public accounting firm. The fact that he or she could not refile client folders may not disqualify him or her, given that that function could be assigned to someone else (Chait, 1992). A key consideration here is the number of other employees who can perform a particular job function or among whom that job function can be distributed.

Intentional and Unintentional Discrimination Under the ADA

The ADA expressly prohibits intentional discrimination against people with disabilities. Employers can not rely on assumptions and stereotypes about what people with disabilities can and cannot do. Rather, they are required to consider, on a case-by-case basis, the job-relevant capabilities of each applicant or employee with a disability.

Employers violate the ADA when they refuse to make a needed accommodation or avoid hiring an applicant in order to sidestep the accommodation requirement. However, an accommodation does not have to be made if doing so would present an undue hardship to the employer. I will elaborate on this shortly.

Adverse impact (unintentional) discrimination also violates the ADA. Employment testing is particularly vulnerable to charges of unintentional discrimination. For example, a preemployment test must accurately measure the skills that a person actually needs to perform a job and not merely reflect a disability. For example, a person with a disability might not pass a business math test, even though he or she knows the material, because of a physical impairment that prohibits him or her from holding a writing instrument. The employer would have to make reasonable accommodation for that condition, unless holding a writing instrument was an essential function of the job and no reasonable accommodation could be made (Chait, 1992).

The previous example related to a physical disability. However, suppose an individual has a mental disability that makes managing time pressures and deadlines difficult. Use of a clerical aptitude test that imposes strict time limits on various sections of the test, when the requirements of the job in question impose no such time limits (e.g., a filing clerk in a library), would be impermissible under the ADA. Although abilities such as spelling and perceptual accuracy (e.g., number checking) may well be important on the job, the test itself reflects the candidate's disability (by imposing strict time limits). It does not measure the abilities needed to perform the job in question in the manner in which such abilities actually are used (i.e., within relaxed time limits).

What Is "Reasonable" Accommodation?

There are three categories of reasonable accommodation (Bruyere, 1992):

1. Modifications or adjustments to a job application process that enable a qualified individual with a disability to compete for a job. Providing hearing-impaired candidates with sign-language interpreters for testing sessions or implementing awareness training for employment interviewers to dispel myths about people with disabilities are examples of such accommodations.
2. Modifications or adjustments to the work environment that enable a qualified individual with a disability to perform the essential functions of that position. Installing telephone amplifiers for hearing-impaired individuals or magnifying glasses for sight-impaired individuals are examples.
3. Modifications or adjustments that provide employees with disabilities with the same benefits and privileges of employment as similarly situated employees without disabilities. Drinking fountains and rest rooms on every floor of a building are examples of benefits that employees without disabilities may take for granted. Lowered drinking fountains and wheelchair-accessible rest rooms on every floor of a building would allow employees with disabilities to enjoy the same benefits.

Examples of these include:

- restructuring a job so that another employee does the nonessential tasks that a person with a disability cannot do
- modifying work hours or work schedules so that a person with a disability can commute during off-peak periods or can attend therapy sessions
- reassigning a worker who develops a disability and is unable to perform the essential functions of his or her current position to a vacant position that he or she is able to perform
- acquiring or modifying equipment or devices (e.g., providing a telecommunications device for the deaf [TDD])
- making appropriate adjustments or modifications of examinations, training materials, or human resource policies, such as those pertaining to sick leave
- providing qualified readers or interpreters.

How Does an Employer Determine Reasonable Accommodations?

The employer is responsible for analyzing the particular job involved to determine its purpose and essential functions. After consulting with the applicant or employee to determine the precise, job-related limitations imposed by his or her disability, the two parties should identify potential accommodations and assess the relative strengths of each in enabling the individual to perform the essential functions of the job.

Employers must make accommodations only to the known disabilities of a job applicant or employee. It is the responsibility of the applicant or employee to identify himself or herself as having a disability that needs accommodation. Once an applicant or employee does this, the employer must make a good-faith effort to accommodate the disability. It is important to emphasize that during the hiring process, the qualifications of a candidate with a disability must be evaluated with the reasonable accommodations that the prospective employee would require to be taken into account. Employers may not legally turn away an applicant with a disability simply because he or she needs reasonable accommodations (Department of Health, Education, and Welfare, 1978). Finally, the employer should consider the preferences of the affected individual before implementing any particular accommodation.

There are both practical and legal reasons why the employer should consult with the applicant or employee. From a practical perspective, the person with the disability may be in the best position to suggest to an employer what can be done to help him or her perform the essential functions of the job in question. Legally, the CRA provides for the award of compensatory and punitive damages in cases wherein an employer has engaged in intentional discrimination. If an employer has communicated with an applicant or employee with respect to possible accommodations that might be needed and can show a good-faith effort to provide reasonable accommodation for the disability, those actions can serve as a defense to an award of compensatory and punitive damages in the event that a charge of unlawful discrimination is made ("ADA," 1993).

Practices to Assist in Making Accommodations

According to Cornell University's National Materials Development Project on the ADA Employment Provisions (Bruyere, 1992), employers with accommodation experience have reported that the following practices have facilitated successful accommodation:

- expressions of commitment by top management to accommodating workers with disabilities
- assignment of a specialist within the equal employment opportunity/affirmative action section of the organization to focus on equal access for people with disabilities
- centralizing recruiting, intake, and monitoring of hiring decisions
- identifying jobs or task assignments in which a specific disability does not bar employment
- developing an orientation process for workers with disabilities and their supervisors and co-workers
- publicizing successful accommodation experiences within and outside of the organization
- providing in-service training to all employees and managers about the employer's equal access policy
- outreach recruitment to organizations that can refer job applicants with disabilities
- reevaluating accommodations on a regular basis.

Examples of accommodations that have been made for physical disabilities include the following (Mancuso, 1990):

- installing ramps, curb cuts, or handrails to assist applicants or employees who have mobility impairments
- rearranging a work site to make an office accessible to an employee using a wheelchair
- providing specialized equipment, such as a talking calculator or a large-type computer display for workers with visual impairments

- paying for a reader, interpreter, personal care attendant, driver, or other supportive assistance.

Recent developments in computer technology have greatly expanded employment opportunities for people with disabilities. For example, Apple Computer offers a valuable collection of products called Macintosh Disability Resources (call 800-795-1000 for voice or 800-755-0601 for TDD for more information). Some of these include

- a membrane keyboard called On:Board that reacts to touch instead of pressure and is adjustable for a light or a heavy hand. This is useful for persons with limited finger control because it allows complete keyboard and mouse emulation. There is even a programmable speech option for all keys, so operators can listen to their keystrokes to verify their accuracy.
- ScreenDoors, a software program that puts a keyboard on the screen and can be used with any point-and-click device, from a mouse to a head pointer. This is useful for people who cannot use a conventional computer keyboard because of limited use of their hands. A built-in word predictor learns the person's vocabulary as he or she types and then completes words based on the first few letters entered. This increases the speed and accuracy of text input.
- a program called outSPOKEN, which provides a talking interface for a graphics-based computer by replacing visual icons with spoken words. Once a person selects a folder, outSPOKEN reads its name aloud. If a person opens a document, he or she hears it spoken by letter, word, or line. If a person pulls down a menu, he or she hears a list of commands. This program works with any Macintosh text-based software, such as word processing, spreadsheet, database, and telecommunications programs.

Reasonable Accommodation and Undue Hardship

Accommodation is not expected when it would result in an undue hardship for an employer. The act defines *undue hardship* as that requiring significant difficulty or expenses. In determining whether an undue hardship exists, the nature and cost of the accommodation is taken into account, along with the nature of the facility and the overall financial resources of the employer. This ultimately requires a case-by-case decision (Chait, 1992). In general, "too expensive" is not an acceptable excuse, unless such modifications will lead an employer to go out of business or to suffer losses to the point at which significant layoffs will occur. Remodeling an office or a store room, including significant structural modifications, may not be required of a small company but may well be considered a reasonable accommodation for a large company with substantial financial resources.

Impact of the ADA on Preemployment Inquiries and Physicals

Under the ADA, employers are not permitted to ask general questions of job applicants regarding their disabilities, physical limitations, or past workers' compensation claims. However, after describing essential job functions, an employer may ask whether the applicant can perform the job in question. The following is an example of the difference between these two types of inquiries: "Do you have any back problems?" clearly violates the ADA because it is not job specific. However, the employer could state the following: "This job involves lifting equipment weighing up to 50 pounds at least once every hour of an eight-hour shift. Can you do that?"

Under the ADA (Sections 1630.13 and 1630.14), employers may no longer require medical examinations prior to hiring an individual. However, an employer can make an offer of employment conditional on the candidate passing a medical examination. To do so, three conditions must be met:

1. The examination must be job related; that is, it must focus on conditions that would prevent a person from doing the specific job for which he or she is being considered.
2. It must be administered to all applicants, regardless of their physical conditions; that is, people who appear to be "strong" or "healthy" may not be exempted.
3. Results of medical examinations must be kept confidential and separate from other personnel records.

After hire, employers may not require routine physical examinations unless they are job related and the results are kept confidential. However, under the ADA, employers may offer voluntary physical examinations as part of a wellness program, again with the provision that the results be kept confidential.

Finally, the ADA notes specifically that a drug test is not considered to be a medical examination. Hence, an employer may administer drug tests before (or after hire), and the employer may refuse to hire individuals who test positive.

Enforcement, Defenses, and Remedies Under the ADA

The employment provisions of the ADA are enforced under the same procedures currently applicable to race, gender, national origin, and religious discrimination under Title VII of the Civil Rights Act of 1964. The enforcement agency is the EEOC. In the first 11 months after the law took effect, 11,760 complaints of discrimination on the basis of disability were filed with the agency. Roughly 20% of the cases were resolved during that time period, and claimants collected over $11 million (Labor Letter, 1993). More than 8 of 10 complaints filed fell into one of three areas: discharge (48%), failure of the employer to accommodate a disability (21%), and hiring (15%) (ADA Update, 1993).

How should an individual proceed if he or she believes that he or she has been discriminated against unlawfully on the basis of a disability? The first step is to contact the EEOC within 180 days of the alleged discrimination. However, if there is a state or local law that provides relief for discrimination on the basis of disability, an individual may have 300 days to file a complaint (U.S., 1992). By law, the EEOC must proceed in three phases: (a) investigation to determine if there is "reasonable cause" to conclude that unlawful discrimination has occurred, (b) voluntary reconciliation by the aggrieved party, and, if all else fails, (c) litigation. The EEOC has the right to sue either on its own behalf or on behalf of a claimant.

When confronted with a charge of discrimination under the ADA, there are several defenses available to an employer. First, the employer can argue that its application of qualification standards, tests, or selection criteria is job related and consistent with business necessity and that performance cannot be accomplished by reasonable accommodation.

Alternatively, an employer may require as a qualification standard that an individual not pose a direct threat to the health and safety of himself or herself or others. *Direct threat* means a significant risk of substantial harm to the health or safety of the individual or others that cannot be eliminated or reduced through reasonable accommodation. Such a determination should be based on an assessment of an individual's present ability to perform the essential functions of a job. Factors to consider include the duration of the risk, the nature and severity of the potential harm, the likelihood that the potential harm will occur, and the imminence of the potential harm (Bruyere, 1992).

If an employer is found guilty of violating the ADA, available remedies include hiring, reinstating, awarding back pay, and proceeding with court orders to stop the discrimination. These are the same remedies available under Title VII. However, as I shall show, under the CRA an individual with a disability who is the victim of intentional discrimination may seek a jury trial. In addition, if the employer is found guilty of acting "with malice or reckless indifference" to the protected rights of a person with a disability (or a class of people with a disability), then compensatory and punitive damages are available.

Legal Requirements of the CRA

Perhaps the best way to appreciate the requirements of the 1991 act is to understand the main holdings of six Supreme Court decisions, five of which were handed down in 1989, that made it more difficult for plaintiffs in employment discrimination lawsuits to win. These six decisions were

- *Wards Cove Packing Co. v. Antonio* (1989), which limited the ability of workers to sue their employers for unintentional discrimination against minorities or women
- *Patterson v. McLean Credit Union* (1989), which restricted previous protections against race discrimination in hiring, promotion, firing, and harassment to hiring only
- *Price Waterhouse v. Hopkins* (1989), which permitted a discriminatory action if the employer could show an additional legitimate motive
- *Martin v. Wilks* (1989), which permitted reopening of previously concluded cases intended to resolve claims of job discrimination by individuals who were not parties in those cases
- *Lorance v. AT&T Technologies* (1989), which severely restricted the time period during which certain discriminatory practices can be challenged
- *EEOC v. Arabian American Oil Co. and Aramco Service Co.* (1991), which held that Title VII of the 1964 Civil Rights Act does not apply to discrimination by U.S. employers against U.S. citizens overseas.

These decisions directly led to passage of the CRA, which overruled more Supreme Court decisions than any other single piece of legislation. As stated by Senator Danforth (cosponsor of the act), "What was wrong in 1989 was not simply that the Supreme Court wrongly decided a half a dozen cases, some of them dealing with technical issues such as how to define business necessity. What was wrong was that in the year 1989 the Supreme Court chose to turn the clocks back, and that can never happen in civil rights; it can never be allowed to happen" (Danforth, 1991, Section 15500). Following are some key provisions in the CRA that are likely to have the greatest impact in the context of employment.

Adverse Impact (Unintentional) Discrimination Cases

A major provision of this act is that it clarifies each party's obligation in such cases. Under the law, when an adverse impact charge is made, the complaining party (the plaintiff) must identify a specific employment practice as the cause of discrimination. If the plaintiff is successful in demonstrating adverse impact, then the burden of proof shifts to the employer, who must prove that the challenged practice is "job-related for the position in question and consistent with business necessity" (Section 105). This overturned the Supreme Court's decision in *Wards Cove Packing Co. v. Antonio* (1989).

Monetary Damages and Jury Trials

A second major effect of this act is to expand the remedies in discrimination cases. Individuals who feel they are the victims of intentional discrimination on the basis of gender (including sexual harassment), religion, or disability can ask for compensatory damages for pain and suffering, as well as for punitive damages, and they may demand a jury trial. In the past, only plaintiffs in age-discrimination cases had the right to demand a jury trial. Compensatory damages are intended to reimburse a plaintiff for injuries or harm. Punitive damages are awarded in civil cases to punish or deter a defendant's conduct. Table 1 shows that the amount of compensatory and punitive damages that can be awarded depends on the size of the employer's work force.

Note that because intentional discrimination by reason of disability is a basis for compensatory and punitive damages, the CRA therefore provides the sanctions for violations of the ADA.

Under the CRA, punitive damages are available only from nonpublic employers and only when the employer has engaged in the discriminatory action with "malice or reckless indifference" to the protected rights of the aggrieved individual (Section 102). Compensatory and punitive damages are not available for adverse impact (unintentional) discrimination cases, nor are they available to victims of intentional discrimination by race or national origin. These people may sue under the Civil Rights Act of 1866, which places no limits on compensatory and punitive damages.

Table 1
Maximum Combined Compensatory and Punitive Damages
(in U.S. Dollars) Per Complaint as Related to Size
of Employer's Workforce

Number of employees	Maximum combined damages
15–100	50,000
101–200	100,000
201–500	200,000
>500	300,000

Protection in Foreign Countries

Another provision of the CRA extends protection from discrimination in employment, as defined by Title VII of the 1964 Civil Rights Act and by the ADA, to U.S. citizens employed in a foreign-country facility owned or controlled by a U.S. company. However, the employer does not have to comply with U.S. discrimination law if to do so would violate the law of the foreign country. This provision overturned *EEOC v. Arabian American Oil Co. and Aramco Service Co.* (1991).

Racial Harassment

The Civil Rights Act of 1866 allows for jury trials and for compensatory and punitive damages for victims of intentional racial and ethnic discrimination, and it extends to employers who are too small to be covered under Title VII (i.e., those with fewer than 15 employees). The CRA amends the Civil Rights Act of 1866 so that workers are protected from intentional discrimination in all aspects of employment, not just in hiring and promotion. Thus, racial harassment is covered by this civil rights law. The effect was to overturn *Patterson v. McLean Credit Union* (1989). Furthermore, once a court order or consent decree is entered to resolve a lawsuit, nonparties to the original suit can not challenge such enforcement actions. The effect was to overturn *Martin v. Wilks* (1989).

Mixed-Motive Cases

As I noted earlier, in a mixed-motive case, an employment decision is based on a combination of job-related factors as well as on unlawful factors, such as race, gender, religion, or disability. Under the CRA, an employer is guilty of discrimination if it can be shown that a prohibited consideration was a motivating factor in a decision, even though lawful factors also were used. However, if the employer can show that the same decision would have been reached, even without the unlawful considerations, the court may not assess damages or require hiring, reinstatement, or promotion. This overturned *Price Waterhouse v. Hopkins* (1989).

Seniority Systems

The CRA provides that a seniority system that intentionally discriminates against the members of a protected group can be challenged at any of three points: (a) when the system is adopted, (b) when an individual becomes subject to the system, or (c) when a person is injured by the system. This provision overturned the Supreme Court's decision in *Lorance v. AT&T Technologies* (1989).

"Race Norming" and Affirmative Action

Section 106 of the CRA makes it unlawful "to adjust the scores of, use different cutoff scores for, or otherwise alter the results of employment-related tests on the basis of race, color, religion, sex, or national origin." This provision was added in reaction to public sentiment that different standards were being used for different groups in the interpretation of test scores. Prior to the passage of this act, within-groups percentile scoring (so-called "race norming") had been used extensively to adjust the test scores of minority candidates to make them more comparable to those of nonminority candidates.

When race norming is used, each individual's percentile score on a selection test is computed relative only to others in his or her racial or ethnic group, not relative to the scores of all examinees who took the test. Then a single, merged list of percentiles is developed from the percentiles that were developed within each group, rank-ordered from highest to lowest. As a result, the same raw score (e.g., 85) may have a very different percentile referent, depending on whether it is derived by comparing it with the scores of White examinees, African-American examinees, or all other examinees. Individuals responsible for making employment decisions see only the merged list of percentiles, not the raw scores from which the percentiles were derived.

Even though the prohibitions of Section 106 are absolute, there may yet be some room for flexibility. Section 116 of the act states, "Nothing in the amendments made by this title shall be construed to affect court-ordered remedies, affirmative action, or conciliation agreements that are in accordance with the law." Although it could be argued that the act would permit individual employers to make test-score adjustments as part of court-ordered affirmative action plans or when a court approves a conciliation agreement, it is not yet clear that courts will interpret Section 116 so broadly (Arnold & Thiemann, 1992).

Retroactivity of the Act

The CRA became effective on November 21, 1991, the day that President Bush signed it. However, a key unresolved issue in the law itself was whether the law applied to cases that were pending when the statute was enacted. The EEOC has taken the position that the law applies only to discrimination that takes place after November 21, 1991. To date, six different appeals courts have ruled that the law is to be applied prospectively. However, the ninth circuit has ruled that it is to be applied retroactively. The Supreme Court has now agreed to hear arguments on this issue in fall 1993 in cases from Ohio and Texas. It is expected to issue a ruling in 1994. If the court determines that the act should be applied retroactively, then employers could be faced with the prospect of punitive and compensatory damages that were not applicable before the 1991 law was enacted (Barrett, 1993).

Issues Under the ADA and the CRA With Special Relevance to Psychologists

Professional psychologists work in a variety of capacities that are relevant to the implementation of these two laws. They include clinical psychologists, industrial and organizational psychologists, neuropsychologists, and rehabilitation psychologists. Although a number of issues raised by the laws are potentially relevant to psychological practice, the remainder of this chapter will focus on five specific issues: job analysis under the ADA, accommodation for mental disabilities under the ADA, preemployment personality tests and the ADA, psychometric issues posed by altering test conditions to make reasonable accommodations, and test scoring under the CRA.

Job Analysis Under the ADA

The term *job analysis* describes the process of obtaining information about jobs. Although it may be collected in several ways (e.g., by observation, interview, structured questionnaire, or actual job performance), it usually includes information about the tasks to be done on a job and the personal characteristics (e.g., education, training, specialized experience) necessary to do the tasks. Professional practice dictates that thorough job analyses always be done given that they provide a deeper understanding of the behavioral requirements of jobs. This, in turn, creates a solid basis on which to make job-related employment decisions.

Job analyses are not required under the ADA, but sound professional practice suggests that they be done for several reasons. First, the law makes it clear that job applicants must be able to understand what the essential functions of a job are before they respond to the question, Can you perform the essential functions of the job for which you are applying? Job analysis is a systematic procedure that can help to identify essential job functions.

Second, existing job analyses may need to be updated to reflect additional dimensions of jobs, namely, the physical demands, environmental demands, and mental abilities required to perform essential functions. Most job analyses focus on only two aspects of jobs: task requirements (what gets done) and the personal characteristics (knowledge, skills, abilities, and other characteristics) necessary to do the work.

Third, once job analyses are updated as described, a summary of the results is normally prepared in writing in the form of a job description. What may work better under the ADA, however, is a video job description that provides concrete evidence to applicants of the physical, environmental (e.g., temperatures, noise level, working space), or mental (e.g., irate customers calling with complaints) demands of jobs. Psychological research in actual company settings has indicated consistent results when such information is communicated clearly to applicants (Premack & Wanous, 1985). That is, when the unrealistically positive expectations of job applicants are lowered to match the reality of the actual work setting before hire, job acceptance rates among candidates who receive such realistic job previews tend to be lower; job performance, however, is unaffected, and job satisfaction and employee retention rates are higher.

These conclusions have held up across different organizational settings (e.g., manufacturing vs. service jobs) and different realistic job preview techniques (e.g., plant tours vs. slide presentations). In fact, meta-analysis indicates that realistic job previews improved retention rates by an average of 9% (McEvoy & Cascio, 1985).

Given the value of a job analysis, the following are several strategies that can be incorporated into existing job analysis approaches:

- After explaining what essential job functions are under the ADA, have subject-matter experts (job incumbents or immediate supervisors) provide independent judgments of essential and nonessential functions with respect to each task identified.
- Include independent ratings from subject-matter experts regarding relative time spent performing each task, as well as the consequences of nonperformance or error with respect to each task. The latter may require a redefinition of the rating scale for importance. Essential tasks are those that require relatively more time and have serious consequences of error or nonperformance associated with them. Given the language in the ADA, one might consider redefining critical tasks as essential job functions.
- To ensure job relatedness, be able to link required knowledge, skills, abilities, and other characteristics (i.e., measures of which candidates actually are assessed on) to essential job functions.
- Recognize that under the ADA, it is imperative that distinctions between essential and nonessential functions be made before announcing a job or interviewing applicants (Donnoe, 1992).

Accommodation for Mental Disabilities Under the ADA

As a group, employers tend to impose more severe stigmas against people with mental or psychiatric disabilities than they do against those with physical disabilities (Combs & Omvig, 1986). Unfortunately, such beliefs do not match evidence that shows that with support, such people perform as well on the job as do those without these disabilities (Howard, 1975).

A review of the literature on accommodation revealed that textbooks, government publications, and journal articles generally neglect to mention mental or psychiatric disabilities, focusing instead on accommodations for people with physical disabilities (Mancuso, 1990). To a large extent, this is understandable given employers' beliefs and stereotypes about people with mental impairments and the desires of people with mental impairments to secure and retain employment. It may well be the case that those who are offered jobs choose to forego the protection of the law to avoid disclosure of their mental disabilities and the stigmatization that may follow. Mancuso (1990) showed that from 1988 to 1990, of 8,270 cases reported by the Job Accommodation Network, mental illness was identified as the primary impairment in only about 1% of the cases.

Moreover, it may be difficult for employers and vocational service providers to develop accommodations to mental disabilities because such disabilities are less tangible. Typically, accommodations involve modifications in work schedules or interpersonal interactions, rather than in adaptive equipment, as is often the case with physical disabilities. Examples of mental disabilities (Mancuso, 1992) include difficulty in

- maintaining concentration over time
- screening out external stimuli
- maintaining stamina over time
- managing time pressure and deadlines
- initiating interpersonal contact
- focusing on multiple tasks simultaneously
- responding to negative feedback
- formulating and executing a plan of action
- overcoming unexpected obstacles
- maintaining orientation in unfamiliar surroundings.

The following are examples of reasonable accommodations that have been made for people with mental disabilities (Mancuso, 1990, 1992).

Modifications to the Supervisory Process

- arranging for a work request to be put in writing for a worker who becomes confused when given verbal instructions or has short-term memory loss
- scheduling daily planning sessions with a co-worker at the start of each day to develop hourly goals for workers who function best with added time structure

Job Modification

- arranging for someone who cannot drive or use public transportation to work at home (i.e., to telecommute)
- restructuring a job to eliminate nonessential tasks that pose problems for a worker with a disability by exchanging those tasks for some of another worker's tasks

Modification of the Physical Environment

- assigning an enclosed office to a worker who loses concentration and accuracy in a noisy room
- installing room dividers for a data-entry operator who loses concentration (and thus accuracy) in an open work area

Schedule Modification

- flexible scheduling, telecommuting, job-sharing, and other part-time arrangements

Modification of Human Resource Policies

- use of sick leave for emotional and cognitive reasons, not just for physical reasons

Perhaps the most fundamental lesson in all attempts to provide reasonable accommodation is that for the process to work properly, there must be a thorough understanding of (a) the needs of the individual worker, (b) the management skills and personal style of the supervisor, and (c) the requirements for successful performance in the work setting (Mancuso, 1990). As these examples show, there are vast opportunities for creative applications of the reasonable accommodation concept.

Appropriately trained psychologists can and should take a lead role in that process.

Preemployment Personality Tests and the ADA

As I noted earlier, Section 102 (c)(3) of the ADA specifies that an employer may not "conduct medical examinations or make inquiries" about the existence, nature, or severity of a disability of a job applicant until after making a conditional offer of employment, and then only when the results of the medical examination are job related. Although the EEOC has indicated that intelligence and aptitude tests probably will not be treated as medical examinations or disability inquiries (W. Camara, personal communication, July 26, 1993), as of this writing it has not yet decided how to treat preemployment personality tests.

The issue focuses on the fact that personality tests are sometimes used in clinical settings to assist in diagnosing a person's psychiatric condition. However, because the EEOC has not yet taken a position on this issue, we must be guided by existing case law, where applicable. One of the most relevant cases regarding the preemployment use of personality tests is *Daley v. Koch* (1989), a case that rose under Section 504 of the Rehabilitation Act. The case is relevant because it demonstrates that the purpose and use of a test (i.e., prediction of future job behavior vs. diagnosis of disability), rather than the type of test, is the most important consideration in determining whether its use is permissible under the ADA.

In *Daley*, a candidate for the New York City Police Department was refused employment on the basis, in part, of test results from the California Psychological Inventory and the Minnesota Multiphasic Personality Inventory. On the basis of these tests, the department concluded that the applicant had the personality traits of "poor judgment, irresponsible behavior, and poor impulse control," which rendered him "unsuitable to be a police officer" (Id. at 1078). The applicant was not diagnosed as having any specific mental disorder. Nevertheless, the plaintiff claimed that the police department had "regarded" him as having a mental disability. The district court agreed with the employer, and court of appeals affirmed that decision. The Second Circuit held that

> [p]oor judgment, irresponsible behavior, and poor impulse control do not amount to a mental condition that Congress meant to be considered as an impairment which substantially limits a major life activity, and therefore a person having those traits or perceived as having those traits cannot be considered a handicapped person within the meaning of the Act. (Id. at 1079)

However, in its interpretive guidance for its ADA regulations, the EEOC states that certain personality traits, such as poor judgment or poor impulse control, are considered impairments if they are symptoms of a mental or psychological disorder. Under this interpretation, a person whose poor judgment or poor impulse control is a result of a traumatic brain injury would be protected by the ADA.

Case law focuses not so much on the specific preemployment personality test that is used as on the purpose and use to which the test (or scale of the test) is put. Courts have routinely acknowledged that personality tests can help select the best candidates from among qualified applicants for key occupations such as air traffic controllers, police officers, and fire fighters (*McKenna v. Fargo*, 1979; *Soroka v. Dayton Hudson Corporation*, 1991). Thus, I agree with others who have concluded that employers may legally assess a broad set of personality characteristics during preemployment screening as long as the purpose of the assessment is to predict necessary, job-related behavior, rather than to diagnose disability (Bernard, 1992; Flanagan, 1991; Potter & Reesman, 1992). However, the EEOC may rule differently.

Psychometric Issues Posed by Altering Test Conditions to Make Reasonable Accommodations

The *Standards for Educational and Psychological Testing* (1985) address a number of practical and psychometric issues associated with using standardized tests with individuals who have disabilities. A more recent treatment of the psychometric and assessment issues raised by the ADA was provided by the Division for Evaluation, Measurement, and Statistics, Division 5 of the American Psychological Association (APA, 1993). Perhaps the most basic principle in this area is that all of the standards that apply to the administration and use of tests with populations of individuals without disabilities also apply to populations of individuals with disabilities.

As the *Standards* note, modifications in the way a test is administered sometimes alter the medium in which the test instructions and questions are presented to the test takers. For example, modifications of tests for people with hearing impairments often include having an interpreter who signs or otherwise interprets test instructions and, occasionally, test questions.

The method used to record a response may also need to be modified, for example, for individuals who cannot use their hands. This might be done by having them speak answers into a tape recorder or, in the case of computer-administered tests, using a pointing device or a touch-sensitive computer display.

Modifications in the time allowed for testing are also considered appropriate test accommodations. However, as the *Standards* noted,

> there are few data available to support any conclusions about the effects of modifications in time, number of sittings, or number of recesses on the test results. Furthermore, little is known about how much time people with various handicapping conditions actually need, because records of the time actually used are rare, and empirical studies to set time limits are even more rare. (p. 77)

Changes in test content are sometimes necessary for people with visual or hearing impairments. Items may be unnecessarily difficult for visually impaired people if they use visual stimuli to measure knowledge acquired through other senses. Alternatively, certain test items may cause problems if they measure knowledge, skills, or concepts learned primarily through vision.

Substitution of other types of items may be inappropriate, however, when the content or mode of response on the altered test is not identical to that required on a job. For example, suppose a test item requires an examinee to analyze critical features of a photograph or scene and then to make decisions based on the characteristics identified. It may not be possible to alter the stimulus (e.g., by substituting a spoken description) if an employee in an actual job situation is expected to "size up" a scene before deciding how to deploy people and equipment, as would be the case with police or fire lieutenants. In such cases, applicants who are severely visually impaired would not be able to perform the job. Hence, modification of test content is not necessary.

Even in situations wherein substitute items are appropriate, it is important to note that the psychometric characteristics of the substitute items may differ from those of the original items. As a result, the same constructs may not be measured in the original and altered forms of a test. Hence, direct comparison of scores across examinees may not be possible.

The *Standards* (1985) noted that, despite the history of attempts to modify tests for people with disabilities, significant (some would say intractable) problems remain. First, there have been few empirical investigations of the effects of special accommodations on the resulting scores or on their reliability and validity. As a result, it is simply not known if a modified test "works" in the same manner as its unmodified counterpart. The *Standards* noted that "strictly speaking, unless it has been demonstrated that the psychometric properties of a test, or type of test, are not altered significantly by some modification, the claims made for the test by its author or publisher cannot be generalized to the modified version" (p. 78).

As Division 5 (APA, 1993) noted, there is no mathematically or scientifically traditional way of equating tests modified to accommodate people with disabilities with the standardized tests for which the modifications were made. The classical method of equating two forms of a test is to select two groups of individuals at random from a larger group and administer one form to one group and another form to the other group. Scores on the two forms are considered equivalent if they yield equal percentiles in the groups that took the different forms or if they correspond to equal standard-score deviates in the groups that took the two forms.

The critical feature of the experimental design is the random selection of individuals to form the two groups. In the case at hand, however, the two groups are prechosen in that one is composed of individuals with disabilities whereas the other is not. The two groups are therefore nonrandom, and they may differ systematically in other important dimensions as a result of disability. When groups, as well as test items, are different, then any observed differences in scores are confounded because they may result either from differences in the difficulty levels of test forms or from differences in the ability levels of the groups.

When the groups are equivalent, however (a condition facilitated by random selection into groups), then any resulting differences in performance on two forms of a test can only be attributed to differences in difficulty levels of the test forms. Although there are approximate solutions to this problem, none is completely satisfactory, and the original problem remains, namely, how to know that tests modified for people with disabilities produce results that are equivalent to the standardized versions of the same tests.

Why has such research not been done? The major reason is the relatively small number of test takers with a given disabling condition. For example, the most comprehensive review of the performance of individuals with disabilities on modified versions of the Scholastic Aptitude Test and the Graduate Record Examination was carried out with some of the largest testing populations in the world (Willingham, 1988). However, some of the samples were as small as 35 (tests modified for persons with visual impairments). As Division 5 (APA, 1993) noted, "it is extremely unlikely that employers, faced with the prospect of administering tests under modified conditions, will be able to conduct separate validity studies for each type of accommodation" (p. 10). The conclusion is that the appropriateness of inferences made from scores on modified employment tests is likely to be highly suspect.

A second problem is that when tests are given to people with conditions that affect cognitive functioning, the modified test may be measuring a different construct given that tests are operational definitions of the constructs they purport to measure. Division 5 (APA, 1993) noted that an integral part of any operational definition is the standardized conditions of administration. Changing the conditions changes the operational definition and may change what is being measured. For example, a test that measures oral comprehension could be modified for applicants with hearing impairments by substituting written instructions and questions. However, the construct measured would now be written comprehension. Similarly, a speed test for clerical aptitude could be administered with relaxed time limits to applicants with orthopedic disabilities. However, it is likely that the test would no longer measure the same ability, and, in many cases, it would be less useful for predicting job performance.

According to Division 5 (APA, 1993), the little research available on this issue indicates that the scores on a modified version of a test may be less valid and possibly unfair and that the nature and degree of unfairness may depend on the defined disability, the type of test modification, and the construct being measured. In short, scores on a modified test may not be fully interpretable.

In addition to more research from the psychological profession, employers clearly need more explicit guidelines to help them determine when they should make accommodations for applicants with disabilities. The EEOC noted that waiving the test is a possible reasonable accommodation. In its place, a situational assessment could be done, assuming that its use and format can be justified in light of job analysis results. This is an area in which some psychologists have relevant training and expertise.

A third problem, and the one that is perhaps most difficult to deal with, concerns whether the reporting of scores from nonstandard administrations (often called "flagging" of test scores) violates professional principles, misleads test users, and perhaps even harms test takers with disabilities whose scores do not accurately reflect their abilities. Some people with disabilities argue that identification of their scores as resulting from nonstandard administrations (thereby identifying them as having a disability) denies them the opportunity to compete on the same grounds as test takers without disabilities. They argue that such a practice is inequitable.

Much appears to depend on who has access to the flagged scores (APA, 1993). Although employers should keep records about the nature of any accommodations made in administering a test, there are legal questions about how much information about nonstandard test administration should be given to those who actually make employment decisions. A flagged score is an immediate indication that the applicant is a person with a disability. Because the ADA prohibits asking an applicant about a disability, legal problems may arise if flagged scores are given to hiring supervisors. There may also be legal problems in some states regarding invasion of privacy. The ethical question of whether flagging scores results in unfair discrimination toward people with disabilities has not been answered definitively (Willingham et al., 1988).

Division 5 (APA, 1993) identified other complex questions associated with flagging scores. Should different flags be used for different modifications? What should an examinee be told about the meaning of his or her test score? What if a job applicant asks for accommodation on a test, qualifies, and then does not ask for accommodation on the job (or even mention the disability after he or she is hired)? As a result, a supervisor may be unaware of the need for accommodation and may well focus on unproductive ways to improve the employee's job performance. Unfortunately, the current body of psychological research does not provide direct answers to these questions.

Advice from the *Standards* (1985) is not encouraging:

> Until test scores can be demonstrated to be comparable in some widely accepted sense, there is little hope of happily resolving from all perspectives the issue of reporting test scores with or without special identification. Professional and ethical considerations should be weighed to arrive at a solution, either as an interim measure or as continuing policy. (p. 78)

An Alternative Method for Achieving Workforce Diversity Goals

It is important to note that a thorough legal analysis of the CRA concluded that "the legislative history of the Civil Rights Act of 1991 contains no indication that the drafters of the Act had any intention of abolishing affirmative action programs" (Norris & Holmes, 1992, p. 28). As I mentioned earlier, however, Section 106 of the CRA makes it unlawful to adjust the scores of, use different cutoff scores for, or otherwise alter the results of employment-related tests on the basis of race, color, religion, sex, or national origin. The term *test* is used in the broad sense here to refer to any basis for an employment decision, such as an interview, an assessment of behavior in structured or unstructured situational exercises, an assessment of training and experience (sometimes called an *unassembled examination*), or the use of biographical information. It does not imply that written tests are the only bases for employment decisions.

When written, paper-and-pencil aptitude tests are used in employment settings, however, mean differences in test scores by race (and also in terms of job performance) have been found consistently (Hartigan & Wigdor, 1989). To reduce such differences, and thus to improve the likelihood that minorities will be offered jobs, score adjustments sometimes have been used. As a basis for discussion, I will review the methods and justification for the use of such adjustments, as described in a report by the Scientific Affairs Committee of the Society for Industrial and Organizational Psychology (Murphy, 1993).

In general, there are three ways to adjust test scores: (a) by adding points to the test scores of specific groups (e.g., veterans); (b) by using different standards to compute norm-referenced scores (e.g., percentiles) for members of different groups, which are then used to compare examinees ("race-" or "gender-norming"); and (c) by using different scoring or prediction equations for members of different groups. For example, in using biographical data to predict turnover, separate scoring schemes might be developed for men and women. The major objection to the use of such score adjustments is that they could change the rank order of individuals who received the same test score.

There is evidence that the use of separate norms by gender does produce modest increases in the validity and usefulness of measures of vocational interests (Tracy & Rounds, 1993), personality measures (Cattell, Eber, & Tatsuoka, 1970), and possibly biographical data instruments (Owens & Schoenfeldt, 1979). Thus, at least in certain cases, there is a scientific justification for test-score adjustment procedures.

However, some score-adjustment procedures designed to reduce differences between the scores of White and minority examinees might decrease the overall validity and utility of the test (Schmidt, Mack, & Hunter, 1984). For example, race-norming tends to reduce Black–White score differences, but it does so at a modest cost in validity (Hartigan & Wigdor, 1989).

In light of these results, the Society for Industrial and Organizational Psychology concluded that test score adjustments that either fail to increase the validity of tests or decrease the validity of tests do not have a firm scientific justification, although they may be justifiable on the grounds of advancing specific public policies (Murphy, 1993). One such public policy objective is the achievement of affirmative action goals.

Assuming that at least some employers regard the achievement of affirmative action or workforce diversity goals as important social and business objectives, what can be done? Does psychological research inform us about alternatives for implementing affirmative action programs? One alternative is the use of the sliding-band technique (Cascio, Outtz, Zedeck, & Goldstein, 1991).

The sliding-band technique is not a score-adjustment procedure because measurement considerations determine which scores are considered to be reliably different from each other, not racial considerations (Cascio, 1992). It uses the standard error of the difference between scores (SED, where SED equals two times the standard error of measurement) as a basis for testing the hypothesis that the test scores of two or more individuals differ reliably from each other. Gulliksen (1950) demonstrated that the SED may be used to determine reasonable limits for the difference between the true scores of two individuals.

Beginning with the top score in a distribution of test scores (the score of the candidate who ordinarily would be offered employment first), a band is formed that includes the top score plus all of the scores that fall within, say, one SED from that top score. The odds are therefore 2:1 that the true difference in test scores falls within that band. All scores within the band are considered statistically indistinguishable from each other; those outside the band are considered to be reliably different from the top score in the band.

For example, if the top score in a distribution is 97 and the bandwidth (one SED) is six points, all scores between 97 and 91 compose the first band. All scores lower than 91 are considered to be reliably different from the top score of 97. Because scores within the first band are statistically indistinguishable, it does not matter which one is chosen. If the first score chosen is the highest score (97), then the band "slides" down to the highest remaining score in the distribution (say, 96), and a second band is formed that includes all scores between 96 and 90. Such a procedure represents a continuous adjustment for the effects of measurement error in test scores. However, if the first score chosen is not the highest score in the band, then the band cannot slide. Additional scores are chosen until the highest score is chosen; at that point, the band slides.

Certainly, the procedure that is statistically optimal and that maximizes validity and economic utility for the employer is top-down selection. It yields the highest average test score among selectees. Banding acknowledges economic utility, but it also allows an employer to take workforce diversity into account during the selection process. For example, the City of San Francisco won court approval to use the sliding-band technique in a promotional examination. In making selections within the band, the city "bundled" three criteria in addition to race: professional conduct, education, and training and experience. The district court, and later the 9th Circuit Court of Appeals, declared banding and the proposed selection criteria "legally sound" under Section 107 (a) of the CRA (*Officers for Justice v. Civil Service Commission of San Francisco*, 1992).

In general, as long as the variability of minority and nonminority test scores is approximately equal, a top-down, minority-preference strategy within bands will yield a higher percentage of minority hires (and, therefore, substantially reduce adverse impact) than will strict top-down selection (Cascio et al., 1991; Cascio & Veres, 1993; Sackett & Roth, 1991). This represents a minimax strategy, where the objective of selection is to minimize the maximum loss in utility while attempting to achieve social goals.

The logic of the sliding-band model has been criticized, as has been the appropriateness of statistical significance testing of predictor scores in the context of the traditional, optimizing selection model (Schmidt, 1991). Such criticisms have been the subject of a lively debate (Zedeck, Outtz, Cascio, & Goldstein, 1991), but on one issue there is no further debate: the legality of the sliding-band method with racial preference in cases wherein past discrimination has been demonstrated. In 1993, the U.S. Supreme Court declined to review the November 1992 decision of the 9th Circuit Court of Appeals in this matter (*Officers for Justice*, 1993). Thus, the appeals court decision stands. The court noted that

> [i]n 1989, following decades of concededly discriminatory promotional procedures, the City in concert with the Union, minority job applicants, and the court finally devised a selection process which offers a facially neutral way to interpret actual scores and reduce adverse impacts on minority candidates while preserving merit as the primary criterion for selection. Today we hold that the banding process is valid as a matter of constitutional and federal law ... we find that the efforts exerted in this process culminated in a unique and innovative program which succeeds in addressing past harm to minorities while minimizing future harmful effects on non-minority candidates. The successful efforts of all parties and the district court in reaching this resolution are to be lauded. (979 F.2d 728)

This decision demonstrates that psychological research, while informing the court, also can contribute to the achievement of economic and social goals.

Summary and Conclusion

The ADA and the CRA represent major steps forward in assuring civil rights protections for Americans in employment settings. Although it is unlikely that unlawful discrimination can be rooted out entirely in our society or that the attitudes of all people will change toward valuing workforce diversity and individual merit (rather than group membership), these two laws ensure that the behavior of individuals responsible for employment decisions will change. More specifically, the laws make it unlawful to discriminate against individuals with disabilities and against individuals who are members of other protected groups in all employment practices: recruitment, hiring, job assignments, performance reviews, pay, layoffs, firing, training, promotions, benefits, and leave. This includes both types of unlawful discrimination, disparate treatment (intentional) discrimination and adverse impact (unintentional) discrimination.

The laws also present numerous challenges and opportunities for psychologists. This chapter focused on five key areas that are ripe for additional research and for enlightened insight from professional practice:

1. Job analysis, the key challenge of which is to link required knowledge, skills, and abilities to essential job functions

2. Accommodation for mental disabilities, the key challenge for which is developing innovative ways to modify jobs, schedules, supervisory processes, physical environments, and human resource policies in ways that maximize productivity

3. Preemployment personality testing under the ADA, the key challenge of which is to be able to demonstrate that the purpose of the assessment is to predict job behavior, rather than to diagnose disability

4. Psychometric issues posed by altering test conditions to make reasonable accommodations, the key challenges of which are to develop ways to equate tests that have been modified for people with disabilities with the standardized tests for which the modifications were made and to develop appropriate methods for handling "flagged" scores so as to satisfy the mutual interests of test takers and employers

5. Test scoring under the CRA, the key challenge of which is to develop alternative means for achieving workforce diversity other than score adjustment procedures based on race, ethnic group, or gender.

This list is not exhaustive. Indeed, new issues relevant to the ADA and the CRA will arise over time. Such issues will provide an ongoing challenge for psychologists to contribute to a more just and inclusive society.

References

ADA—Reasonable accommodations and the disabled employee. (1993, June). *Mountain States Employers Council Bulletin*, p. 2. Denver, CO: Author.

ADA update: The first year in review. (1993, July). *HRfocus*. New York: American Management Association.

American Psychological Association, Division of Evaluation, Measurement, and Statistics. (1993, January). Psychometric and assessment issues raised by the Americans With Disabilities Act (ADA). *Score, 15*(4), 1, 2, 7–15.

Americans With Disabilities Act of 1990, Public Law No. 101–336, 104 Stat. 328 (1990). Codified at 42 U.S.C. , Section 12101 *et seq.*

Apple Computer, Inc. (1993, summer). *The Apple catalog* (pp. 42–44). Clearwater, FL: Author.

Arnold, D. W., & Thiemann, A. J. (1992, December). Test scoring under the Civil Rights Act of 1991. *PTC Quarterly, 8*(4), 1–2.

Barrett, P. M. (1993, February 23). Justices to decide if 1991 job-bias law applies to cases pending when enacted. *Wall Street Journal*, p. A3.

Bernard, S. (1992). *Pre-employment personality tests and the ADA*. Unpublished manuscript, Atlanta, GA.

Bruyere, S. M. (1992, November). *An overview of the ADA employment provisions.* Paper presented at the conference on the ADA and Mental Health in the Workplace, Washington, DC.

Carey, J. H. (1990, August 15). Americans With Disabilities Act of 1990. *Employment Testing, 4*(13), 629–633.

Cascio, W. F. (1992). Reconciling economic and social objectives in personnel selection. In D. Saunders (Ed.), *New approaches to employee management: Fairness in employee selection* (Vol. 1, pp. 61–86). Greenwich, CT: JAI Press.

Cascio, W. F., Outtz, J., Zedeck, S., & Goldstein, I. L. (1991). Statistical implications of six methods of test score use in personnel selection. *Human Performance, 4,* 233–264.

Cascio, W. F., & Veres, J. G., III. (1993, May). *Implications of alternative methods of test score use in personnel selection.* Paper presented at the eighth annual conference of the Society for Industrial and Organizational Psychology, San Francisco.

Cattell, R. B., Eber, H. W., & Tatsuoka, M. M. (1970). *Handbook for the Sixteen Personality Factors Questionnaire.* Champaign, IL: Institute for Personality and Ability Testing.

Chait, H. N. (1992). Employment discrimination and the Americans With Disabilities Act of 1990. In H. N. Chait (Ed.), *HRM Update* (pp. 1–3). New York: McGraw-Hill.

Civil Rights Act of 1991, Public Law No. 102–166, 105 Stat. 1071 (1991). Codified as amended at 42 U.S.C., Section 1981, 2000e *et seq.*

Clymer, A. (1991, October 31). Senate approves rights bill, ending bitter job-bias rift. *New York Times,* p. A10.

Combs, I. H., & Omvig, C. P. (1986). Accommodation of disabled people into employment: Perceptions of employers. *Journal of Rehabilitation, 52*(2), 42–45.

Daley v. Koch, 51 Fair Employment Practice Cases 1077, 1079 (2nd Cir. 1989).

Danforth, J. (1991, October 30). *Congressional Record* (daily edition), *137,* Section 15500.

Department of Health, Education, and Welfare. (1978). *Section 504 of the Rehabilitation Act of 1973: Handicapped persons' rights under federal law.* Washington, DC: Office of the Secretary, Office for Civil Rights.

Donnoe, W. E. (1992, March 26–27). *Job analysis requirements under the ADA.* Paper presented at the spring conference of the Personnel Testing Conference of Northern California, Berkeley, CA.

EEOC v. Arabian American Oil Co. and Aramco Service Co., 111 S. Ct., 1227, 113 L. Ed. 2d 274 (1991).

Flanagan, C. L. (1991, December). The ADA and police psychology. *Police Chief,* 14, 16.

Gulliksen, H. (1950). *Theory of mental tests.* New York: Wiley.

Hartigan, J. A., & Wigdor, A. K. (1989). *Fairness in employment testing: Validity generalization, minority issues, and the General Aptitude Test Battery.* Washington, DC: National Academy Press.

Hazelwood School District v. U.S., 433 U.S. 299 (1977).

Howard, G. (1975). The ex-mental patient as an employee: An on-the-job evaluation. *American Journal of Orthopsychiatry, 45,* 479–483.

International Brotherhood of Teamsters v. U.S., 331 U.S. 324 (1979).

Labor letter. (1993, July 27). *The Wall Street Journal,* p. A1.

Lorance v. AT&T Technologies, 490 U.S. 900, 104 L. Ed. 2d 961, 109 S. Ct. 2261 (1989).

Mancuso, L. (1990). Reasonable accommodation for persons with psychiatric disabilities. *Psychosocial Rehabilitation Journal, 14*(2), 3–19.

Mancuso, L. (1992, November). *Reasonable accommodation in the workplace for persons with psychiatric disabilities.* Paper presented at the conference on the ADA and Mental Health in the Workplace, Washington, DC.

Martin v. Wilks, 490 U.S. 755, 104 L. Ed. 2d 835, 109 S. Ct. 2180 (1989).

McDonnell Douglas v. Green, 411 U.S. 972 (1973).

McEvoy, G. M., & Cascio, W. F. (1985). Strategies for reducing employee turnover: A meta-analysis. *Journal of Applied Psychology, 70*, 342–353.

McKenna v. Fargo. (1979). 451 F. Supp. 1355, 1381–1382 (D. NJ. 1973), affirmed without opinion, 601 F.2d 575 (3rd Cir. 1979).

Murphy, K. R. (1993, May). *Use of subgroup norms in employment-related tests: Technical issues and limitations.* Unpublished report prepared by the Scientific Affairs Committee of the Society for Industrial and Organizational Psychology.

Norris, J. A., & Holmes, W. F. (1992). *Corporate affirmative action practices and the Civil Rights Act of 1991.* Washington, DC: Employment Policy Foundation.

Officers for Justice v. Civil Service Commission of San Francisco, 92 C.D.O.S. 9052 (1992).

Officers for Justice v. Civil Service Commission, 979 F.2d 721 (9th Cir. 1992), *cert. denied*, 61 U.S.L.W. 3667, 113 S. Ct. 1645 (March 29, 1993).

Owens, W. A., & Schoenfeldt, L. F. (1979). Toward a classification of persons. *Journal of Applied Psychology, 64*, 569–607.

Patterson v. McLean Credit Union, 491 U.S. 164, 105 L. Ed. 2d 132, 109 S. Ct. 2363 (1989).

Potter, E. E., & Reesman, A. E. (1992). *Employment tests are not medical examinations.* Washington, DC: Employment Policy Foundation.

Premack, S. L., & Wanous, J. P. (1985). A meta-analysis of job preview experiments. *Journal of Applied Psychology, 70*, 706–719.

Price Waterhouse v. Hopkins, 490 U.S. 228, 104 L. Ed. 2d 268, 109 S. Ct., 1775 (1989).

Sackett, P. R., & Roth, L. (1991). A Monte Carlo examination of banding and rank order methods of test score use in personnel selection. *Human Performance, 4*, 279–295.

Schmidt, F. L. (1991). Why all banding procedures in personnel selection are logically flawed. *Human Performance, 4*, 265–277.

Schmidt, F. L., Mack, M. J., & Hunter, J. E. (1984). Selection utility in the occupation of U.S. Park Ranger for three modes of test use. *Journal of Applied Psychology, 69*, 490–497.

Soroka v. Dayton Hudson Corporation, 235 Cal. App. 3d, 654, 658–659 (1991).

Standards for educational and psychological testing. (1985). Washington, DC: American Psychological Association.

Tracy, T. J., & Rounds, J. (1993). Evaluating Holland's and Gati's vocational interest models: A structural meta-analysis. *Psychological Bulletin, 113*, 229–246.

U.S. Equal Employment Opportunity Commission. (1992). *The Americans With Disabilities Act: Your employment rights as an individual with a disability.* Washington, DC: Author.

Wards Cove Packing Co. v. Antonio, 490 U.S. 642, 104 L. Ed. 2d 733, 109 S. Ct. 2115 (1989).

Willingham, W. W. (1988). Testing handicapped people—The validity issue. In H. Wainer & H. Braun (Eds.), *Test validity* (pp. 89–103). Hillsdale, NJ: Erlbaum.

Willingham, W. W., Ragosta, M., Bennett, R. E., Braun, H., Rock, D. A., & Powers, D. E. (1988). *Testing handicapped people.* Needham Heights, MA: Allyn & Bacon.

Zedeck, S., Outtz, J., Cascio, W. F., & Goldstein, I. L. (1991). Why do "Testing experts" have such limited vision? *Human Performance, 4,* 297–308.

EARN CONTINUING EDUCATION CREDITS THROUGH HOME STUDY PROGRAMS BASED ON THE APA MASTER LECTURES

The Master Lectures, presented each year at the APA Convention, can be used to earn Continuing Education (CE) Credits through the successful completion of a test developed to accompany most volumes of this series. The following Home Study Programs are available:

1993 — "PSYCHOLOGY AND THE LAW"

1992 — "A CENTENNIAL CELEBRATION — FROM THEN TO NOW: PSYCHOLOGY APPLIED"

1991 — "PSYCHOPHARMACOLOGY"

1990 — "PSYCHOLOGICAL PERSPECTIVES ON HUMAN DIVERSITY IN AMERICA"

1989 — "PSYCHOLOGICAL ASPECTS OF SERIOUS ILLNESS"

1988 — "THE ADULT YEARS: CONTINUITY AND CHANGE"

1987 — "NEUROPSYCHOLOGY AND BRAIN FUNCTION"

For more information about the Home Study Programs, detach and mail the form below (please print, type or use pre-printed label), or telephone 202/336-5991, 9 a.m.–5 p.m. EST/EDT.

- ✂

Please send me more information about APA's Home Study Programs for Continuing Education Credit.

Name: _____

Address: _____

_____

_____

(City)   (State)   (Zip code)

Daytime phone: _____ / _____
             Area Code

Mail this form to the following address:

Continuing Education Home Study Programs
American Psychological Association
750 First Street, NE
Washington, DC 20002
202/336-5991